Teaching Students To Be Peacemakers

David W. Johnson

Roger T. Johnson

INTERACTION BOOK COMPANY

7208 Cornelia Drive
Edina, Minnesota 55435

(612) 831-9500

© Johnson & Johnson

Copyright © 1987, 1991 by David W. Johnson

This book is dedicated to our wives, Linda Mulholland Johnson and Anne Earle Johnson, who keep our conflict skills in practice.

ISBN: 0-939603-15-2

Table of Contents

Preface

How students may be taught the procedures and skills they need to resolve conflicts constructively has been a relatively ignored issue in teaching. Despite the amount of time teachers and students waste in dealing with destructively managed conflicts, and despite the considerable research evidence indicating that the constructive management of conflict will increase the productivity of the classroom, teachers receive very little training in how to use conflict for instructional purposes and how to teach students the procedures and skills involved in constructive conflict management. In essence, teachers have been implicitly taught to avoid and suppress conflicts and to fear them when they burst forth and cannot be denied. Conflicts cannot be suppressed or denied. Trying to do so makes them worse.

This book is about students learning to be peacemakers. If students are to learn and master the procedures and skills required for constructive conflict management, they must do so in the classroom. This book includes many practical strategies as well as specific suggestions to teach conflict procedures and skills to students. Doing so will not be easy. It will take training, perseverance, and support. The training that has been planned to go with this book will provide a good start, but it may take a year or two of actual experience in the classroom before teaching students conflict procedures and skills becomes a natural part of your teaching. The results for your students are well worth your efforts.

It has taken us nearly 30 years to build the theory, research, and practical experience required to write this book. In the 1960's we began by reviewing the research, conducting our initial research studies, and training teachers in the classroom use of constructive conflict (Johnson, 1970). Since then our work has proliferated. Our more recent writings on constructive conflict include **Reaching Out** (Johnson, 1990), **Joining Together** (Johnson & F. Johnson, 1991), and **Productive Organizational Conflict**. We have made a video to accompany this book (**Training Students To Be Peacemakers**). Related work in cooperative learning includes **Cooperation in the Classroom** (Johnson, Johnson, & Holubec, 1984/1991), **Learning Together and Alone** (Johnson & Johnson, 1975/1991) and **Circles of Learning** (Johnson, Johnson, & Holubec, 1984/1990). Yet the concept of constructively managed conflict is much, much older than our work. Our roots reach back to Morton Deutsch and then to Kurt Lewin. We wish to acknowledge our indebtedness to the work of both of these social psychologists. We are also indebted to our two sisters, Edythe Johnson Holubec and Helen Johnson Misener, who have significantly contributed to this book and our understanding of conflict.

Many teachers have taught us procedures for training students to be peacemakers and have field tested our ideas in their classrooms with considerable success. We have been in their classrooms and we have taught beside them. We appreciate their ideas and celebrate their successes. In addition, we have had many talented and productive graduate students who have conducted research studies that have made significant contributions to our understanding of cooperation. We feel privileged to have worked with them.

Our debt to Judy Bartlett is unmeasurable. Her talents, her dedication, and her work beyond the call of duty have all contributed to the completion of this book. We are continually impressed with and are grateful for her work. She also believes in peacemaking and cooperative learning and is dedicated to ensuring they are shared with students in the classroom. We wish to thank Thomas Grummett for most of the drawings in this book. A few of the drawings were contributed by Nancy Waller to whom we are also grateful.

 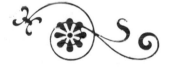

1   What Are Constructive Conflicts?

Peace In The Classroom

> *If we are to reach real peace in the world we shall have to begin with children; and if they will grow up in their natural innocence, we won't have to struggle; we won't have to pass fruitless ideal resolutions, but we shall go from love to love and peace to peace, until at last all the corners of the world are covered with the peace and love for which consciously or unconsciously the whole world is hungering.*
>
> Gandhi

Does this sound familiar? "Roger, why did you hit David?" "He hit me first." "He says you hit him first." "I didn't. He hit me first." "That still doesn't answer my question. Why did you hit him?" "He hit me first." Conflicts occur all the time in school. They are a natural, inevitable, potentially constructive, and normal part of school life. Students disagree over who to sit by at lunch, which game to play during recess, when to work and when to play, when to talk and when to listen, who is going to pick the paper up off the floor, whose turn it is to use the computer, and who has done the most work on a group project. Students put each other down, call each other names, and torment and even physically attack each other. Overt conflicts are not the only conflicts that need to be resolved within schools and classrooms. More frequent, and perhaps even more disruptive to classroom learning, are covert conflicts, in which students sit and "fester" about perceived grievances. Until covert conflicts are made overt and resolved, students cannot focus their attention on learning. Both overt and covert conflicts occur all the time in classrooms and schools.

Teachers cannot teach and students cannot learn unless there is peace and order in the classroom. Teachers (and administrators) are expected to ensure that peace and order reigns. While schools teach math, reading, social studies, and science, perhaps the most important thing for students to learn is how to interact effectively and peacefully with each other and the world at large. If students are putting each other down, teasing each other, trying to hurt each other emotionally and physically, their energies are focused on issues other than learning. The anger and hostility that are aftermaths of destructively managed conflicts are serious barriers to learning. The more energy students put into attack and defense, the less energy they have for learning. It is only when classrooms become cooperative, peaceful, orderly places that students can learn to their fullest capacity.

Absence Of Procedures And Skills For Managing Conflicts

> *What dismays me is not bloodshed per se in fighting, it is the native cowardice and abysmal crudity of the American fighting style. Most Americans will avail themselves of any sneaky excuse to avoid a fight in the first place. But if cornered they begin clobbering away at one another like dull-witted Neanderthals. They are clumsy, weak-kneed, afflicted with poor aim, rotten timing, and no notion of counterpunching. What is more, they fight dirty. Their favorite weapons are the low blow and the rock-filled glove.*

George Bach

The procedures and strategies students use to manage their conflicts are quite often inadequate and destructive, making things worse rather than better. DeCecco and Richards (1974), for example, conducted a seven-year study in which they interviewed more than 8,500 persons (8,000 students and 500 faculty) in more than sixty junior and senior high schools in the New York City, Philadelphia, and San Francisco areas. They found that both school personnel and students avoided verbal expression of anger and open negotiation of conflicts. But ignoring the conflicts did not make them go away. The avoidance and denial of conflicts seemed to make the schools angry places in which students questioned every rule and committed acts of defiance astonishing in their destructiveness. School personnel would then react with strict punishments, armed hallway guards, and other forms of repression. The outcomes of 61 percent of the conflicts reported by students were perceived by them as bad. In only 9 percent of the conflicts did students believe that constructive outcomes resulted. In 91 percent of the conflicts, students reported that their tension level was not lowered by the way in which the conflict was managed. Conflicts that are not openly expressed and constructively resolved will be expressed indirectly at great cost to the group or organization, and the indirect expression of conflicts will persist far longer than would open confrontation and settlement of the conflicts (Walton, 1986).

When conflicts are not avoided, they are often managed destructively. Each year over $200 million is spent repairing damage to school property in the United States. Each month over 100,000 teachers and 2 million students report a theft of their property in school; over 5,000 teachers and 250,000 students report being physically attacked (Bybee & Gee, 1982). The problem of violence and vandalism in schools is national; schools across the nation have security budgets, often security forces (Committee on the Judiciary of the United

States Senate, 1975). Between 1984 and 1989 the number of youths arrested for murder nationwide more than doubled. Youths under 18 now make up more than 10 percent of all homicide arrests, according to federal statistics. The rate of violence to teenagers is greater in school than any other single place.

Most students simply do not know how to manage their conflicts constructively. The violence and destruction in inner-city schools illustrates the current absence of procedures and skills for managing conflicts. Even in the best of schools, students do not know how to manage their conflicts constructively (Johnson, Johnson, & Dudley, 1991a, 1991b). Suburban, middle-class students engaged in frequent conflicts involving put-downs, teasing, insults, playground conflicts involving winning/losing and not playing fair, access to objects such as computers and possession of objects such as books or even pencils, physical fights, who was doing the most work on a joint project, and taking turns. Students referred the majority of conflicts to the teacher, used destructive strategies that tended to escalate the conflict rather than resolve it, and lacked knowledge of how to negotiate. The students tended to view conflict as fights that always resulted in a winner and a loser. They viewed the teacher as being responsible for resolving conflicts. When the students did not refer the conflict to the teacher, they tended to use destructive strategies (such as repeating their request and trying to force the other person to give in) that escalated the conflict and increased the likelihood that the teacher would have to intervene. Students never indicated they would negotiate a solution to the conflicts and seemed completely unable to do so. Almost half of the students could not even state what they wanted in a conflict.

In his dissertation at the University of Minnesota, Brett Laursen queried over 700 high school sophomores and juniors about conflicts they had experienced the preceding day. He was surprised to find that 85 percent of the conflicts occurred within close relationships (family, friends, girlfriend/boyfriend). This was true even when the amount of time spent together was controlled out. He concluded that adolescents tend not to fight unless there is "something special about the relationship." A person has to be important enough to bother with. Conflicts with teachers and other adults tended to be about rules and responsibilities. Conflicts with peers tended to be about annoyances, putdowns, and romantic relationships. Laursen found that stu-

dents rarely negotiated solutions to the conflicts. Either they escalated the conflict into more destructive forms or else they disengaged, walking away from the conflict and leaving it unresolved.

Diversity Of Students

America has always been a nation of many cultures, races, languages, and religions. In the last eight years alone, over 7.8 million people journeying from over 150 different countries and speaking dozens of different languages came to make the United States their new home. The school is the meeting ground for children from different cultural, ethnic, social class, and language backgrounds. They come to know each other, appreciate the vitality of diversity, and internalize a common heritage of being an American that will bind them together. While this diversity represents a source of creativity and energy that few other countries have, it also provides a series of problems concerning how conflicts are managed in the classroom. A wide variety of assumptions about conflict and methods of managing conflict can be found in almost any classroom.

Conflicts are often complex and take time to resolve. Not every conflict can be resolved in a few minutes. Sometimes when the conflict is between individuals from different ethnic, cultural, or social class backgrounds, students' assumptions about each other have to be changed. Suspicions and fears of each other may need to be expelled. Differences may need to be recognized and adjusted to. Agreements have to be reached that both solve the problem and change the relationship among students so that future conflicts are prevented and easier to resolve. Within schools, participants in conflicts have an ongoing, long-term relationship with each other. How any conflict is resolved lays the groundwork for resolving future conflicts. New skills, understandings, and insights must be attained as part of the conflict resolution process. To resolve a conflict in ways that clarify and strengthen the relationship and improve skills in managing future conflicts takes time and effort. Participants need both patience and perseverance to discuss conflicts until truly constructive resolutions are achieved that solve the problem, strengthen the relationship, and improve conflict resolution skills.

Need For Co-Orientation

Different students have quite different ideas about how conflicts should be resolved. Some rely on physical dominance through threats and violence. Other students use procedures such as verbal attack, the cold shoulder, giving in, or getting back at the other person in some way in the future. The multiple procedures for managing conflicts within the classroom create some chaos. This is especially true when students are from different cultural, ethnic, social class, and language backgrounds.

In order for education to proceed and learning to occur, students need to be **co-oriented** so that everyone understands and uses the same procedures for managing conflicts. All students need to operate under the same norms and adhere to the same conflict resolution procedures. **Norms** are shared expectations about the behavior that is appropriate within the situation. Conflict resolution begins with a common set of norms concerning what behaviors are appropriate and what procedures are to be used. These norms must be clearly and publicly established. Physical violence against oneself or another person, public humiliation and shaming, and lying and deceit should be outlawed. Conflicts among students should be skillfully negotiated to solve the problem and improve the relationship. There are norms for appropriate social conduct that students (and school personnel) are expected to follow without exception.

What is needed is a training program that creates a shared set of procedures and strategies for managing conflicts constructively. Such a program is primarily established and maintained day-to-day by classroom teachers.

Peacemakers In The Classroom

Teachers and principals can spend large amounts of time restoring peace and dealing with the residual anger and hostility. The teacher can be a **police officer** and take students to the principal's office to be punished. This may suppress the public display of the conflict, but will not resolve it, and will add new conflicts with the teacher and principal on the top of the current conflict between the two students. A police officer resolves conflict by arresting one or more of the parties. The teacher can be an **arbitrator** who listens to each side's presentation and then renders a verdict as to who is right and who is wrong. This would make one student happy and the other resentful and angry toward the teacher. An arbitrator has to decide who is right and who is wrong and what each student has to do to end the conflict. The teacher can provide **teacher mediation** and assist students in negotiating a resolution to their conflict. Or, the teacher can refer students to a **peer mediator** who assists them in resolving their conflict and restoring their friendship. For many reasons, mediation is to be preferred over suppressing or arbitrating conflicts. And for many reasons, peer mediators are preferable to adult mediators. Teachers should be training students to mediate conflicts among classmates and, thereby, creating peacemakers.

1 : 5

The procedures and strategies students use to manage their conflicts are quite often inadequate and destructive, making things worse rather than better. Most students simply do not know how to manage their conflicts constructively. Wide diversity exists among students. Different students have quite different ideas about how conflicts should be managed. Under these circumstances, conflict can produce chaos. Teachers can respond by being police officers, arbitrators, or mediators. Ideally, however, **teachers will co-orient students by teaching them the procedures and skills required to manage conflicts constructively.**

When students are taught how to manage conflicts constructively, and see themselves as part of a learning community, they become peacemakers. Part of every student's responsibilities becomes managing his or her conflicts constructively and helping schoolmates do likewise. Many students have never thought of themselves as being peacemakers. But conflicts, no matter what, occur all the time and only students themselves can restore order and peace.

What Is Conflict?

If civilization is to survive, we must cultivate the science of human relationships--the ability of all peoples, of all kinds, to live together, in the same world at peace.

Franklin Delano Roosevelt

Can you live without conflict? No. Conflict is a natural part of life. Everyone has conflicts. You usually know when you are in a conflict. Yet the concept has not been an easy one for psychologists to define. Some psychologists have focused on frustration, others have focused on decisions among attractive or unattractive alternatives, and some have concentrated on the feelings of the people involved (rage, anger, distrust, and rejection). According to the **World Book Dictionary**, a conflict is a fight, struggle, battle, disagreement, dispute, or quarrel. A conflict can be as small as a disagreement or as large as a war. Probably the most influential definition is that of Deutsch (1969), who states that a **conflict** exists whenever incompatible activities occur. An activity that is incompatible with another activity is one that prevents, blocks, or interferes with the occurrence or effectiveness of the second activity. Incompatible activities may originate in one person, between two or more people, or between two or more groups. If, for example, you wish to spend Saturday afternoon both sleeping and studying, you are in conflict with yourself. If you wish to cross the street and someone decides to prevent, block, or interfere with your doing so, you are involved in an interpersonal conflict. If your group decides to win a football game and the other group decides it also wants to win the game, your group is in conflict with the other group.

Types Of Conflicts

Four types of Conflicts

There are at least four important types of conflicts: controversies, conceptual conflicts, conflicts of interests, and developmental conflicts. A **controversy** exists when one person's ideas, information, conclusions, theories, and opinions are incompatible with those of another and the two seek to reach an agreement. An example of a controversy is when students are placed in groups of four. Two students argue that all nuclear energy plants should be closed while the other two students argue that nuclear energy is vital to meet our nation's energy needs in a safe way. The group must write one report on nuclear energy giving their best thinking on the subject.

A **conceptual conflict** occurs when incompatible ideas exist simultaneously in a person's mind or when information being received does not seem to fit with what one already knows (Berlyne, 1957, 1966). An example is when the same amount of water is poured into two glasses--one is tall and skinny and the other is short and fat. The student knows that each glass holds the same amount of water but at the same time believes that the tall glass has more water in it.

A **conflict of interests** exists when the actions of one person attempting to maximize his or her wants and benefits prevent, block, or interfere with another person maximizing his or her wants and benefits. When two students both want the same library book at the same time, a conflict of interests exists. When merit pay is given to the "best" teacher in the school, a conflict of interests exists. Each teacher attempts to prove that he or she is a better teacher than the other teachers in the school. When teachers place students in competition with each other over grades, a conflict of interests exists. When needs, values, and goals are incompatible, when certain resources (such as power, time, space, popularity, money, and position) are scarce, and when competition for rewards and privileges is taking place, a conflict of interests exists.

A **developmental conflict** exists when recurrent incompatible activities between adult and child based on the opposing forces of stability and change within the child cycles in and out of peak intensity as the child develops cognitively and socially. An example is when one year a child is dependent on the teacher and wants to be noticed and approved of by the teacher all the time. The next year the child is independent and does not want the teacher to express approval or liking. The student does not choose to be dependent or independent, there are social developmental imperatives that demand that he or she be so. These imperatives are pushed to the extreme until a teacher (or parent) sets limits and communicates social reality.

Conflicts Have Value

Conflicts are inevitable. You will always be involved in conflicts with someone. Conflicts will occur no matter how inconspicuous and unoffensive you try to be. The occurrence of conflicts, however, is not a cause for despair. Conflicts are often valuable.

First, intellectual conflicts (known as controversies) are essential to good instruction. Conflicts among students' thinking can result in higher achievement, more higher-level reasoning, and more creative problem solving.

Second, conflicts are essential to promoting caring and committed relationships among students. Conflicts can deepen and enrich relationships, strengthening each person's conviction that the relationship can hold up under stress, communicating the commitments and values of each person that the other must take into account, and generally keeping the relationship clear of irritations and resentments so that positive feelings can be experienced fully. Conflicts make us more aware of problems in our relationships that need to be solved and energize us to deal with them. Conflicts increase our awareness of what the problems are, who is involved, and how the problems can be solved. The irritations of relating to others is reduced when we become aware of the specific problems causing them. A good argument may do a lot to resolve the small tensions of interacting with others. And resolving conflicts creates a sense of joint identity and cohesiveness within the relationship. Conflicts, furthermore, energize and increase our motivation to deal with relationship problems. Awareness of conflict can trigger a great deal of physical energy and an intensity of psychological focus, which in turn result in a strong motivation to resolve the conflict and put one's plans into action.

Nothing divides humans more than poorly managed conflicts. Nothing brings humans together more than constructively managed conflicts. Like all communities, classrooms and schools are cooperative enterprises within which diverse and heterogeneous individuals work together to achieve mutual goals. Conflicts will occur, and when they are constructively managed, the quality of community life within schools is enhanced.

3   **Third, conflicts are essential for healthy social development.** It is through conflicts that relationship issues are resolved at various stages of growth. Many times, there are developmental imperatives that require conflicts between children/adolescents and adults (see Chapter 7).

4   **Fourth, conflicts are essential for having an interesting and fun life.** Being in a conflict often sparks curiosity and stimulates interest. Arguments about politics, sports, work, and societal problems make interpersonal interaction more intriguing and less boring. Skillful bargaining is a form of entertainment. The disagreement of others with your ideas may inspire you to find out more about the issue. Conflicts can be fun when they are not taken too seriously. Many persons seek out conflicts through such activities as competitive sports and games, movies, plays, books, and teasing. They do so because they enjoy being involved in such conflict situations.

5.   **Fifth, conflicts help you understand what you are like as a person and how you need to change.** What makes you angry, what frightens you, what is important to you, and how you tend to manage conflicts are all highlighted when you are in conflict with someone. Being aware of what you are willing to argue about and how you act in conflicts can help you learn a great deal about yourself. Such awareness encourages change. There are times when things need to change, when new skills need to be learned, when old habits need to be modified.

6.   **Finally, skills in managing conflicts constructively make you more employable, will enhance your career success, and generally increase the quality of your life.** The current opinion of many business leaders is that schools often provide a distorted view of work because students do not learn the importance of being part of a cooperative team and managing conflicts skillfully in order to "get the job done." Through experiencing numerous conflicts and perfecting the procedures and skills required to manage them effectively, you will be able to maintain higher quality friendships and family relationships, will be able to maintain higher quality relationships on the job with superiors, peers, and subordinates, and will be able to advance to management and leadership positions more readily.

The energy that students put into being angry and upset could be focused on learning when conflicts are resolved constructively. The benefits gained from learning how to manage conflicts constructively far outweigh the cost of learning time lost by students being upset and angry. **From a cost-analysis perspective, one of the soundest investments**

educators and students can make in classroom and school productivity is teaching students how to manage conflicts constructively. When teachers want to maintain the focus on learning rather than on hurt feelings, ensuring that the conflicts currently being dealt with are managed constructively is the most useful thing teachers can do. The **aggressive-passive mentality** where students believe that either they must dominate through force or are passive victims is prevented and avoided when students are empowered to resolve conflicts constructively by being taught the needed procedures and skills.

Conflicts Can Bring Destructive Or Constructive Outcomes

Every conflict has at least two sides. A conflict is a moment of truth, a crisis that can weaken or strengthen interpersonal relationships. When conflicts go bad, each side is convinced he or she is right, people get their feelings hurt, people can be physically injured, people can lose their possessions, and people can feel more frustrated and angry. Lasting resentment, smoldering hostility, and physical and psychological scars can result. When conflicts go well, each side seeks an agreement that benefits everyone, people become better friends, everyone gains, and people feel more satisfied and happy. Creative insight, closer relationships, and increased unity and cooperation can result. Conflicts can bring aggression or mutual understanding. It is not the presence of conflicts, but the way in which they are managed, that determines whether they are destructive or constructive. **Conflicts are constructive to the extent that they:**

1. Strengthen the relationship among participants so that they are better able to interact or work cooperatively with each other with increased liking, respect, and trust for each other.

2. Result in an agreement that allows all participants to achieve their goals. The agreement maximizes joint outcomes, benefits everyone, and is in all participants' best interests.

3. Increase participants' ability to resolve future conflicts with each other constructively.

Managing Conflicts Constructively

What people know about managing conflicts is usually learned at a very early age within the family. Children manage conflicts the same way their parents and older siblings do. The authors initially learned how to manage conflicts from our older sister, Helen. Helen was an early maturing female in a family of late maturing males (she was 5'4" when we were 2'6"). Her basic rule was, "Save time, see it my way now!" In conflicts she tended to strike out emotionally, accusing and blaming us in ways to induce guilt and shame. "You did it, it's all your fault, if you were not such a rotten person, then I would not have obliterated you," were some of her favorite statements. Most characteristic of all, she gleefully believed with all her heart that all our hostile actions were caused by our nasty and vicious personalities while any hostile be-

havior she (a remarkably sweet, gentle, and kind person) engaged in was the result of circumstances and situational factors (this is called the **fundamental attribution error**). She loved to "demonize" us. "Let's discuss your degree of rottenness," was one of her favorite topics of conversation. Helen, of course, now works for a professional football team, ruling the players with an iron fist. While she taught us how to bully and blame others, make the fundamental attribution error, and demonize our enemies, none of that has helped us live happy and fulfilling lives. We, like so many other people, have had to relearn how to manage conflict constructively.

It is a mistake to avoid conflicts. Conflicts are pervasive. They cannot be avoided or suppressed. Even if conflicts could be suppressed, no one would want to do so. Without conflict there would be no creativity, high-level reasoning, and cognitive development. Conflicts lead to growth, development, and change. This is true of individuals, groups, organizations, and even societies. Because of the highly constructive potential of conflicts, all students need to learn the procedures and skills required to resolve conflicts constructively.

In a series of studies on resilience in the face of adversity, Ann Mastern and Norman Garmezy at the University of Minnesota found problem-solving skills and qualities such as empathy to be directly related to children and adolescents' long-term coping with adversity. Mastern states that both problem-solving skills and empathy can be improved through training in conflict management. There are a number of challenges that adolescents face. One is processes such as changes associated with puberty, poverty, disabilities or handicaps, or racial prejudice. Another is catastrophes such as the death of a family member or friend. In addition, there are a variety of everyday conflicts. Competent adolescents tend to be more cooperative (as opposed to disruptive) and more proactive and involved (as opposed to withdrawn). **The more students learn how to take a cooperative approach to managing**

conflicts through joint problem-solving, the healthier psychologically they tend to be and the better able they are to deal with stress and adversity. Adolescents who cannot cope with the challenges they face tend to not know what to do when faced with conflicts and misfortune. **Negotiation skills are carried with the adolescent wherever he or she goes and, once acquired, cannot be taken away.** Having procedures and skills to negotiate solutions to joint problems prepares children and adolescents to handle conflict and cope with life's challenges and unforeseen adversities.

Students need to learn constructive ways of managing conflict. Violence, fear, intimidation, threat, acquiescence, and abuse have no place within classrooms and schools. Yet without direct training in how to manage conflicts constructively, many students will never become able to do so. Classrooms need to become places where destructive conflicts are prevented and where constructive conflicts are structured, encouraged, and utilized to improve the quality of instruction and classroom life.

Each teacher may make a contribution to students' competencies in managing conflicts constructively. This does not mean that all conflicts will become constructive and all students will quickly learn the necessary skills. Remedial goals may often need to be modest. Sigmund Freud once said, "Much is gained by having transformed hysterical misery into common unhappiness." Each contribution to making students more skillful in managing conflicts constructively is valuable and worthwhile.

There is a marked lack of training for students (and school personnel) in how to manage conflicts constructively. Such training will not only improve the quality of life within the classroom and school, but also benefit students their whole life long. If students are to learn how to manage conflicts constructively:

1. They have to be directly taught the required procedures and skills.

2. The classroom and school norms and values have to support the use of the procedures and skills.

Classrooms need to become places where destructive conflicts are prevented and where constructive conflicts are structured, encouraged, and utilized to improve the quality of instruction and classroom life.

 There are five steps in teaching students the procedures and skills they need to manage conflicts constructively.

Step 1: Creating A Cooperative Context

The best way I know how to defeat an enemy is to make him a friend.

Abraham Lincoln

The first step in managing conflicts constructively is to establish a cooperative classroom environment. Classroom conflicts may be prevented, reduced, and managed constructively through the establishment of a cooperative context. The more cooperative the relationships among students, the more constructively conflicts will be managed. The easiest way to create a cooperative environment is to use cooperative learning procedures the majority of the day (Johnson, Johnson, & Holubec, 1990). Since cooperative learning increases achievement and promotes a number of other important instructional outcomes (Johnson & Johnson, 1989a), there will be little objection to doing so. In addition to its overall positive effects, cooperative learning promotes a long-term time perspective and enhances the learning of social skills. The constructive resolution of conflict within the classroom and school requires students and staff to recognize that their long-term relationships are more important than is the result of any short-term conflict. In order for their long-term mutual interests to be recognized and valued, individuals must perceive their mutual interdependence and be invested in each other's well-being. The cooperative environment also establishes the context within which to teach students the procedures and skills they need to manage conflicts constructively. Finally, the overuse and inappropriate use of competitive and individualistic learning procedures should be avoided. The more competitive the relationships among students, and the more students tend to focus on their own self-interests, the more frequently conflicts will occur, and the more destructive conflicts will tend to be.

Step 2: Instructional Use Of Academic Controversies

It's best that we should not all think alike. It's difference of opinion that makes horse races.

Mark Twain

The second step is to frequently promote intellectual controversies to increase the quantity and quality of academic learning. Controversies promote conceptual conflicts. In order to maximize student achievement, student critical thinking, and student use of higher-level reasoning strategies, teachers need to engage students in intellectual conflicts within which they have to prepare intellectual positions, present them, advocate them, criticize opposing intellectual positions, view the issue from a variety of perspectives, and synthesize the various positions into one position. The frequent use of academic controversies allows students to practice their conflict skills daily.

Step 3: Teaching Students To Negotiate Resolutions To Conflicts-Of-Interests

| *A soft answer turneth away wrath.*

Bible

The third step is to teach students how to negotiate constructive resolutions to their conflicts. When two students both want to use the computer at the same time, a conflict of interests exists. Conflicts of interests deal more with wants, needs, values, and goals rather than differences in information and conclusions. When such conflicts occur, settlements must be negotiated. Students, therefore, have to be taught the procedures and skills of negotiating.

Step 4: Teaching Students To Mediate Schoolmates' Conflicts

The fourth step is to mediate students' conflicts when they are unable to negotiate a constructive resolution by themselves. When students are unable to negotiate an acceptable agreement, they will turn to the teacher (or a student mediator) for help. **Mediation** exists when a neutral third person--a mediator--intervenes to help resolve a conflict between two or more people in a way that is acceptable to them. A mediator listens carefully to both sides and helps the disputants move effectively through each step of the negotiation sequence in order to reach an agreement that both believe is fair, just, and workable. Mediation is an extension of the negotiation process and is a collection of strategies aimed at promoting more efficient and effective negotiations. The main difference between negotiating and mediating is that a third party, the mediator, ensures that both persons engage in each step of the negotiation process. While the teacher may mediate conflicts among students, the teacher may also train all students to be mediators, each day (or week) select a pair of class mediators, and then refer to them all conflicts. It is important that all students are given the opportunity to be a mediator

as it will increase students' negotiation skills. Peer mediation gives students an opportunity to resolve their dispute themselves, in mutually satisfactory ways, without having to engage the attention of a teacher. This empowers the students who sometimes feel like they are victims of the "arbitrary" whims of the teacher. It also reduces the demands on the teacher, who can devote less time to arbitration and discipline in general, and more time to teaching.

Step 5: Arbitrating Students' Conflicts

The fifth step is to arbitrate student conflicts. When mediation fails, the teacher or principal may have to decide. **Arbitration** is the submission of a dispute to a disinterested third party (such as a teacher or principal) who makes a final and binding judgment as to how the conflict will be resolved. The arbitrator carefully listens to both sides and makes a decision. The process of having a teacher or principal decide who is right and who is wrong seldom satisfies anyone, leaving at least one student with resentment and anger toward the arbitrator. More importantly, it reinforces students' beliefs that they are not capable of working out future disputes themselves. For these reasons, arbitration is the last resort for resolving conflicts within the classroom and school. In a way, arbitration is a threat to encourage the success of negotiations and mediation.

Your Challenge

Your challenge is to learn how to make conflicts go well. Most people spend a lot of time and energy in conflicts. They often do not understand what causes conflicts or how they can be settled. People worry about the conflicts they are in and are afraid when conflicts take place. What they do not realize is that conflicts offer the chance to see a problem more clearly, get new ideas, make better friends, see things in a new way, and motivate change for the better. History is filled with many exciting examples of constructive conflicts. It is not possible to eliminate conflict from your life. It is, however, possible to learn how to make conflict enrich rather than disrupt your life. The better you and everyone else understands how to make conflicts go well, the better your life will be. A better life, and a more peaceful world, begins with you.

Learning Conflict Skills

Reading a book on physical conditioning exercises will not make you physically fit. Studying books on golf, horse-back riding, or swimming will not make you an expert.

Learning the procedures and skills required to manage conflicts constructively is no different. Successful conflict managers are not born, they are trained. You first must **see the need** for becoming a skilled conflict manager, then **understand how to manage** conflicts skillfully, and finally **practice, practice, practice** until skillful management of conflict is an automatic reflex that does not require conscious thought or practice.

With most skills there is a period of slow learning, then a period of rapid improvement, then a period where performance remains the same, and then another period of rapid improvement, then another plateau, and so forth. Individuals have to practice the conflict skills long enough to make it through the first few plateaus and integrate the skills into their behavioral repertoires. There is a set of **stages** that most skill development goes through:

1. **Awareness** that the skill is needed.

2. **Understanding** of what the skill is.

3. Self-conscious, **awkward engagement** in the skill. Practicing any new skill feels awkward. The first few times someone throws a football, plays a piano, or paraphrases, it feels strange.

4. Feelings of **phoniness** while engaging in the skill. After a while the awkwardness passes and enacting the skill becomes more smooth. Many individuals, however, feel unauthentic or phony when performing the skill. Encouragement is often needed to move individuals through this stage.

5. **Mechanical use** of the skill.

6. Automatic, **routine use** where the skill is fully integrated into the person's behavioral repertoire and seems like a natural action to engage in.

You learn any skill (tennis or managing conflict) by:

1. Taking a risk by engaging in a challenging action, that is, experimenting to increase one's competence.

2. Obtaining feedback on the success or failure of one's efforts.

3. Engaging in self-reflection and analysis of the effectiveness of the actions taken.

4. Modifying one's actions, and trying again.

5. Recycling to Step 2 over and over again.

In learning any skill it is helpful to remember the following advice. "You have to sweat on the practice field before you perform on the playing field!" "You gotta study the lessons before you get the grades!" "You gotta make the call before you get the sale!"

While reading this book you will be expected to learn the procedures and skills you need to manage conflict constructively. You will be asked to try out procedures, assess the effectiveness of your actions, reflect on how you could behave more competently in conflict situations, then try again in a modified way. You will be asked to support and encourage the efforts of your classmates to do likewise. Improving your competence is an exciting and exhilarating experience, but in doing so it is often helpful to remember the stages of skill learning involved. Do not worry about feeling awkward the first time you negotiate or mediate. Persevere and practice and soon the awkwardness will pass.

Being A Peer Mediator

Betty finished changing out of her gym clothes and was ready to return to class. She was blocked from exiting from her row in the lockerroom because another student, Carol, had her foot up on a locker and was tying her shoe. Betty said "pardon me" to Carol twice, but Carol kept tying her shoe without any effort to let Betty by. Betty lost her temper and tried to knock Carol's leg out of her way. Carol jumped up and pushed Betty yelling that Betty had better keep her hands to herself.

Betty and Carol need help in resolving their conflict. Students come to mediators with real problems. They may have been physically fighting on the playground. They may have been trading cutting remarks because they are jealous. One may have been pressuring the other into something the other person does not want to do. One may have problems with parents that resulted in a striking out at a classmate because he was the nearest target. It is not enough to want to help others when they are in pain and distress. You must be prepared and skilled in how to help them. You must know how to negotiate and how to mediate. Being a mediator is fun. Helping others is very satisfying and something to be proud of. But mediation is far more than "common sense." Mediators must always know exactly what they are doing and why they are doing it.

A peer mediator first separates Betty and Carol and helps them cool down. She then explains the process of mediation and asks both students to commit themselves to solving their problem. The mediator leads Betty and Carol through the steps of negotiation. When an agreement is reached, the mediator writes it down, has both students sign it, and states that she will check back with the students in a few days to see if the agreement is working. Given the help of a mediator, Betty and Carol agree to say "pardon me" when trying to pass someone, move out of the way when someone is trying to pass, and avoid physical fighting.

Learning how to manage conflicts constructively requires that you learn how to establish a cooperative relationship, negotiate, and mediate. You must be trained to mediate. You must gain practical experience actively mediating conflicts. In order to do so, you must understand the steps of negotiating. You must understand how to build a cooperative context. In order to ensure that conflicts are managed constructively, schools should be predominately cooperative places where all students are trained to negotiate to solve interpersonal problems. When they are unable to do so, they should first turn to peer mediators for help and assistance before seeking the help of a teacher.

In this book the five steps of managing conflicts constructively will be discussed. Chapter 2 will focus on how to create a cooperative context so that constructive conflict procedures and skills may be taught. Chapters 3 and 4 will present an overall problem-solving negotiation procedure. One of the most problematic emotions connected with conflicts is anger. Chapter 5 focuses on how to manage anger. Chapter 6 presents the peer mediation program and the procedures and skills students need to learn to mediate classmates' conflicts. Chapter 7 discusses recurrent conflicts that occur among students and between students and faculty as part of students' cognitive and social development.

Summary

Conflicts occur all the time. They are a natural, inevitable, potentially constructive, and normal part of school life. Students disagree over who to sit by at lunch, which game to play during recess, when to work and when to play, when to talk and when to listen, and who is going to pick the paper up off the floor. Overt conflicts are not the only conflicts that need to be resolved within schools and classrooms. More frequent, and perhaps even more disruptive to classroom learning, are covert conflicts, in which classmates sit and "fester" about your perceived grievances. To focus students' attention on learning, covert conflicts have to be made overt and resolved.

While classrooms are filled with conflict, the procedures and strategies most students use to manage these conflicts are often quite inadequate and destructive, making things worse rather than better. Students generally have received very little training in how to manage conflicts constructively. Different students have different ideas about how conflicts should be resolved. Students may get angry, fight, hurl verbal abuse at each other, verbally harass each other, ignore the conflict, take their anger out on someone/something else, play head-games, or fantasize how to get revenge. These methods generally provide little chance of resolving any problems and often result in alienating students from their peers and the school staff. What is needed is a training program that creates a shared set of procedures and strategies for managing conflicts constructively.

Actually, conflict is a natural part of life and is ever present in relationships. Everyone has conflicts. That is, the actions of one person frequently prevent, block, or interfere with another person's attempts to achieve his or her goals. There are four major types of conflicts. When one person's ideas or conclusions are incompatible with those of another person, and the two must reach an agreement, a **controversy** occurs. When a person has two incompatible ideas, a **conceptual conflict** exists. When one person strives to achieve his or her goals and another person blocks him or her from doing so, a **conflict of interests** exists. When recurrent incompatible actions occur between a child and an adult as part of the child's social development, a **developmental conflict** exists.

All four types of conflicts have value. They promote learning, problem solving, healthy social development, change, and success as well as make life more interesting and fun. The value of conflicts only occurs, however, if participants have the procedures and skills required to manage conflicts constructively. You know that a conflict has been constructive when it solves the problem, strengthens the relationships among participants, and increases their ability to resolve their conflicts constructively in the future. Students learn how to achieve these outcomes when (a) a cooperative context for relationships is created through the extensive use of cooperative learning, (b) academic controversies are structured by the teacher, (c) all students learn a basic negotiation procedure, (d) all students learn how to mediate their classmates' conflicts, and (e) teachers arbitrate as a last resort.

Conflicts can only be managed constructively within a cooperative context. The first step to ensuring that students learn how to deal with their conflicts in helpful and beneficial ways is to make the classroom and school a cooperative enterprise. This will only happen when cooperative learning is used the majority of the time. In the next chapter we will learn what cooperative learning is and how it may be used to create a constructive context for effectively managing conflicts.

⟶⟨ Creative Conflict Contract ⟩⟶

Major Learnings	Implementation Plans

Date _____ Date of Progress Report Meeting _____

Participant's Signature _____

Signatures of Other Group Members _____ _____

_____ _____ _____

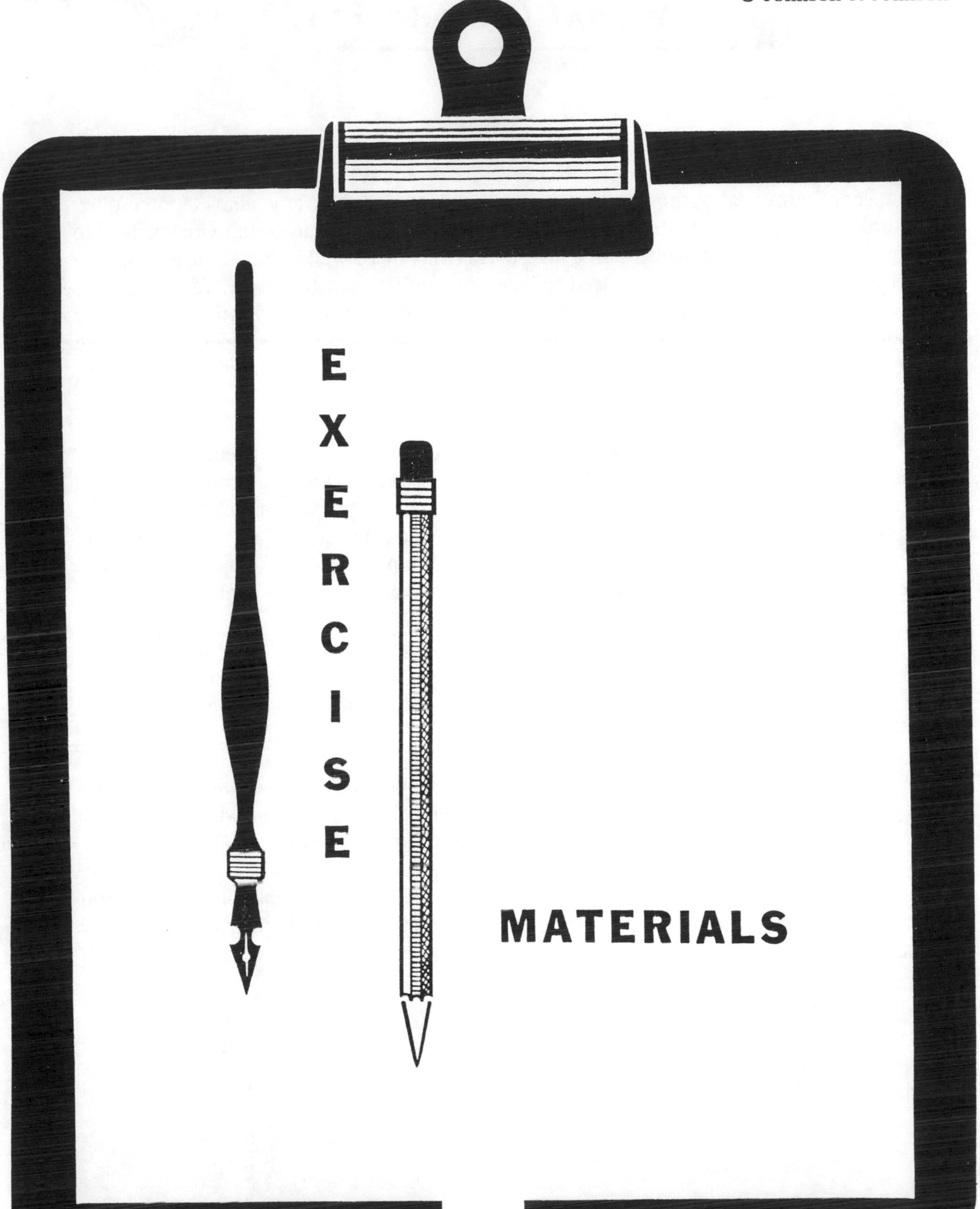

EXERCISE

MATERIALS

1 : 21

STEPS of MANAGING CONFLICT

1. **Create A Cooperative Context**: The constructive resolution of conflict within an ongoing organization such as a school and classroom requires participants to recognize that their long- term relationship is more important than the result of any short- term conflict. In order for long-term mutual interests to be recognized and valued, individuals have to perceive their interdependence and be invested in each other's well-being. To teach students the procedures and skills they need to manage conflicts constructively, furthermore, a cooperative classroom environment must be established. The easiest way to do so is to use cooperative learning procedures at least 60 percent of the day. Since cooperative learning increases achievement and promotes a number of other important instructional outcomes, there will be little objection to doing so.

2. **Structure Academic Controversies**: In order to maximize student achievement, student critical thinking, and student use of higher-level reasoning strategies, engage students in intellectual conflicts within which they have to prepare intellectual positions, present them, advocate them, criticize opposing intellectual positions, view the issue from a variety of perspectives, and synthesize the various positions into one position. The frequent use of academic controversies allows students to practice their conflict skills daily.

3. **Teach Students How To Negotiate**: In order to resolve conflicts of interests and developmental conflicts constructively, students have to be taught the procedures and skills of negotiating. Student time on task will improve when they are not preoccupied with unresolved conflicts.

4. **Teach Students How To Mediate Conflicts**: When students cannot successfully negotiate a constructive resolution to their conflicts, mediators should be available to assist. Experience as a mediator, in addition, will increase negotiation skills.

5. **Arbitrate Student Conflicts**: When mediation fails, the teacher or principal arbitrates the conflict. As a last resort, when students cannot negotiate their conflicts and a mediator is unable to assist them to negotiate effectively with each other, the teacher or principal will have to decide. This is a last resort because typically it involves deciding who is right and, therefore, at least one student may be left with resentment and anger toward the arbitrator.

CHAPTER VOCABULARY

Working with a partner, learn the definitions of the following words.

1. Define each word in two ways.

   First, write down what you think the word means.
   Second, look it up in the book and write down its definition.
   Note the page on which the definition appears.

2. For each word write a sentence in which the word is used.

3. Make up a story in which all of the words are used.

4. Learn how to spell each word. They will be on your spelling test.

Dictionary

Word List

- conflict
- conceptual conflict
- developmental conflict
- mediate
- co-orientation
- controversy
- conflict of interests
- negotiate
- arbitrate
- norms

Pair Reading of the Chapter

Your **task** is to read and comprehend the material in the chapter. To do this you must establish the meaning of each paragraph and then integrate the meaning of the paragraphs into the meaning of the chapter (and book) as a whole.

Form pairs. Work **cooperatively**. Ensure that both you and your partner become experts on the material. Agree on the meaning of each paragraph. Formulate one summary from the two of you. Both must be able to explain the meaning of the assigned material. Use the following procedure:

1. Read all the section heads in the chapter to get an overview.

2. One of you will be the **summarizer** and one will be the **accuracy checker**. These roles are rotated after each paragraph.

   a. Both members silently read the first paragraph.

   b. The **summarizer** summarizes in his or her own words the content of the paragraph.

   c. The **accuracy checker** listens carefully, corrects any misstatements, and adds anything left out. Then he or she tells how the material relates to something they already know.

   d. Move on to the next paragraph, switch roles, and repeat the procedure. Continue until you have read the whole chapter.

3. Work **cooperatively with other groups**. Whenever it is helpful, check procedures, answers, and strategies with another pair.

Name _____ Date _____

CONFLICT RESOLUTION

WORD HUNT

WORDS FOUND

_____ _____

_____ _____

_____ _____

_____ _____

_____ _____

_____ _____

_____ _____

_____ _____

_____ _____

_____ _____

_____ _____

For this activity, you and your partner have to put your heads together to find as many words as you can from the phrase CONFLICT RESOLUTION. You may use as few or as many letters in each word as you like, arranged in any order, as long as the letter appears in CONFLICT RESOLUTION. Write each of the words you find in the columns on the left. You may also write each word in the Bonus Column if you can write a sentence on the back of this sheet using the word. THE SENTENCE MUST HAVE SOMETHING TO DO WITH CONFLICT. Good luck in your conflict word hunt!

EXAMPLE: You and your partner find the word it. Write it in a Words Found space. On the back of your paper you write the sentence: When Sue called me "fatty," I told her I would like to talk about it. (Any sentence you write will count as long as it deals with conflict in some way.)

BONUS WORDS

_____

_____

_____

_____

_____

_____

_____

_____

_____

_____

_____

_____

_____

Name _____   Date _____

PUZZLING CONFLICTS

Let's see if you and your partner can do some puzzle solving. The words below are all ones we've used lately in talking about Conflict Resolution. See if the two of you can fit the words into this crossword puzzle. (If you need some help, turn the page upside down and you will see a list of the words used.)

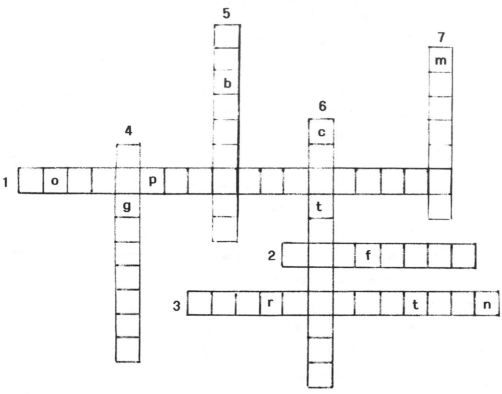

WORD LIST

negotiate
mediate
coorientation
controversy
conflict
conceptual conflict
arbitrate

Across

1. A conflict of incompatible ideas (2 words)
2. Another word for a fight, disagreement, or even a war.
3. Operating under the same norms and adhering to the same procedure.

Down

4. Settle an argument in five steps.
5. Submit a dispute to a disinterested third party who makes a final and binding judgment.
6. Intellectual conflict within which students prepare positions, present them, advocate them, take a variety of perspectives and synthesize the positions into one.
7. Help others to settle their conflicts or disagreements.

∽ **Conflict Journal** ∽

You are to make a conflict journal in which you record what you are learning about yourself and how you behave in conflict situations. A **journal** is a personal collection of your significant thoughts about conflict. Include specific information you have learned about conflict resolution, effective behavior in conflict situations, and the extent to which you have mastered the conflict skills. Personalize it with art, poetry, cartoons, and creative writing. The most important thing about journal writing is to express your ideas freely without judging them. Whatever you write is OK. Spelling, grammar, and neatness do not count. The only thing that matters is writing freely about your experiences and ideas.

The purposes of the journal are to collect (a) thoughts that are related to the book's content (the best thinking often occurs when you are riding to or from school, about to go to sleep at night, and so forth) and (b) newspaper and magazine articles and references that arc relevant to resolving conflicts constructively.

Entries

1. Each day find a conflict in the newspaper or on television and describe it in your journal.

2. Each day describe one conflict you werc involved in during the day:

   a. What was the conflict about?

   b. Who was involved?

   c. What strategies did you use to manage the conflict?

   d. How did you feel?

   e. How was it resolved?

   f. What did you learn about managing conflicts constructively?

(Note: If you publish your journal as did John Holt, Hugh Prather, and others, all we ask is a modest 10 percent of the royalties.)

Journal Entry One

Conflicts always occur, and you can profit from them if you have the necessary skills. It is important, therefore, to master the skills necessary for resolving conflicts constructively. The first step for doing so is to become more aware of your most frequently used strategies for managing conflicts.

Think back over the interpersonal conflicts you have been involved in during the past few years. These conflicts may be with students, administrators, parents, or colleagues.

1. Describe a recent conflict with a schoolmate, teacher, administrator, or parent.

2. What kind of emotional reaction do you have to these or other classroom or school-related conflicts? Check the ones that are appropriate.

___ Anger   ___ Resentment   ___ Depression

___ Frustration   ___ Fear   ___ Excitement

___ Annoyance   ___ Exasperation   ___ Sadness

___ Resignation

3. What were the strategies you used to resolve the conflicts?

4. Compare your answers with those of the person next to you.

CONFLICT DETECTIVE

Conflicts go on continually everywhere. As a conflict detective you need to investigate conflicts daily. The two major sources of conflicts are the newspaper, TV entertainment programs, and TV news programs.

1. **Investigate the newspaper each day.** Find an example of a conflict in an article. It can be a small conflict (neighbors quarreling about a barking dog) or a large conflict (nations disagreeing). Bring in the article for the Conflict Bulletin Board. Or you can put the article in your Conflict Journal.

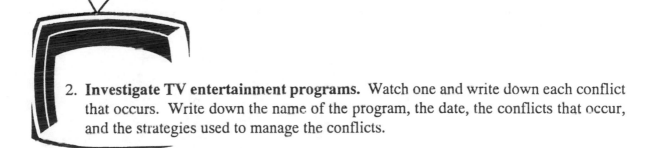

2. **Investigate TV entertainment programs.** Watch one and write down each conflict that occurs. Write down the name of the program, the date, the conflicts that occur, and the strategies used to manage the conflicts.

3. **Investigate TV news programs.** Watch one and write down each conflict that is discussed. Write down who is involved in the conflict and what strategies they are using to resolve it.

WHAT IS CONFLICT?

Working as a pair, write out your answers to the following questions. There should be one set of answers for the two of you, both of you have to agree on the answers, and both of you have to be able to explain your answers to the teacher or the entire class. When you have finished, find another pair and compare answers. Take some of their ideas and make your answers better.

1. Conflict begins when two people want the same thing. When one person says, "I want the ice cream bar" and another person says, "I want the ice cream bar," a conflict exists. What do you think a conflict is? Define the word **conflict** in your own words, using your own ideas.

2. Are conflicts good _____ or bad _____?

Fill in the table on the next page to discover conflict in your life!

WHAT IS CONFLICT? (continued)

Give three examples of good conflicts. Give three examples of bad conflicts. Then list three small and three large conflicts you know about. Finally, list three conflicts at home and three conflicts at school.

	Good	Bad
1		
2		
3		

	Small	Large
1		
2		
3		

	Home	School
1		
2		
3		

3. What is more important:

_____ Getting what you want   _____ Maintaining a good relationship with the other person.

(What lasts longer, a cookie or a friend?)

Name _____   Date _____

What CONFLICT Means to Me

Think of what CONFLICT means to you. Is it scary or exciting? Is it interesting or yukky? Write in the circles words that come into your mind when you think of conflict. [Make additional circles if you need to.]

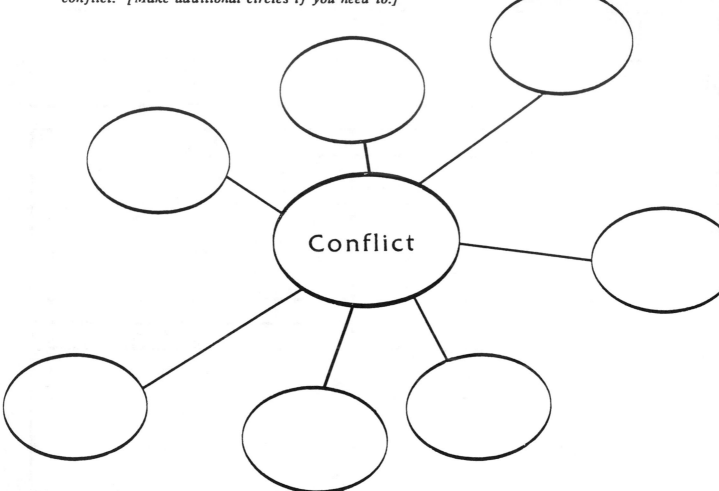

Now compare your words with those of the other members of your group. Decide as a group what conflict means and write the meaning below.

_____

_____

ASSOCIATIONS MAPPING FOLLOW-UP

Cooperative Task:

1 What elements do all conflicts have in common?

2 What causes conflict?

3 What makes conflicts destructive?

4 What makes conflicts constructive?

Individualistic Task:

Write down answers to the following:

1 What did you learn about your associations with conflict.

2 What did you learn about the nature of conflict and how most people perceive it?

Conflict Self-Assessment

1. Rate your ability to resolve conflicts constructively on the criteria given in the table below.

Low 1--2--3--4--5--6--7--8--9--10 High

2. Then rate the ability of your classmates (students) to resolve conflicts constructively.

Low 1--2--3--4--5--6--7--8--9--10 High

3. Share ratings with partner. Compare your ratings of yourself and others.

Rating of Me	Criteria	Rating of Others
	Engage In Conflicts Frequently	
	Knowledge of Negotiation Procedure	
	Overall Level of Negotiation Skills	
	Able to Negotiate Agreements That Achieve Both Own And Other's Goals	
	Able to Negotiate So That Relationship Is Improved (Liking, Trust, Respect Increased)	
	Able to Improve Negotiation Skills Every Time A Conflict Is Resolved	

I   am _____
   am not _____   satisfied with the way I now solve conflicts.

I   would _____
   would not _____   like to learn ways to solve conflicts.

Name _____ Date _____

YOU'VE WON!!

Congratulations!

Your group has just won an all-expense-paid field trip for one week to the destination of your choosing. It can be anywhere in the world. Since it is a field trip, you will have no school for that week. Now comes the hard part -- where will your group choose to go?

1. Think of three places you would like to go. Write down your reasons for wanting to go there.

	Place	**Reason**
Place 1		
Place 2		
Place 3		

2. In order to make that choice, form pairs. Each pair will think up a list of three places that would be special to them to visit. The pairs will write down their choices and talk over reasons why they think their choices are wise ones. (A trip to someone's grandparent's house may be a fine choice, if that person can suggest things that all the group members would enjoy there.)

   a. Person A states where he or she wants to go. Person B states where he or she wants to go.

   b. Person A states his or her reasons. Person B states his or her reasons.

   c. The two reach an agreement as to where they would like to go as a pair and why.

3. After each pair has made its selection of places, two pairs combine to make a group of four. The group meets to choose a field-trip destination. The group must reach consensus in order to claim their prize.

4. Divide into two pairs. Working as a pair, define the words negotiate, negotiating, and negotiations.

DIVIDING OUR MONEY Exercise

Some conflicts begin because there is only so much of something several people want, and no one can have as much as he or she would like. Salaries, promotions, office space, supplies, and even food are often the sources of such conflicts. Where there is only so much money and several people have definite plans about how it should be used, not everyone has his or her plans adopted by the total group. This exercise focuses on such a conflict. It requires three people to divide some money two ways. If you participate actively in this lesson, you will become more aware of how you manage such conflicts. You will also be able to give other participants feedback on how they act during such conflicts. The specific procedure is as follows.

1. Divide into groups of three. Each person contributes one dollar to the group; the three dollars is placed in a pool.

2. The triad decides how to divide the money between two people. The majority rules. Only two people can receive money. The group has fifteen minutes to make this decision. The group cannot use any sort of "chance" procedure such as drawing straws or flipping a coin to decide which two people get what amounts of money. Side agreements--for instance, to buy a soda for the person left out--are not allowed. It is all right for one person to end up with all the money. A clear decision must be reached as to how the money is to be divided between not more than two people.

3. The purpose of this exercise is to get as much money for yourself as you can. Try to convince the other two members of your triad that you should receive all the money. Tell them you are broke, poor, smarter than they are, or more deserving of the money. Tell them you will put it to better use or will give it to charity. If the other two people make an agreement to divide the money between themselves, offer one of them a better deal. For example, if they agree to split the money fifty-fifty, tell one person that you will let that person have two dollars and will take only one dollar if he or she agrees to split the money with you.

4. The majority rules. Whenever two people make a firm agreement to split the money a certain way, the decision is made. Be sure, however, to give the third person a chance to offer one of the two a better deal.

 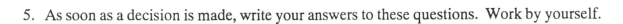

5. As soon as a decision is made, write your answers to these questions. Work by yourself.

   a. What were my feelings during the negotiations?

   b. How would my conflict strategies be described? Did I give up? Did I try to persuade others to my point of view? Did I try to take the money by force?

   c. What strategies did the other two individuals use in trying to get the money?

   d. What did I learn about how I manage conflicts?

6. In your group of three, give each other feedback describing how you saw each other's actions during the decision making. Use the rules for constructive feedback. Make sure all members of your triad receive feedback.

7. Combine into a group of six and discuss the following questions.

   a. What were the feelings present in each triad during the decision making?

   b. How did members act in each triad during the decision making?

   c. What conflict styles were present in each triad during the decision making?

   d. What did we learn about conflict from the lesson?

Abe Absentmind can't find his history book. He is convinced that Harry Findandkeep has two books and one of them is Abe's. Harry denies having Abe's book. In history class Abe walks by Harry's desk and suddenly grabs the history book in Harry's hands. Harry jumps up and tries to grab the book back, but Harry holds tight to the book and insists that it is his. Harry shoves Abe and demands the book back. Abe starts yelling that he is going to "get" Harry if he does not stop it.

Abe and Harry are in your class. In order to restore peace to the class without getting Abe and Harry in serious trouble, you wish to mediate the conflict. Your **task** is to explain how you would do so.

This is a **cooperative** assignment. Formulate one plan from the three of you, everyone must agree, everyone must be able to explain the group's plan.

NONVERBAL CONFLICTS Exercise

Thumb Wrestling: Lock fingers with another person with your thumbs straight up. Tap your thumbs together three times and then try to pin the other's thumb so that the other cannot move it.

Slapping hands: Person A puts her hands out, palms down. Person B extends his hands, palms up, under Person A's hands. The object of the exercise is for Person B to try to slap the hands of Person A by quickly moving his hands from the bottom to the top. As soon as Person B makes a move, Person A tries to pull her hands out of the way before Person B can slap them.

What Might YOU Do?

Here are three problems. You are to pretend you are the person in the conflict. You are to guess what you might do in the same situation. Write out your answer.

1 Another student is playing with a ball you would really like to use. You ask him nicely if you can have the ball and he says "no." You still want to play with it. What might you do?

2 You are reading a book. A classmate wants you to join their game. You want to be left alone. What might you do?

3 During lunch a classmate calls you "stupid." Your feelings are hurt. What might you do?

Form pairs. Share your answers. Come to an agreement as to what the person in each conflict should do. Write out your answers. One member will be choosen at random to present the pair's answers to the class.

1:39

How Conflicts Should Be Managed

1. Working with a partner, write out five rules for resolving your conflicts. There should be one set of answers for the two of you, both of you have to agree on the answers, and both of you have to be able to explain your answers to the teacher or the entire class.

   1.

   2.

   3.

   4.

   5.

2. Combine with another pair. Share your rules. Listen carefully to theirs. Use their ideas to improve your list.

   1.

   2.

   3.

   4.

   5.

Here is a list from another class:

1. Deal with the present, not the past (ancient history does not count).
2. No name calling (it only makes things worse).
3. No pushing, shoving, or hitting (physical violence makes things worse).
4. Stand up for yourself (You have a perfect right).
5. Talk to each other face-to-face (not behind each other's back).
6. Do not spread the conflict (keep it between the two or you).
7. Attack problems, not people.

What Are The Four Types Of Conflicts?

Working with a partner, write out in your own words the definitions of the types of conflict.

1. Conflict:

2. Controversy:

3. Conceptual Conflict:

4. Conflict Of Interests:

5. Developmental Conflict:

Name the type of conflict each of the following examples represents:

1. The same amount of water is poured into two glasses. One glass is tall and skinny and the other glass is short and fat. The student knows that each glass holds the same amount of water but at the same time believes that the tall glass has more water in it.

2. The grade is "A" is given to the "best" students in the class. Each student attempts to prove that he or she is a better student than the other students in the class.

3. Students are placed in groups of four. Two students argue that all nuclear energy plants should be closed. The other two students argue that nuclear energy is vital to meet our nation's energy needs in a safe way. The group must write one report on nuclear energy giving their best thinking on the subject.

4. One year a child is dependent on the teacher and wants to be noticed and approved of by the teacher all the tiime. The next year the child feels independent and does not want the teacher to express approval or liking.

Me and My Conflicts

Describe what you would do and feel in each of the situations given below.

Conflict	I Am Likely To:	I Feel:
When someone takes something of mine and will not give it back		
When someone tells me to do something I do not want to do .		
When someone pushes me or hits me for no reason .		
When someone calls me names .		
When someone blames me for something I did not do .		
When someone talks behind my back and says things that are lies		

Find a partner and form a pair. Compare your answers. If they are different, each should explain why he or she would act and feel that way. Then you should come to an agreement about what would be best to do.

Then make three conclusions about how conflicts should be managed.

1.

2.

3.

2 Creating a Cooperative Classroom Environment

The First Step

Throughout history, people have come together to accomplish feats that any one of them could not achieve alone and to share their joys and sorrows. Having children, hunting, building pyramids and cathedrals, and sending rockets to the moon are examples. Social interdependence is as old as the human species. Among the hominids, the almost modern **Homo sapiens** appeared at least 300,000 years ago, and the anatomically modern **Homo sapiens sapiens**, 40,000 years ago (Renshberger, 1984). From small tribes, to small communities, to small states and countries, to large countries, to a world-wide community, there has been an unmistakable increase in the size of the "we-group" within which murder is considered a crime among humans (Bigelow, 1972). It is only 10,000 years ago that agricultural communities began, marking the birth of civilization. Today there is no nation independent from the rest of the world. Raw materials, manufactured goods, consumers and markets, monetary systems, and preservation of the environment all cross national borders and illustrate the interdependence existing among humans throughout the world. The management of human interdependence on a global, national, regional, organizational, community, family, and interpersonal level is one of the most pressing issues of our time.

Interdependence carries the seeds of conflict. As diverse individuals and groups work together their interdependence creates conflicts. Conflict also threatens interdependence, for if conflict is managed destructively, relationships and coalitions can be destroyed, eliminating all possibility of cooperative efforts. When two people are in conflict, they always face the possibility that the relationship will be so damaged that all potential for future cooperation will be ended. If they plan to continue the relationship, conflict will be managed in constructive and caring ways. If they plan never to interact in the future, conflict may be managed in destructive and hurtful ways.

The first step in managing conflict effectively is to establish a constructive context. The context within which conflicts occur largely determines whether the conflict is managed constructively or destructively (Deutsch, 1973; Johnson & Johnson, 1989; Tjosvold & Johnson, 1983; Watson & Johnson, 1972). There are two possible contexts for conflict: cooperative and competitive (in individualistic situations individuals do not interact and, therefore, no conflict occurs).

Competitive Context

For competition to exist, there must be scarcity. I must defeat you to get what I want. Rewards are restricted to the few who perform the best. In a **competitive** situation, individuals work against each other to achieve a goal that only one or a few can attain. You can attain your goal if and only if the other people involved cannot attain their goals. Thus, competitors seek outcomes that are personally beneficial but detrimental to all others in the situation.

Conflicts usually do not go well in a competitive context. Within competitive situations, individuals typically have a short-term time orientation where all energies are focused on winning. Little or no attention is paid to maintaining a good relationship. Within competitive situations:

1. Communication tends to be avoided and when it does take place it tends to contain misleading information and threats. Threats, lies, and silence do not help students resolve conflicts with each other. Competition gives rise to espionage or other techniques to obtain information about the other that the other is unwilling to communicate, and "diversionary tactics" to delude or mislead the opponent about oneself.

2. There are frequent and common misperceptions and distortions of the other person's position and motivations that are difficult to correct. Students engage in **self-fulfilling prophecies** by perceiving another person as being immoral and hostile and behaving accordingly, thus evoking hostility and deceit from the other person. Students see small misbehaviors of opponents while ignoring one's own large misbehaviors (**mote-beam mechanism**). **Double standards** exist. Because preconceptions and expectations influence what is perceived, and because there is a bias towards seeing events in a way that justifies one's own beliefs and actions, and because conflict and threat impair perceptual and cognitive processes, the misperceptions are difficult to correct.

3. In a competitive situation, individuals have a suspicious, hostile attitude toward each other that increases their readiness to exploit each other's wants and needs and to refuse each other's requests.

4. In a competitive situation, individuals tend to deny the legitimacy of others' wants, needs, and feelings and to consider only their own interests.

Cooperative Context

For cooperation to exist there must be mutual goals that all parties are committed to achieving. I am not successful unless you are successful. The more successful you are, the more I benefit and the more successful I am. In a **cooperative** situation students work together to accomplish shared goals. Students seek outcomes that are beneficial to everyone involved. They are committed to each other's, as well as their own, well-being and success.

Conflicts usually go well in a cooperative context. Within cooperative situations, individuals typically have a long-term time orientation where energies are focused both on achieving goals and on building good working relationships with others. Within cooperative situations:

1. Effective and continued communication is of vital importance in resolving a conflict. Within a cooperative situation, the communication of relevant information tends to be open and honest, with each person interested in informing the other as well as being informed. Communication tends to be more frequent, complete, and accurate.

2. Perceptions of the other person and the other person's actions are far more accurate and constructive. Misperceptions and distortions such as self-fulfilling prophecies and double standards occur less frequently and are far easier to correct and clarify.

3. Individuals trust and like each other and, therefore, are willing to respond helpfully to each other's wants, needs, and requests.

4. Individuals recognize the legitimacy of each other's interests and search for a solution accommodating the needs of both sides. Conflicts tend to be defined as mutual problems to be solved in ways that benefit everyone involved.

Conclusions

Conflicts cannot be managed constructively within a competitive context. When competitive and individualistic learning dominates a classroom and school, conflicts will inevitably be destructive. Instead of trying to solve interpersonal problems, students will think short-term and go for the "win."

In order to resolve a conflict constructively there must be a clear perception of the other's positions and motivations, accurate and complete communication, a positive and trusting attitude toward the other, and a definition of the conflict as a mutual problem. It is only within a cooperative context that such conditions tend to exist.

If students are to learn how to manage conflicts constructively, a cooperative context must exist within the school. A cooperative context is established by structuring the majority of learning situations cooperatively. When cooperative learning is used over 50 percent of the time, students will develop the relationships and long-term perspective required to solve interpersonal problems effectively. While this chapter introduces cooperative learning, a more complete and thorough discussion may be found in **Circles of Learning** (Johnson, Johnson, & Holubec, 1990).

Types Of Interdependence

Teachers may structure academic lessons so that students are (a) in a win-lose struggle to see who is best, (b) learning individually on their own without interacting with classmates, or (c) learning in pairs or small groups helping each other master the assigned material. When lessons are structured **competitively**, students work against each other to achieve a goal that only one or a few students can attain. When lessons are structured **individualistically**, students work by themselves to accomplish learning goals unrelated to those of their classmates. When lessons are structured **cooperatively**, students work together to accomplish shared goals. Students are assigned to small groups and instructed to learn the assigned material and to make sure that the other members of the group also master the assignment. Individual performance is checked regularly to ensure all students are learning. A criteria-referenced evaluation system is used. In a cooperative learning situation, students' goal achievements are positively

correlated; students perceive that they can reach their learning goals if and only if the other students in the learning group also reach their goals. Thus, students seek outcomes that are beneficial to all those with whom they are cooperatively linked. Students discuss material with each other, help one another understand it, and encourage each other to work hard.

Basic Elements Of Cooperative Learning

Together we stand, divided we fall.

Watchword Of The American Revolution

In a classroom the teacher is trying out learning groups. "This is a mess," she thinks. In one group students are bickering over who is going to do the writing. In another group a member sits quietly, too shy to participate. Two members of a third group are talking about football while the third member works on the assignment. "My students do not know how to work cooperatively," the teacher concludes.

What is an teacher to do in such a situation? Simply placing students in groups and telling them to work together does not mean that they know how to cooperate or that they will do so even if they know. Many teachers believe that they are implementing cooperative learning when in fact they are missing its essence. **Putting students into groups to learn is not the same thing as structuring cooperation among students.** Cooperation is **not**:

1. Having students sit side by side at the same table and talk with each other as they do their individual assignments.

2. Having students do a task individually with instructions that the ones who finish first are to help the slower students.

3. Assigning a report to a group where one student does all the work and others put their name on it.

Cooperation is much more than being physically near other students, discussing material with other students, helping other students, or sharing materials with other students, although each of these is important in cooperative learning.

In order for a lesson to be cooperative, five basic elements are essential (Johnson, Johnson, & Holubec, 1990). In a math class, for example, an teacher assigns her students a set of math problems to solve. Students are placed in groups of three. The **instructional**

task is for students to solve each story problem correctly and understand the correct strategy for doing so. The teacher must now implement five basic elements. The first element of a cooperative lesson is **positive interdependence**. Students must believe that they are linked with others in a way that one cannot succeed unless the other members of the group succeed (and vice versa), that is, they "sink or swim together." Within the math lesson, the teacher creates positive goal interdependence by requiring group members to agree on the answer and the strategies for solving each problem. Positive role interdependence is structured by assigning each student a role. The **reader** reads the problems aloud to the group. The **checker** makes sure that all members can explain how to solve each problem correctly. The **encourager** in a friendly way encourages all members of the group to participate in the discussion, sharing their ideas and feelings. Resource interdependence is created by giving each group one copy of the problems to be solved. All students work the problems on scratch paper and share their insights with each other. Positive reward interdependence is structured by giving each group five points if all members score above 90 percent correct on the test given at the end of the unit. The most important type of interdependence is goal interdependence. All cooperative learning starts with a mutually shared group goal.

The second element of a cooperative lesson is **face-to-face promotive interaction** among students, which exists when students help, assist, encourage, and support each other's efforts to learn. Students promote each other's learning by orally explaining to each other how to solve problems, discussing with each other the nature of the concepts and strategies being learned, teaching their knowledge to each other, and explaining to each other the connections between present and past learning. In the math lesson, the teacher must provide the time, knee-to-knee seating arrangement, and teacher encouragement for students to exchange ideas and help each other learn.

The third element is **individual accountability**, which exists when the performance of each individual student is assessed and the results given back to the group and the individual. It is important that group members know (a) who needs more assistance in completing the assignment and (b) they cannot "hitch-hike" on the work of others. Common ways of structuring individual accountability include giving an individual test to each student and randomly selecting one student's work to represent the efforts of the entire group.

The fourth element is **social skills**. Groups cannot function effectively if students do not have and use the needed leadership, decision-making, trust-building, communication, and conflict-management skills. These skills have to be taught just as purposefully and precisely as academic skills. Many students have never worked cooperatively in learning situations and, therefore, lack the needed social skills for doing so. In the math lesson the teacher emphasizes the skill of "checking to make sure everyone understands." The teacher defines

the skill as the phrases and the accompanying nonverbal behaviors to be used by the checker. The group roles are rotated each day. When the teacher sees students engaging in the skill, she verbally praises the group and/or records the instance on an observation sheet. Procedures and strategies for teaching students social skills may be found in Johnson (1990, 1991), Johnson and F. Johnson (1991), and Johnson, Johnson, and Holubec (1990).

Finally, the teacher must ensure that **groups process** how well they are achieving their goals and maintaining effective working relationships among members. At the end of the math period the groups **process** their functioning by answering two questions: (1) What is something each member did that was helpful for the group and (2) What is something each member could do to make the group even better tomorrow? Such processing enables learning groups to focus on group maintenance, facilitates the learning of social skills, ensures that members receive feedback on their participation, and reminds students to practice the small group skills required to work cooperatively. Some of the keys to successful processing are allowing sufficient time for it to take place, making it specific rather than vague, varying the format, maintaining student involvement in processing, reminding students to use their social skills while they process, and ensuring that clear expectations of the purpose of processing have been communicated. Often, each group is required to turn in a summary of their processing that is signed by all group members.

These five elements are what differentiates (a) cooperative learning groups from traditional discussion groups and (b) a well-structured cooperative learning lesson from a poorly structured one. The five elements are discussed in detail in Chapter 3. There are three broad types of cooperative learning groups that are structured through the use of the five basic elements. They are discussed in Chapters 4, 5, and 6.

Types of Cooperative Learning Groups

These problems are endemic to all institutions of education, regardless of level. Children sit for 12 years in classrooms where the implicit goal is to listen to the teacher and memorize the information in order to regurgitate it on a test. Little or no attention is paid to the learning process, even though much research exists documenting that real understanding is a case of active restructuring on the part of the learner. Restructuring occurs through engagement in problem posing as well as problem solving, inference making and investigation, resolving of contradictions, and reflecting. These processes all mandate far more active learners, as well as a different model of education than the one subscribed to at present by most institutions. Rather than being powerless and dependent on the institution, learners need to be empowered to think and learn for themselves. Thus, learning needs to be conceived of as something a learner does, not something that is done to a learner.

Catherine Fosnot (1989)

Students often feel helpless and discouraged, especially when facing a difficult class or when they have just entered a new school. Giving them cooperative learning partners provides hope and opportunity. Perhaps the most important aspect of faculty life is empowering students by organizing them into cooperative teams. It is social support from and accountability to valued peers that motivates committed efforts to achieve and succeed. Cooperative learning groups empower their members by making them feel strong, capable, and committed. If classrooms are to be places where students care about each other and are committed to each other's success in academic endeavors, a cooperative structure must exist. A cooperative structure consists of the integrated use of three types of cooperative learning groups.

Cooperative learning groups may be used to teach specific content (**formal cooperative learning groups**), to ensure active cognitive processing of information during a lecture (**informal cooperative learning groups**), and to provide long-term support and assistance for academic progress (**cooperative base groups**). Any assignment in any curriculum may be done cooperatively. In **formal cooperative learning groups** the teacher structures the learning groups (deciding on group size and how to assign students to groups); teaches the academic concepts, principles, and strategies that the students are to master and apply; assigns a task to be completed cooperatively; monitors the functioning of the learning groups and intervenes to (a) teach collaborative skills and (b) provide assistance in academic learning when it is needed; and then evaluates student learning and guides the processing by learning groups of their effectiveness.

During a lecture **informal cooperative learning groups** can be used to focus student attention on the material to be learned, set a mood conducive to learning, help set expectations as to what will be covered in a class session, ensure that students cognitively process the material being taught, and provide closure to an instructional session. Students can summarize in three-to-five minute discussions what they know about a topic in focused discussions before and after a lecture. Short three-to-five minute discussions in cooperative pairs can be interspersed throughout a lecture. In this way the main problem of lectures can be countered: The information passes from the notes of the teacher to the notes of the student without passing through the mind of either one.

Finally, **cooperative base groups** can be used to provide each student the support, encouragement, and assistance he or she needs to make academic progress. Base groups meet daily (or whenever the class meets). They are permanent (lasting from one to several years) and provide the long-term caring peer relationships necessary to influence members consistently to work hard in school. The use of base groups tends to improve attendance, personalize the work required and the school experience, and improve the quality and quantity of learning. The larger the class or school and the more complex and difficult the subject matter, the more important it is to have base groups.

When used in combination, cooperative formal, informal, and base groups provide an overall structure for learning.

Outcomes Of Cooperation

When you are playing with a group of guys, as opposed to a single sport, it's different. You can play tennis and win a championship and know you've accomplished something. But when you can look in the eyes of teammates and can share that feeling, it's something you can't describe.

Bryan Trottier, Pittsburg Penguins Hockey Team

Learning together to complete assignments can have profound effects on students and teachers. A great deal of research has been conducted comparing the relative effects of cooperative, competitive, and individualistic efforts on instructional outcomes (Johnson & Johnson, 1974, 1978, 1983, 1989; Johnson, Johnson, & Maruyama, 1983; Johnson, Maruyama, Johnson, & Skon, 1981; Pepitone, 1980; Sharan, 1980; Slavin, 1983). These research studies began in the late 1800's when Triplett (1897) in the United States, Turner (1889) in England, and Mayer (1903) in Germany conducted a series of studies on the factors associated with competitive performance. The amount of research that has been conducted since is staggering. During the past 90 years over 575 experimental and 100 correlational studies have been conducted by a wide variety of researchers in different decades with different age subjects, in different subject areas, and in different settings (see Johnson & Johnson, 1989a for a complete listing of these studies). In our own research program at the Cooperative Learning Center (University of Minnesota) over the past 25 years we have conducted over 85 studies to refine our understanding of how cooperation works. We know far more about the efficacy of cooperative learning than we know about lecturing, depart-

Figure 2.1

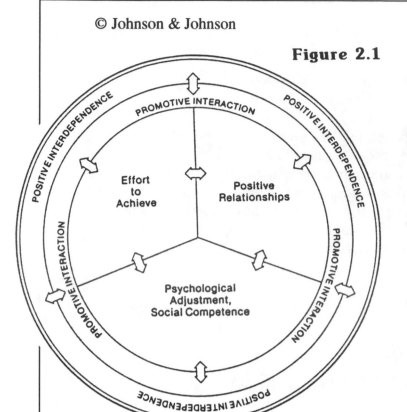

OUTCOMES of COOPERATION

mentalization, the use of technology, or almost any other facet of education. A comprehensive review of all studies and meta-analyses of their results may be found in Johnson and Johnson (1989a).

Building on the theorizing of Kurt Lewin and Morton Deutsch, the premise may be made that the type of interdependence structured among students determines how they interact with each other which, in turn largely determines instructional outcomes. Structuring situations cooperatively results in promotive interaction, structuring situations competitively results in oppositional interaction, and structuring situations individualistically results in no interaction among students. These interaction patterns affect numerous variables, which may be subsumed within the three broad and interrelated outcomes of effort exerted to achieve, quality of relationships among participants, and participants' psychological adjustment and social competence (see Figure 2.1) (Johnson & Johnson, 1989a).

Positive interdependence results in students promoting each other's learning and achievement. **Promotive interaction** may be defined as individuals encouraging and facilitating each other's efforts to achieve, complete tasks, and produce in order to reach the group's goals. While positive interdependence in and of itself may have some effect on outcomes, it is the face-to-face promotive interaction among individuals fostered by the positive interdependence that most powerfully influences efforts to achieve, caring and committed relationships, and psychological adjustment and social competence. Students focus both on increasing their own achievement **and** on increasing the achievement of their groupmates. Promotive interaction is characterized by individuals (Johnson & Johnson, 1989a):

1. Providing each other with efficient and effective help and assistance.

2. Exchanging needed resources such as information and materials and processing information more efficiently and effectively.

3. Providing each other with feedback in order to improve the subsequent performance of their assigned tasks and responsibilities.

4. Challenging each other's conclusions and reasoning in order to promote higher quality decision making and greater insight into the problems being considered.

5. Advocating the exertion of effort to achieve mutual goals.

6. Influencing each other's efforts to achieve the group's goals.

7. Acting in trusting and trustworthy ways.

8. Being motivated to strive for mutual benefit.

9. Having a moderate level of arousal characterized by low anxiety and stress.

Negative interdependence typically results in students opposing and obstructing each other's learning. **Oppositional interaction** occurs as students discourage and obstruct each other's efforts to achieve. Students focus both on increasing their own achievement **and** on preventing any classmate from achieving higher than they do. **No interaction** exists when students work independently without any interaction or interchange with each other. Students focus only on increasing their own achievement and ignore as irrelevant the efforts of others.

Different learning outcomes result from the student-student interaction patterns promoted by the use of cooperative, competitive, and individualistic goal structures (Johnson & Johnson, 1989a). The numerous outcomes of cooperative efforts may be subsumed within three broad categories: effort to achieve, positive interpersonal relationships, and psychological adjustment. Since research participants have varied as to economic class, age, sex, and cultural background, since a wide variety of research tasks and measures of the dependent variables have been used, and since the research has been conducted by many different researchers with markedly different orientations working in different settings and in different decades, the overall body of research on social interdependence has considerable generalizability.

Achievement

Over 375 studies have been conducted over the past 90 years to give an answer to the question of how successful competitive, individualistic, and cooperative efforts are in promoting productivity and achievement (Johnson & Johnson, 1989a). When all of the studies were included in the analysis, the average student cooperating performed at about 3/4 a standard deviation above the average student learning within a competitive (effect size = 0.67) or individualistic situation (effect size = 0.64). When only high-quality studies were included in the analysis, the effect sizes were 0.88 and 0.61, respectively. The effect sizes are higher for the studies using pure operationalizations of cooperative learning than for studies using mixed operationalizations (cooperative vs. competitive, pure = 0.71 and mixed = 0.40, cooperative vs. individualistic, pure = 0.65 and mixed = 0.42). Cooperative learning, furthermore, resulted in more higher-level reasoning, more frequent generation of new ideas and solutions (i.e., **process gain**), and greater transfer of what is learned within one situation to another (i.e., **group to individual transfer**) than did competitive or individualistic learning.

Interpersonal Attraction And Cohesion

Cooperative learning experiences, compared with competitive, individualistic, and "traditional instruction," promote considerably more liking among students (effect sizes = 0.66 and 0.60, respectively) (Johnson & Johnson, 1989a; Johnson, Johnson, & Maruyama, 1983). Students who studied cooperatively, compared with those who studied competitively or individualistically, developed considerably more commitment and caring for each other no matter what their initial impressions of and attitudes toward each other were. When only the high quality studies were included in the analysis, the effect sizes were 0.82 (cooperative vs. competitive) and 0.62 (cooperative vs. individualistic) respectively. The effect sizes were higher for the studies using pure operationalizations of cooperative learning than for studies using mixed operationalizations (cooperative vs. competitive, pure = 0.79 and mixed = 0.46, cooperative vs. individualistic, pure = 0.66 and mixed = 0.36). Students learning cooperatively also liked the teacher better and perceived the teacher as being more supportive and accepting academically and personally. In addition, when students are heterogeneous with regard to ethnic, social class, language, and ability differences, cooperative learning experiences are a necessity for building positive peer relationships.

Psychological Health

When students leave school, they need the psychological health and stability required to build and maintain career, family, and community relationships, to establish a basic and meaningful interdependence with other people, and to participate effectively in society. We have conducted a series of studies on the relationship between cooperation and psychological health. Our studies (see Johnson & Johnson, 1989a) indicate that **cooperativeness** is positively related to a number of indices of psychological health, namely: emotional maturity, well-adjusted social relations, strong personal identity, and basic trust in and optimism about people. **Competitiveness** seems also to be related to a number of indices of psychological health, while **individualistic attitudes** tend to be related to a number of indices of psychological pathology, such as emotional immaturity, social maladjustment, delinquency, self-alienation, and self-rejection. Schools should be organized cooperatively to reinforce those traits and tendencies that promote students' psychological well-being.

Social perspective taking is the ability to understand how a situation appears to another person and how that person is reacting cognitively and emotionally to the situation. The opposite of perspective taking is **egocentrism**, the embeddedness in one's own viewpoint to the extent that one is unaware of other points of view and of the limitation of one's perspective. Cooperative learning experiences tend to promote greater cognitive and affective perspective taking than do competitive or individualistic learning experiences (Johnson & Johnson, 1989a).

Cooperation tends to promote higher levels of self-esteem than do competitive and individualistic efforts (effect sizes = 0.58 and 0.44, respectively). Within **competitive** situations self-esteem tends to be based on the contingent view of one's competence that, "If I win, then I have worth as a person, but if I lose, then I have no worth." Within **individualistic** situations, students are isolated from one another, receive little direct comparison with or feedback from peers, and perceive evaluations as inaccurate and unrealistic. A defensive avoidance, evaluation apprehension, and distrust of peers results. Within **cooperative** situations, individuals tend to interact, promote each other's success, form multi-dimensional and realistic impressions of each other's competencies, and give accurate feedback. Such interaction tends to promote a basic self-acceptance of oneself as a competent person. High self-esteem seems desirable as individuals with low self-esteem tend to (Johnson & Johnson, 1989a):

1. Have low productivity due to setting low goals for themselves, lacking confidence in their ability, and assuming that they will fail no matter how hard they try.

2. Be critical of others as well as themselves by looking for flaws in others and trying to "tear them down."

3. Withdraw socially due to feeling self-conscious, awkward, and vulnerable to rejection.

4. Be conforming, agreeable, highly persuasible, and highly influenced by criticism.

5. Develop more psychological problems such as anxiety, nervousness, insomnia, depression, and psychosomatic symptoms.

Reciprocal Relationships Among The Three Outcomes

The reason we were so good, and continued to be so good, was because he (Joe Paterno) forces you to develop an inner love among the players. It is much harder to give up on your buddy, than it is to give up on your coach. I really believe that over the years the teams I played on were almost unbeatable in tight situations. When we needed to get that six inches we got it because of our love for each other. Our camaraderie existed because of the kind of coach and kind of person Joe was.

Dr. David Joyner

Efforts to achieve, positive interpersonal relationships, and psychological health are reciprocally related (see Figure 2.1). Within cooperative situations, the causal arrows connecting the three outcomes are all bidirectional. Each induces the others.

Joint efforts to achieve mutual goals create caring and committed relationships; caring and committed relationships among group members increase their effort to achieve (Johnson & Johnson, 1989a). From working together to accomplish academic tasks, students develop camaraderie and friendships. As students strive together, helping each other, sharing materials, exchanging ideas and information, and encouraging each other's efforts they get to know each other, become committed to each other, and develop friendships. Caring relationships come from mutual accomplishment, mutual pride in joint work, and the bonding that results from joint efforts. **At the same time**, caring and committed relationships promote joint efforts to achieve mutual goals. Individuals seek out opportunities to work with those they care about. As caring increases, so does regular attendance, commitment to learning and achievement, personal responsibility to do one's share of the work, willingness to take on difficult tasks, motivation and persistence in working toward goal achievement, willingness to listen to and be influenced by groupmates, and willingness to endure pain and frustration on behalf of the group (Johnson & F. Johnson,

1991; Johnson & R. Johnson, 1989; Watson & Johnson, 1972). All these contribute to group productivity. The most successful leaders in business and industry are ones that build teams with such personal closeness that team members feel like a family (Kouses & Posner, 1987).

Joint efforts to achieve mutual goals promote psychological health and social competence; the more healthy psychologically group members are, the more able they are to contribute to the joint effort (Johnson & Johnson, 1989a). Cooperating involves contributing to others' success and well-being, knowing there are others who contribute to your success and well-being, and being involved in a joint effort greater than oneself. Working together to complete academic tasks increases a person's social competencies, success, sense of meaning and purpose, ability to cope with failure and anxiety, self-esteem, and self-efficacy. Contributing to others' success has been found to cure the blues (i.e., decrease depression). Knowing that one's efforts contribute to the success of others as well as oneself gives added meaning and value to academic work. **At the same time**, the healthier psychologically individuals are, the better able they are to work with others to achieve mutual goals. States of depression, anxiety, guilt, shame, and fear interfere with ability to cooperate and decrease the energy a person has to devote to a cooperative effort. Joint efforts require coordination, effective communication, leadership, and conflict management which, in turn, require social competencies.

The more caring and committed the relationships among group members, the greater their psychological health and social competencies tend to be; the healthier members are psychologically, the more able they are to build and maintain caring and committed relationships (Johnson & Johnson, 1989a). Psychological health is built on the internalization of the caring and respect received from loved-ones. Psychological health and the ability to cope with stress are built through internalization of positive relationships, direct social support, shared intimacy, and expressions of caring. Friendships are developmental advantages that promote self-esteem, self-efficacy, and general psychological adjustment. Destructive relationships, and even the absence of caring and committed relationships, tend to increase psychological pathology. **At the same time**, the healthier people are psychologically (i.e., free of psychological pathology such as depression, paranoia, anxiety, fear of failure, repressed anger, hopelessness, and meaninglessness), the more able they are to initiate, build, and maintain caring and committed relationships.

With the amount of research evidence available, it is surprising that classroom practice is so oriented toward individualistic and competitive learning. It is time for the discrepancy to be reduced between what research indicates is effective in teaching and what teachers actually do.

The Teacher's Role: Being "A Guide On The Side"

Each class session teachers make the choice of being "a sage on the stage" or "a guide on the side." In doing so they might remember that the challenge in teaching is not **covering** the material **for** the students, it's **uncovering** the material **with** the students.

One of Roger's favorite demonstration science lessons is to ask students to determine how long a candle burns in a quart jar. He assigns students to groups of two, making the pairs as heterogeneous as possible. Each pair is given one candle and one quart jar (resource interdependence). He gives the instructional task of timing how long the candle will burn and the cooperative goal of deciding on one answer that both pair members can explain. Students are to encourage each other's participation and elaborate what they are learning to previous lessons (social skills). Students light their candle, place the quart jar over it, and time how long the candle burns. The answers from the pairs are announced. Roger then gives the pairs the task of generating a number of answers to the question, "How many factors make a difference in how long the candle burns in the jar?" The answers from the pairs are written on the board. The pairs then repeat the experiment in ways that test which of the suggested factors do in fact make a difference in how long the candle burns. The next day students individually take a quiz on the factors affecting the time a candle burns in a quart jar (individual accountability) and their scores are totaled to determine a joint score that, if high enough, earns them bonus points (reward interdependence). They spend some time discussing the helpful actions of each member and what they could do to be even more effective in the future (group processing).

Science experiments are only one of the many places cooperative learning may be used. Cooperative learning is appropriate for any instructional task in any subject area and with any age student. Whenever the learning goals are highly important, the task is complex or conceptual, problem solving is required, divergent thinking or creativity is desired, quality of performance is expected, higher level reasoning strategies and critical thinking are needed, long-term retention is desired, or when the social development of students is one of the major instructional goals--cooperative learning should be used (Johnson & Johnson, 1989a).

The teacher's role in using formal cooperative learning groups includes five parts (Johnson & Johnson, 1991; Johnson, Johnson, & Holubec, 1990):

1. Specifying the objectives for the lesson.

2. Making decisions about placing students in learning groups before the lesson is taught.

3. Explaining the task and goal structure to the students.

4. Monitoring the effectiveness of the cooperative learning groups and intervening to provide task assistance (such as answering questions and teaching task skills) or to increase students' interpersonal and group skills.

5. Evaluating the students' achievement and helping students discuss how well they collaborated with each other.

Specifying the Instructional Objectives

There are two types of objectives that a teacher needs to specify before the lesson begins. The **academic objective** needs to be specified at the correct level for the students and matched to the right level of instruction according to a conceptual or task analysis. The **social skills objective** details what interpersonal and small group skills are going to be emphasized during the lesson. A common error many teachers make is to specify only academic objectives and to ignore the social skills objectives needed to train students to cooperate effectively with each other.

Preinstructional Decisions

Deciding on the Size of the Group

Once the objectives of the lesson are clear, the teacher must decide which size of learning group is optimal. Cooperative learning groups typically range in size from 2 to 4. In selecting the size of a cooperative learning group remember that the shorter the amount of time available, the smaller the group should be; the larger the group, the more resources available for the group's work but the more skills required to ensure that the group works productively. Sometimes the materials or equipment available or the specific nature of the task may dictate a group size.

Assigning Students to Groups

Teachers often ask four basic questions about assigning students to groups:

1. **Should students be placed in learning groups homogeneous or heterogeneous in member ability?** There are times when cooperative learning groups homogeneous in ability may be used to master specific skills or to achieve certain instructional objectives. Generally, however, we recommend that teachers maximize the heterogeneity of students, placing high- , medium-, and low-achieving students within the same learning group. More elaborative thinking, more frequent giving and receiving of explanations, and greater perspective taking in discussing material seems to occur in heterogeneous groups, all of which increase the depth of understanding, the quality of reasoning, and the accuracy of long-term retention.

2. **Should nontask-oriented students be placed in learning groups with task-oriented peers or be separated?** To keep nonacademically-oriented students on task it often helps to place them in a cooperative learning group with task-oriented peers.

3. **Should students select whom they want to work with or should the teacher assign students to groups?** Teacher-made groups often have the best mix since teachers can put together optimal combinations of students. Random assignment, such as having students "count off" is another possibility for getting a good mix of students in each group. Having students select their own groups is often not very successful. Student-selected groups often are homogeneous with high-achieving students working with other high-achieving students, white students working with other white students, minority students working with other minority students, and males working with other males. Often there is less on-task behavior in student-selected than in teacher-selected groups. A useful modification of the "select your own group" method is to have students list whom they would like to work with and then place them in a learning group with one person they choose and one or two or more students that the teacher selects.

4. **How long should the groups stay together?** Actually, there is no formula or simple answer to this question. Some teachers keep cooperative learning groups together for an entire year or semester. Other teachers like to keep a learning group together only long enough to complete a task, unit, or chapter. Sooner or later, however, every student should work with every other classmate. Our best advice is to allow groups to remain stable long enough for them to be successful. Breaking up groups that are

having trouble functioning effectively is often counterproductive as the students do not learn the skills they need to resolve problems in collaborating with each other.

Arranging the Room

How the teacher arranges the room is a symbolic message of what is appropriate behavior and it can facilitate the learning groups within the classroom. Members of a learning group should sit close enough to each other that they can share materials, maintain eye contact with all group members, and talk to each other quietly without disrupting the other learning groups. The teacher should have a clear access lane to every group. Within each learning group students need to be able to see all relevant task materials, see each other, converse with each other without raising their voices, and exchange ideas and materials in a comfortable atmosphere. The groups need to be far enough apart so that they do not interfere with each other's learning.

Planning the Instructional Materials to Promote Interdependence

Materials need to be distributed among group members so that all members participate and achieve. When a group is mature and experienced and group members have a high level of interpersonal and small group skills, the teacher may not have to arrange materials in any specific way. When a group is new or when members are not very skilled, however, teachers may wish to distribute materials in carefully planned ways to communicate that the assignment is to be a joint (not an individual) effort and that the students are in a "sink or swim together" learning situation. Three of the ways of doing so are:

1. **Materials Interdependence**: Give only one copy of the materials to the group. The students will then have to work together in order to be successful. This is especially effective the first few times the group meets. After students are accustomed to working cooperatively, teachers can give a copy of the materials to each student.

2. **Information Interdependence**: Group members may each be given different books or resource materials to be synthesized. Or the materials may be arranged like a jigsaw puzzle so that each student has part of the materials needed to complete the task. Such procedures require that every member participate in order for the group to be successful.

3. **Interdependence from Outside Enemies**: Materials may be structured into a tournament format with intergroup competition as the basis to promote a perception

of interdependence among group members. Such a procedure was introduced by DeVries and Edwards (1973). In the teams-games-tournament format students are divided into heterogeneous cooperative learning teams to prepare members for a tournament in which they compete with the other teams. During the intergroup competition the students individually compete against members of about the same ability level from other teams. The team whose members do the best in the competition is pronounced the winner by the teacher.

All of these procedures may not be needed simultaneously. They are alternative methods of ensuring that students perceive that they are involved in a "sink or swim together" learning situation and behave collaboratively.

Assigning Roles to Ensure Interdependence

Positive interdependence may also be structured through the assignment of complementary and interconnected roles to group members. In addition to their responsibility to learn, each group member can be assigned a responsibility to help groupmates work together effectively. Such roles include a **summarizer** (who restates the group's major conclusions or answers), a **checker of understanding** (who ensures that all group members can explicitly explain how to arrive at an answer or conclusion), an **accuracy coach** (who corrects any mistakes in another member's explanations or summaries), an **elaborator** (who relates current concepts and strategies to material studied previously), a **researcher-runner** (who gets needed materials for the group and communicates with the other learning groups and the teacher), a **recorder** to write down the group's decisions and edit the group's report, an **encourager of participation** who ensures that all members are contributing, and an **observer** who keeps track of how well the group is cooperating. Assigning such roles is an effective method of teaching students social skills and fostering positive interdependence.

Roles such as checking for understanding and elaborating are vital to high-quality learning but are often absent. The role of checker, for example, focuses on periodically asking each groupmate to explain what is being learned. From their research review, Rosenshine and Stevens (1986) concluded that "checking for comprehension" was significantly associated with higher levels of student learning and achievement. Wilson (1987) conducted a three-year, college teaching-improvement study and found that the teaching behavior faculty and students perceived faculty needing the most help on was "knows if the class is understanding the material or not." Wilson found that checking for understanding was highly correlated with overall effectiveness as an teacher. While the teacher cannot continually check the understanding of every student in the class (especially if there are 300

students in the class), the teacher can engineer such checking by having students work in cooperative groups and assigning one member the role of checker.

Structuring The Task And Positive Interdependence

Explaining the Academic Task

Teachers explain the academic task so that students are clear about the assignment and understand the objectives of the lesson. Direct teaching of concepts, principles, and strategies may take place at this point. Teachers may wish to answer any questions students have about the concepts or facts they are to learn or apply in the lesson. Teachers need to consider several aspects of explaining an academic assignment to students:

1. **Set the task so that students are clear about the assignment.** Most teachers have considerable practice with this already. Instructions that are clear and specific are crucial in warding off student frustration. One advantage of cooperative learning groups is that they can handle more ambiguous tasks (when they are appropriate) than can students working alone. In cooperative learning groups students who do not understand what they are to do will ask their group for clarification before asking the teacher.

2. **Explain the objectives of the lesson and relate the concepts and information to be studied to students' past experience and learning to ensure maximum transfer and retention.** Explaining the intended outcomes of the lesson increases the likelihood that students will focus on the relevant concepts and information throughout the lesson.

3. **Define relevant concepts, explain procedures students should follow, and give examples to help students understand what they are to learn and do in completing the assignment.** To promote positive transfer of learning, point out the critical elements that separate this lesson from past learnings.

4. **Ask the class specific questions to check the students' understanding of the assignment.** Such questioning ensures thorough two-way communication, that the assignment has been given effectively, and that the students are ready to begin completing it.

Explaining Criteria for Success

Evaluation within cooperatively structured lessons needs to be criterion-referenced. Criteria must be established for acceptable work (rather than grading on a curve). Teachers may structure a second level of cooperation by not only keeping track of how well each group and its members are performing, but also by setting criteria for the whole class to reach. Improvement (doing better this week than one did last week) may be set as a criterion of excellence.

Structuring Positive Interdependence

Communicate to students that they have a group goal and must work cooperatively. We cannot overemphasize the importance of communicating to students that they are in a "sink or swim together" learning situation. In a cooperative learning group students are responsible for learning the assigned material, making sure that all other group members learn the assigned material, and making sure that all other class members successfully learn the assigned material, in that order. Teachers can do this in several ways.

1. **Structure positive goal interdependence by giving the group the responsibility of ensuring that all members achieve a prescribed mastery level on the assigned materials.** Teachers may wish to say, "One answer from the group, everyone has to agree, and everyone has to be able to explain how to solve the problem or complete the assignment." Teachers may establish the prescribed mastery level as (a) individual levels of performance that each group member must achieve in order for the group as a whole to be successful (the group goal is for each member to demonstrate 90 percent mastery on a curriculum unit) or (b) improvement scores (the group goal is to ensure that all members do better this week than they did last week).

2. **Structure positive reward interdependence by providing group rewards and celebrations**. Bonus points may be added to all members' academic scores when everyone in the group achieves up to criterion. Or bonus points may be given to each member when the total of all group members' scores is above a preset criterion of excellence.

Positive interdependence creates peer encouragement and support for learning. Such positive peer pressure influences underachieving students to become academically involved. Members of cooperative learning groups should give two interrelated messages, "Do your work--we're counting on you!" and "How can I help you to do better?"

Structuring Individual Accountability

One of the purposes of a cooperative group is to make each member a stronger individual in his or her own right. This is usually accomplished by maximizing the learning of each member. A group is not truly cooperative if members are "slackers" who let others do all the work. To ensure that all members learn, and that groups know which members to provide with encouragement and help, teachers need to assess frequently the level of performance of each group member. Observing the participation patterns of each group member, giving practice tests, randomly selecting members to explain answers, having members edit each other's work, having students teach what they know to someone else, and having students use what they have learned on a different problem are ways to structure individual accountability.

Structuring Intergroup Cooperation

The positive outcomes found within a cooperative learning group can be extended throughout a whole class by structuring intergroup cooperation. Bonus points may be given if all members of a class reach a preset criteria of excellence. When a group finishes its work, the teacher should encourage the members to find other groups who are finished and compare and explain answers and strategies.

Specifying Desired Behaviors

The word **cooperation** has many different connotations and uses. Teachers will need to define cooperation operationally by specifying the behaviors that are appropriate and desirable within the learning groups. There are beginning behaviors, such as "stay with your group and do not wander around the room," "use quiet voices," "take turns," and "use each other's names." When groups begin to function effectively, expected behaviors may include:

1. Having each member explain how to get the answer.

2. Asking each member to relate what is being learned to previous learnings.

SKILLFUL GROUP MEMBERS ARE MADE – NOT BORN.

3. Checking to make sure everyone in the group understands the material and agrees with the answers.

4. Encouraging everyone to participate.

5. Listening accurately to what other group members are saying.

6. Not changing your mind unless you are logically persuaded (majority rule does not promote learning).

7. Criticizing ideas, not people.

Teachers should not make the list of expected behaviors too long. One or two behaviors to emphasize for a few lessons is enough. Students need to know what behavior is appropriate and desirable within a cooperative learning group, but they should not be subjected to information overload.

Monitoring And Intervening

Monitoring Students' Behavior

The teacher's job begins in earnest when the cooperative learning groups start working. Resist that urge to go get a cup of coffee or grade some papers. Much of your time in cooperative learning situations should be spent observing group members in order to (a) obtain a "window" into students' minds to see what they do and do not understand and (b) see what problems they are having in working together cooperatively. Through working cooperatively students will make hidden thinking processes overt and subject to observation and commentary. You will be able to observe how students are constructing their understanding of the assigned material. A variety of observation instruments and procedures that can be used for these purposes can be found in Johnson and F. Johnson (1991) and in Johnson, Johnson, and Holubec (1991a, 1991b).

Providing Task Assistance

In monitoring the groups as they work, teachers will wish to clarify instructions, review important procedures and strategies for completing the assignment, answer questions, and teach task skills as necessary. In discussing the concepts and information to be learned, teachers will wish to use the language or terms relevant to the learning. Instead of saying, "Yes, that is right," teachers will wish to say something more specific to the assignment, such as, "Yes, that is one way to find the main idea of a paragraph." The use of the more specific statement reinforces the desired learning and promotes positive transfer by helping the students associate a term with their learning. One way to intervene is to interview a cooperative learning group by asking them (a) What are you doing?, (b) Why are you doing it?, and (c) How will it help you?

Intervening to Teach Social Skills

While monitoring the learning groups teachers will also find students who do not have the necessary social skills and groups where problems in cooperating have arisen. **In these cases the teacher will wish to intervene to suggest more effective procedures for working together and more effective behaviors for students to engage in.** Teachers may also wish to intervene and reinforce particularly effective and skillful behaviors that they notice. The social skills required for productive group work, along with activities that may be used in teaching them, are covered in Johnson and F. Johnson (1991) and Johnson (1990, 1991).

Teachers should not intervene any more than is absolutely necessary In the groups. Most of us as teachers are geared to jumping in and solving problems for students to get them back on track. With a little patience we would find that cooperative groups can often work their way through their own problems (task and maintenance) and acquire not only a solution, but also a method of solving similar problems in the future. Choosing when to intervene and when not to is part of the art of teaching. Even when intervening, teachers can turn the problem back to the group to solve. Many teachers intervene in a group by having members set aside their task, pointing out the problem, and asking the group to create three possible solutions and decide which solution they are going to try first.

Evaluating Learning And Processing Interaction

Providing Closure to the Lesson

At the end of the lesson students should be able to summarize what they have learned and to understand where they will use it in future lessons. Teachers may wish to summarize the major points in the lesson, ask students to recall ideas or give samples, and answer any final questions students have.

Evaluating the Quality and Quantity of Students' Learning

Tests should be given and papers and presentations should be graded. The learning of group members must be evaluated by a criterion-referenced system for cooperative learning to be successful.

Processing How Well the Group Functioned

An old observational rule is, **if you observe, you must process your observations with the group.** Even if class time is limited, some time should be spent in **small group processing** as members discuss how effectively they worked together and what could be improved. Teachers may also wish to spend some time in **whole-class processing** where they give the class feedback and have students share incidents that occurred in their groups.

Discussing group functioning is essential. A common teaching error is to provide too brief a time for students to process the quality of their cooperation. Students do not learn from experiences that they do not reflect on. If the learning groups are to function better tomorrow than they did today, members must receive feedback, reflect on how their actions may be more effective, and plan how to be even more skillful during the next group session.

Establishing A Cooperative Relationship

Teachers can create a cooperative context by using cooperative learning the majority of the time. When a conflict occurs, however, you may need to establish a sense of interdependence between you and the other person. Whenever you are involved in a conflict, your first step is to establish the cooperative context. You can do this in several ways:

1. Pointing out to the other person that the two of you share a **common fate** where we both gain or lose depending on what we do. We strive for **mutual benefit** so that both will gain.

2. Recognize that outcomes are **mutually caused**. You can't do it alone. It takes the efforts of both of you. The mutual causation empowers both of you by giving you confidence that whenever "I can't, we can."

3. **You can encourage positive interdependence by "enlarging the shadow of the future":**

   a. Showing that the long-term benefits of cooperation outweigh the short-term benefits of taking advantage of the other group members or of not cooperating. Teachers may wish to demonstrate that sharing the work and helping each other learn is more productive and fun than competing or working alone. The long-term vision must be more compelling than the temptation of short-term personal advantage.

   b. Highlighting the facts that interactions among disputants will be frequent and their relationships will be durable. The shadow of the future looms largest when interactions among students are frequent and durable. **Durability** promotes cooperative efforts because it makes interpersonal relationships long lasting. It ensures that students will not easily forget how they have treated, and been treated by, each other. **Frequency** promotes stability by making the consequences of today's actions more salient for tomorrow's work. When students realize they will work with each other frequently and for a long period of time, they see the need to be cooperative and supportive in current dealings with each other.

4. Build a **shared identity** that includes both of you.

5. Frequently have **joint celebrations** to note the accomplishments you have made.

Processing Agreements

Group processing creates a procedure to examine agreements periodically to see if they are working. The students involved in the conflict (and the mediator if there is one) sit down and discuss (a) how well the agreement is working, (b) how well their relationship is working, and (c) does anything need to change in order to ensure that the conflict has been fruitfully resolved.

Conflict Lessons

As part of this book you will be going through a series of lessons on how to negotiate and mediate effectively. Each of these lessons is structured cooperatively. You can only learn how to negotiate by negotiating. That takes at least two people. You can only learn to mediate by mediating. That takes at least three people. For each lesson you participate in, you should be aware of the positive interdependence, promotive interaction, individual accountability, required social skills, and group processing. Structure each of these elements into every lesson.

Summary

The first step in managing conflict effectively is to establish a constructive context. There are two possible contexts for conflict: cooperative and competitive (in individualistic situations individuals do not interact and, therefore, no conflict occurs). In a **competitive context** a valued commodity (such as grades) is scarce and individuals work against each other to win. Each person tries to defeat others. Within such a context individuals do not share information and are as likely to mislead as to clarify. Competitors are likely to misperceive the other's intentions and distort rival's actions. Competitors tend to be suspicious of and hostile toward each other. They tend to deny the legitimacy of the rival's goals and consider only their own interests. In a competitive context you go for the win and then walk away.

In a **cooperative context** individuals work together to achieve shared goals. The more honestly they communicate with each other, the more accurately they perceive each other's actions, the more they trust each other, and the more committed they are to each other's interests, the better able individuals are to achieve their mutual goals. In a cooperative context problems are solved so that the joint effort to achieve mutual goals can continue.

To create a cooperative context within which conflicts can me resolved constructively, cooperative learning must be used the majority of time during the school day. Any lesson with any age student in any subject area may be taught cooperatively. All it takes is a teacher who is skilled in translating the old competitive and individualistic lessons into cooperative ones. In order to be cooperative, a lesson must include positive interdependence, face-to-face interaction among students, individual accountability, the use of collaborative skills, and the processing of how well the learning groups functioned. When done correctly, cooperative learning tends to promote higher achievement, greater motivation, more positive relationships among students, more positive attitudes toward the subject area and the teacher, greater self-esteem and psychological health, greater social skills, and many other important instructional outcomes. The teacher's role in structuring learning situations cooperatively involves clearly specifying the objectives for the lesson, placing students in learning groups and providing appropriate materials, clearly explaining the cooperative goal structure and learning task, monitoring students as they work, and evaluating students' performance.

Once cooperative learning has been established in the classroom, and a predominantly cooperative environment exists, a teacher is ready to take steps two and three. Step Two is the instructional use of intellectual conflicts. Intellectual conflicts may be promoted through the use of structured academic controversy. This topic is discussed at length in **Creative Conflict** (Johnson & Johnson, 1991). Step Three is teaching all students how to negotiate constructive resolutions to their conflicts of interests. The next chapter focuses on this issue.

⫷ CONTROVERSY CONTRACT ⫸

Major Learnings	Implementation Plans

Date _____   Date of Progress Report Meeting _____

Participant's Signature _____

Signatures of Other Group Members _____   _____

_____   _____   _____

❀ CONTROVERSY PROGRESS REPORT ❀

NAME _____ SCHOOL _____

AGE LEVEL _____ SUBJECT _____

Day and Date	Description of Tasks and Activities Performed	Successes Experienced	Problems Encountered

Description of critical or interesting incidents:

2:31

EXERCISE MATERIALS

* *Vocabulary Sheet*
* *Goal Structures*
* *Basic Elements of Cooperative Learning*
* *Contest of the Codes*
* *Conquering the Codes Together*
* *Concept Induction*
* *What Is It?*
* *When Are You Interdependent?*
* *Establishing Positive Interdependence*
* *The Teacher's Role in Cooperation*
* *Curriculum Adaptation*
* *Best Advice*
* *Breaking Balloons*
* *Blowing Off Steam*
* *Defusing the Bomb Exercise*

VOCABULARY SHEET

Working with a partner, learn the definitions of the words below.

1. Define each word in two ways.

   First, write down what you think the word means.

   Second, look it up in the book and write down its definition.

   Note the page on which the definition appears.

- cooperation

- competition

- individualistic learning

- individual accountability

- group processing

- positive interdependence

- promotive interaction

- goal structure

2. For each word write a sentence in which the word is used.

3. Make up a story in which all of the words are used.

4. Learn how to spell each word. They will be on your spelling test.

GOAL STRUCTURES

A learning **goal** is a desired future state of competence or mastery in the subject area being studied. A **goal structure** specifies the type of interdependence among students as they strive to accomplish their learning goals. Interdependence may be positive (cooperation), negative (competition), or none (individualistic efforts).

Cooperation: We Sink Or Swim Together

Teachers structure lessons so that students work together to maximize their own and each other's learning. Students work together to achieve shared goals.
- Work in small, often heterogeneous groups
- Strive for all group members' success
- What benefits self benefits others
- Joint success is celebrated
- Rewards are viewed as unlimited
- Evaluated by comparing performance to preset criteria

Competition: I Swim, You Sink; I Sink, You Swim

Teachers structure lessons so that students work against each other to achieve a goal only one or a few can attain.
- Work alone
- Strive to be better than classmates
- What benefits self deprives others
- Own success and others' failure is celebrated
- Rewards are limited
- Graded on a curve or ranked from "best" to "worst"

Individualistic: We Are Each In This Alone

Students work by themselves to accomplish learning goals unrelated to those of other students.
- Work alone
- Strive for own success
- What benefits self does not affect others
- Own success is celebrated
- Rewards are viewed as unlimited
- Evaluated by comparing performance to preset criteria

asic Elements Of Cooperative Learning

Positive Interdependence

Students perceive that they need each other in order to complete the group's task ("sink or swim together"). Teachers may structure positive interdependence by establishing **mutual goals** (learn and make sure all other group members learn), **joint rewards** (if all group members achieve above the criteria, each will receive bonus points), **shared resources** (one paper for each group or each member receives part of the required information), and **assigned roles** (summarizer, encourager of participation, elaborator).

Face-to-Face Promotive Interaction

Students promote each other's learning by helping, sharing, and encouraging efforts to learn. Students explain, discuss, and teach what they know to classmates. Teachers structure the groups so that students sit knee-to-knee and talk through each aspect of the assignment.

Individual Accountability

Each student's performance is frequently assessed and the results are given to the group and the individual. Teachers may structure individual accountability by giving an individual test to each student or randomly selecting one group member to give the answer.

Interpersonal And Small Group Skills

Groups cannot function effectively if students do not have and use the needed social skills. Teachers teach these skills as purposefully and precisely as academic skills. Collaborative skills include leadership, decision-making, trust-building, communication, and conflict-management skills.

Group Processing

Groups need specific time to discuss how well they are achieving their goals and maintaining effective working relationships among members. Teachers structure group processing by assigning such tasks as (a) list at least three member actions that helped the group be successful and (b) list one action that could be added to make the group even more successful tomorrow. Teachers also monitor the groups and give feedback on how well the groups are working together to the groups and the class as a whole.

CONTEST OF THE CODES:
Who'll Be the Best?

Your **task** is to solve the following codes. You have a set of coded messages and the same messages decoded. Your task is to identify the pattern so that you are able to write a message with the code.

This is a **competitive** activity. Work by yourself. Try to break the codes faster and more accurately than the other students. At the end of this activity you will be ranked from best to worst in breaking codes.

NEHWEHTGNITTESSIEVITITEPMOCIMIWS

WHENTHESETTINGISCOMPETITIVEISWIM

DNAUOYKNISROIKNISDNAUOYMIWS.

ANDYOUSINKORISINKANDYOUSWIM.

The pattern for this code is _____.

VA N PBBCRENGVIR TEBHC, GUR ZBER FHPPRFFSHY LBH NER
IN A COOPERATIVE GROUP, THE MORE SUCCESSFUL YOU ARE

GUR ZBER V ORARSVG NAQ GUR ZBER FHPPRFFSHY V NZ.
THE MORE I BENEFIT AND THE MORE SUCCESSFUL I AM.

The pattern for this code is _____.

GM   D H A 6 J   A 9 C   K 7 9 C 6 A 10 C 2   10 H   MH K 9 J
MY   G O A L S   A R E   U N R E L A T E D   TO   Y O U R S

L 4 C 7   LC   L H 9 F   E 72 E 11 E 2 KA 6 E J 10 EB A 66 M
W H E N   WE   W O R K   I N D I V I D U A L I S T I C A L L Y.

The pattern for this code is _____.

Conquering the Codes Together

Your **task** is to solve the following codes. You have a set of coded messages and the same messages decoded. Your task is to identify the pattern so that you are able to write a message with the code.

This is a **cooperative** activity. Work together. Encourage and assist each other's learning. Agree on one answer to each question. Every member must be able to explain what the code is and be able to write a message with the code.

---

18 5 13 5 13 2 5 18   20 8 1 20   9 14   1   3 15 15 16 5 18 1 20 9 22 5   7 18 15 21 16

R E M E M B E R   T H A T   I N   A   C O O P E R A T I V E   G R O U P

23 5   1 12 12   19 9 14 11   15 18   19 23 9 13   20 15 7 5 20 8 5 18

W E   A L L   S I N K   O R   S W I M   T O G E T H E R.

The pattern for this code is _____ .

HDFK LQGLYLGXDU PXVQ EH DFFRXQWDEUH IRU KLV/KHU

EACH INDIVIDUAL MUST BE ACCOUNTABLE FOR HIS/HER

RZQ SHUIRUPDQFH ZKHQ ZRUNLQJ FRRSHUDWLYHOB.

OWN PERFORMANCE WHEN WORKING COOPERATIVELY.

The pattern for this code is _____ .

WHN W WRK   CPRTVLY,   W HLP, SHR,

WHEN WE WORK COOPERATIVELY, WE HELP, SHARE,

ND NCRG CH THR T LRN.

AND ENCOURAGE EACH OTHER TO LEARN.

The pattern for this code is _____ .

Concept Induction

Concepts may be taught inductively as well as deductively. Concept formation may be done inductively by instructing students to figure out why the examples have been placed in the different boxes.

Tasks: Analyze the examples the teacher places in each box. Identify the concept represented by each box. Then create new examples that may be placed in the boxes.

Cooperative: Students turn to the person next to them and create an answer they can agree on.

Procedure:
1. Draw two (or three) boxes on the chalkboard. Label them Box 1, Box 2, or Box 3.
2. Place one item in each box.
3. Instruct students to use the **formulate, explain, listen, create** procedure to discuss how the items are different.
4. Place another item in each box and repeat. Tell students not to say outloud to another group or the class how the items are different. Each pair must discover it.
5. Once a pair "has it," the members are to make a definition for each box. They then create new examples that may be placed in the boxes.

The procedure for students is:
1. **Formulate** an individual answer.
2. **Share** their answer with their partner.
3. **Listen** carefully to their partner's answer.
4. **Create** a new answer that is superior to their initial formulations through the processes of association, building on each other's thoughts, and synthesizing.

Expected Criteria For Success: Each student must be able to identify the concept represented by each box.

Individual Accountability: One member from the pair will be randomly chosen to explain the answer.

Expected Behaviors: Explaining, listening, synthesizing by all members.

? What Is It?

Tasks: Analyze the examples the instructor places in each box. Identify the concept represented by each box. Assign each example given below to a box. Then create new examples that may be placed in each box.

Cooperative: Turn to the person next to you and create a joint answer.
1. **Formulate** an individual answer.
2. **Share** your answer with your partner.
3. **Listen** carefully to your partner's answer.
4. **Create** a new answer that is superior to your initial formulations through the processes of association, building on each other's thoughts, and synthesizing.

Expected Criteria For Success: Each person must be able to identify the concept represented by each box.

Individual Accountability: One member from the pair will be randomly chosen to explain the answer.

Expected Behaviors: Explaining, listening, synthesizing by all members.

Examples

1. Strive for everyone's success.
2. Strive to be better than others.
3. Strive for own success only.
4. What benefits self does not affect others.
5. Joint success is celebrated.
6. What benefits self benefits others.
7. Only own success is celebrated.
8. Motivated to help and assist others.
9. What benefits self deprives/hurts others.
10. Motivated only to maximize own productivity.
11. Own success and other's failure is celebrated.
12. Motivated to ensure that no one else does better than oneself.

Box 1

1.

2.

3.

4.

5.

6.

Box 2

1.

2.

3.

4.

5.

6.

Box 3

1.

2.

3.

4.

5.

6.

2:40

When Are You Interdependent?

You can take a walk by yourself. You can only play tennis with another person. Some things we can do by ourselves. Some things can only be through through a joint effort. When a joint effort is required, you are interdependent. You are dependent on others to do their part, they are dependent on you to do your part.

Given below are a sets of activities. Some can be done separately. Some can only be done as part of a joint effort. Classify each activity as being "independent" or "interdependent." Then write down **why** you classified the activity as you did. Finally, name three things you can do by yourself. Add them to the above list. Name three things that require the efforts of you and several other people to accomplish. Add them to the above list.

This is a cooperative task. Work as a pair. Both persons must agree on and be able to explain the answers.

Activity	Separate	Mutual
Win a lottery		
Score a touchdown		
Follow a map from A to Z		
Play in a band		
Run a mile		
Negotiate		
Kick a ball		
Mediate		
Pilot a jet airliner		
Sing in choir		
Form a human circle around a tree		
Have a friend		
Play soccer		
Jump rope 25 times		
Play catch		
Lift 500 pounds		
Get married		
Be a hermit		
Teach math		
Be a family		

Establishing Positive Interdependence

Jim can't find his lunch. It contains two ham sandwiches, a banana, and a plain chocolate candy bar. Jim sees Roger sitting at a lunch table with two ham sandwiches, a banana, and a plain chocolate candy bar. Roger has often grabbed and eaten parts of Jim's lunch in the past. Jim has let it go, but this is too much. Jim says, "Hey! That's my lunch! Give it back!" Roger insists the lunch is his. Jim and Roger start yelling at each other over whose lunch it is.

1. Whenever you are involved in a conflict, your first step is to establish the cooperative context. What can Jim do to remind Roger to take a long-term cooperative perspective on the relationship and therefore help find a solution to the conflict?

2. Role play the following methods of establishing positive interdependence. Alternate roles of actor and listener. The actor plays Jim and presents the appeal for interdependence. The listener plays Roger and responds to the appeal.

3. After all situations have been role played, write down three recommendations for establishing a perception of positive interdependence with the opponent.

Appeals For Interdependence

1. "We share a common fate. We can solve this problem in a way that we both benefit."

2. "You can not succeed without my help and I can't succeed without your help."

3. "Look. We are going to be classmates for years. Let's think about the future as well as about this issue."

   a. "We have more to gain by staying friends and working this out than we have to gain by trying to win over each other. Let's not try to take advantage of each other. Let's solve this problem and stay friends."

   b. "We are in the same classes. Our lockers are near each other. We see each other all the time. And we are going to keep seeing each other for the next three years. We have a long- lasting relationship. We interact frequently. Let's work together to solve this problem."

4. "We are both basketball players. We live in the same neighborhood."

5. "Remember all the times we celebrated our successes? We accomplished a lot together in the past. We can do it again in the future."

The Teacher's Role in Cooperation

Make Decisions

Specify Academic and Collaborative Objectives. What academic and/or collaborative skills do you want students to learn or practice in their groups? Start with something easy.

Decide on Group Size. Students often lack collaborative skills, so start with groups of two or three students; later advance cautiously to fours.

Assign Students to Groups. Heterogeneous groups are the most powerful, so mix abilities, sexes, cultural backgrounds, and task orientations. Assign students to groups randomly or select groups yourself.

Arrange the Room. The closer the students are to each other, the better they can communicate. Group members should be "knee to knee and eye to eye."

Plan Materials. Materials can send a "sink or swim together" message to students if you give only one paper to the group or give each member part of the material to learn and then teach the group.

Assign Roles. Students are more likely to work together if each one has a job which contributes to the task. You can assign work roles such as Reader, Recorder, Calculator, Checker, Reporter, and Materials Handler or skill roles such as Encourager of Participation, Praiser, and Checker for Understanding.

Set the Lesson

Explain the Academic Task. Prepare students by teaching them any material they need to know, then make certain they clearly understand what they are to do in the groups. This might include explaining lesson objectives, defining concepts, explaining procedures, giving examples, and asking questions.

*Structure Positive Interdependence. Students must feel that they need each other to complete the group's task, that they "sink or swim together." Some ways to create this are by establishing mutual goals (students must learn the material and make certain group members learn the material), joint rewards (if all group members achieve above a certain percentage on the test, each will receive bonus points), shared materials and information, and assigned roles.

*Structure Individual Accountability. Each student must feel responsible for learning the material and helping the group. Some ways to ensure this feeling include frequent oral quizzing of group members picked at random, giving individual tests, having everyone in the group write (pick one paper at random to grade), or having students do work first to bring to the group.

Structure Intergroup Cooperation. Having groups check with and help other groups and giving rewards or praise when all class members do well can extend the benefits of cooperation to the whole class.

Explain the Criteria for Success. Student work should be evaluated on a criteria-referenced rather than a norm-referenced basis. Make clear your criteria for evaluating the groups' work.

Specify Expected Behaviors. The more specific you are about the behaviors you want to see in the groups, the more likely students will do them. Make it clear that you expect to see everyone contributing, helping, listening with care to others, encouraging others to participate, and asking for help or clarification. Younger students may need to be told to stay with their group, take turns, share, ask group members questions, and use quiet voices.

*Teach Collaborative Skills. After students are used to working in groups, pick one collaborative skill they need to learn, point out the need for it, define it carefully, have students give you phrases they can say when using the skill, post the phrases (praise, bonus points, stars), and observe for and encourage the use of the skill until students are doing it automatically. Then teach a second skill. Consider praising, summarizing, encouraging, checking for understanding, asking for help, or generating further answers.

Monitor and Intervene

*Arrange Face-to-Face Interaction. The beneficial educational outcomes of cooperative learning groups are due to the interaction patterns and verbal exchanges that take place among students. Make certain there is oral summarizing, giving and receiving explanations, and elaborating going on.

Monitor Students' Behavior. This is the fun part! While students are working, you circulate to see whether they understand the assignment and the material, give immediate feedback and reinforcement, and praise good use of group skills.

Provide Task Assistance. If students are having trouble with the task, you can clarify, reteach, or elaborate on what they need to know.

Intervene to Teach Collaborative Skills. If students are having trouble with group interactions, you can suggest more effective procedures for working together or more effective behaviors for them to engage in. You can ask students to figure out how to work more effectively together. If students are learning or practicing a skill, record on an observation sheet how often you hear that skill, then share your observations with the groups.

Evaluate and Process

Evaluate Student Learning. Assess how well students completed the task and give them feedback.

*Process Group Functioning. In order to improve, students need time and procedures for analyzing how well their group is functioning and how well they are using collaborative skills. Processing can be done by individuals, small groups, or the whole class. To start, have groups routinely list three things they did well in working together today and one thing they will do better tomorrow. Then summarize as a whole class.

Provide Closure. To reinforce student learning you may wish to have groups share answers or paper, summarize major points in the lesson, or review important facts.

CURRICULUM ADAPTATION

Changing lesson plans to include cooperative interaction can be time-consuming at first. Here is a quick lesson plan worksheet which can be used initially to ensure all the critical elements of cooperative learning are incorporated into your lessons. As you use groups more often, this form can be used as a quick self-check.

SUBJECT AREA

I. DECISIONS

LESSON: _____

GROUP SIZE: _____

ASSIGNMENT TO GROUPS : _____

MATERIALS: _____

II. SET THE LESSON

WHAT IS/ARE:

Academic Task:	Criteria for Success:

*Positive Interdependence:	*Individual Accountability:	*Expected Behaviors:

III. *MONITORING

WILL BE DONE BY: Teacher _____   Teacher/Student _____

FOCUS WILL BE ON: Whole Class _____   Individual Groups _____   Individuals _____

OBSERVATION SHEET INCLUDES THE BEHAVIORS OF: _____

_____

_____

*PROCESSING/FEEDBACK: _____

_____

_____

---
*An essential element of cooperative groups   2:45

BEST ADVICE

I. DECISIONS

Lesson: _Start with a short lesson, something you feel comfortable with._

Group Size: _Start small, a pair or a threesome (with larger groups more skills are necessary to be successful)._

Assignment to Groups: _You can randomly choose or assign students depending on the group's task. It is your choice._

Materials: _Give each student materials or the group can have one set of papers. One group set helps create interdependence among members._

II. SET THE LESSON

What Is/Are:

Academic Task:	Criteria for Success:
Clearly state what you want students to do: make a mural, complete the worksheet, answer the questions.	_State how they will know they have been successful with the task:_ _90% Fantastic (A)_ _80% Very Good (B)_

*Positive Interdependence:	*Individual Accountability	*Expected Behaviors:
The groups need to know they have to be concerned with each other's learning. They sink or swim together.	_Students should know they are each responsible for knowing the work -- this can be done by testing each one._	_Specify how you want them to behave while they work. Name specific, observable, describable behaviors._

III. *MONITORING _Start with the teacher as the observer to model how observing should be done._

Will Be Done By: Teacher ___X___   Teacher/Student _____

Focus Will Be On: Whole Class _____   Individual Groups _____   Individuals _____

Observation Sheet Includes the Behaviors Of: _Start small with just two or three behaviors. They should be positive behaviors not negative._

(Taking turns, sharing, praising, checking) (Refer to Expected Behaviors box above)

IV. *PROCESSING/FEEDBACK _Take time to give feedback to your students._

Refer back to the behaviors you asked them to try, pointing out positive behaviors you noticed.

----

*Essential elements of cooperative groups

2:46

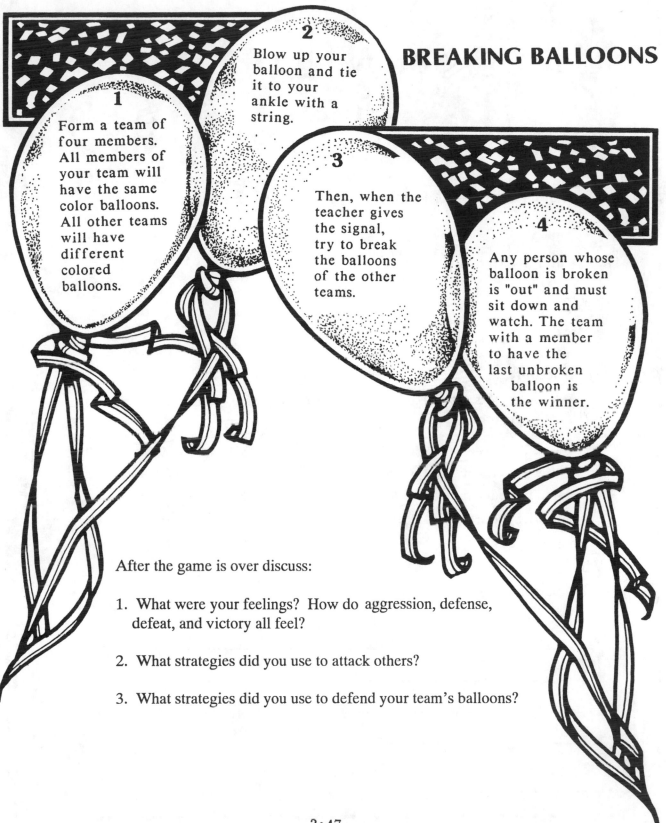

BREAKING BALLOONS

1 Form a team of four members. All members of your team will have the same color balloons. All other teams will have different colored balloons.

2 Blow up your balloon and tie it to your ankle with a string.

3 Then, when the teacher gives the signal, try to break the balloons of the other teams.

4 Any person whose balloon is broken is "out" and must sit down and watch. The team with a member to have the last unbroken balloon is the winner.

After the game is over discuss:

1. What were your feelings? How do aggression, defense, defeat, and victory all feel?

2. What strategies did you use to attack others?

3. What strategies did you use to defend your team's balloons?

2:47

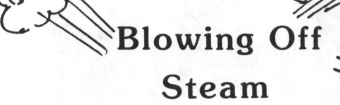

Blowing Off Steam

In order to accomplish this task, you must have a cooperative group!

Materials needed:

table
paper cup
grocery bag

Procedure:

Ask your classmates to kneel around the table, spacing themselves out evenly. Place the paper cup at one end of the table and tape the bag at the other end. At a given signal, join together in blowing the cup to the opposite end of the table. Everyone must work together until the cup drops into the bag. Don't touch the cup with your body. Repeat the task until you can do it more and more quickly.

Describe the activity and how it worked:

_____

_____

_____

_____

3 Negotiating

You Cannot Not Negotiate

> *Not everything that is faced can be changed but*
> *Nothing can be changed until it is faced.*

James Baldwin

Betsy is frustrated. She is a member of a cooperative group that includes Meredith, who is the bossiest student in the class. Whenever Betsy tries to contribute to the group's work, Meredith interrupts her and takes over. No one else gets to contribute ideas and conclusions. Betsy wants to be an equal participant in the group but believes that Meredith will not let her. What is she to do?

Storms are a natural and unavoidable aspect of the earth's weather system. Storms range in intensity from rainstorms to hurricanes. Some are accompanied by gentle rain, others by thunder and lightning. Similarly, interpersonal storms are a natural and unavoidable aspect of life that vary in intensity from mild to severe. Interpersonal storms have their origins in the interdependence existing among students, faculty, and all other members of the school. The interdependence is based on shared goals, a division of labor, complementary roles such as "student" and "teacher," and dependence on each other's resources. Everyone in the school is interdependent. What you do influences what others do. What they do influences what you do. When Meredith interrupts, Betsy cannot contribute. When groupmates do not understand, a member reexplains. When a teacher asks for a conference, students agree. Because teachers, students, administrators, and parents (as well as cooks, custodians, secretaries, and so forth) all share common goals, they are interdependent. But at the same time, they all have somewhat different perspectives, goals, and needs. **The combination of interdependence and differing perspectives creates conflicts of interests, making it impossible for a school or classroom to be free from interpersonal conflicts.**

To understand conflicts of interests, you must first understand what wants, needs, goals, and interests are. There are many things each of us want. A **want** is a desire for something. Each person basically has a unique set of wants. A **need** is a necessity for survival. Needs are more universal. Every person needs to survive and reproduce (water, food, shelter, sex), belong (loving, sharing, cooperating), have power, have freedom, and have fun (Glasser,

1984). On the basis of our wants and needs we set goals. **A goal** is an ideal state of affairs that we value and are working to achieve. Our goals are related through social interdependence. When we have mutual goals we are in a cooperative relationship; when our goals are opposed we are in a competitive relationships. Our **interests** are the potential benefits to be gained by achieving our goals.

Within schools and classrooms the interests of students, teachers, and administrators at times are congruent and at times are in conflict. A **conflict of interests** exists when the actions of one person attempting to reach his or her goals prevent, block, or interfere with the actions of another person attempting to reach his or her goals (Deutsch, 1973). When two students both want the same library book, want to play the same position on an athletic team, want to be elected to the same student-body office, want to date the same person, or even want to use the pencil sharpener at the same time, they have a conflict of interests. In many classrooms teachers create a conflict of interests among students by having them compete for grades. **Both because they occur naturally and because they are deliberately created, conflicts of interests are common among students, between students and faculty, among faculty members, and between faculty and administrators.**

David is very clear about his priorities. He comes to school to see his friends and to have a good time. Schoolwork is unimportant and homework is unthinkable. Class is endured for the few minutes in the hallway when David can interact with his friends. Whenever possible, David will clown around in class in order to enjoy himself more and gain the attention of his peers. He is never mean or hostile. He just never pays attention, does not try to learn, and never does any schoolwork he can avoid. Although there is no anger involved, David is in constant conflict with the school staff. There are some interests shared in common. David wants to be in school and the school staff wants David in school. There are other interests that are opposed. David wants to do no academic work and the school staff wants David to do considerable academic learning. Getting David to learn academic material is a matter of persistent and creative negotiation.

Resolving conflicts of interests requires negotiation. Each person has needs and wants. To meet his/her needs and wants each person makes proposals to others. The other

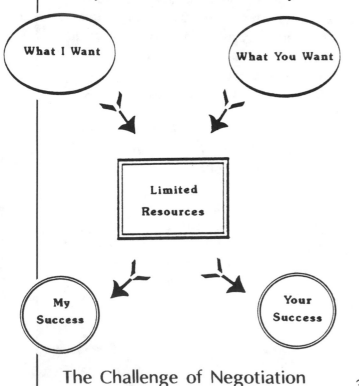

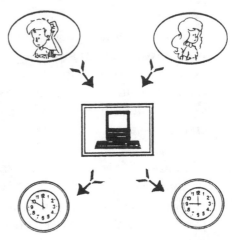

THE CHALLENGE OF NEGOTIATION

persons evaluate the proposal on the basis of how well it meets their needs and wants and either agree or make a counter-proposal. **Negotiation** is a process by which persons who have shared and opposed interests and want to come to an agreement try to work out a settlement (Johnson & F. Johnson, 1991). In order to resolve their different interests and continue to relate to each other in productive and fulfilling ways, negotiations must take place.

You spend a great deal of time negotiating, even when you do not think of yourself as doing so. Every day you (and all the other students, teachers, and administrators in the school) face the choice of negotiating agreements or engaging in hostilities. Negotiating occurs continually throughout the school day. Most of your negotiating occurs informally without you being fully aware that it is going on. Conflicts continually occur, resolutions are negotiated, and individuals live with the consequences of the agreements they have made.

Two Types Of Negotiating

Two students, Meg Mine and Nennah Notyours have lost their pencils. Meg, in searching the floor, finds a pencil under Nennah's desk and proclaims that she has found her lost pencil. "Hey," Nennah says, "that's my pencil! I can tell by the teeth marks!" "Not a chance," replies Meg. "See these scratch marks on the side of the pencil? I always do that with my finger nail!" In negotiating for the pencil Meg and Nennah have a choice as to how they will negotiate with each other. They can each try to get the pencil (and see who wins) or they can try to find a mutually satisfying solution to their problem. You can negotiate in two ways. You can go for a "win" or you can try to solve the "problem." Both are appropriate under certain circumstances.

Type 1: Win-Lose Negotiations

People...are trying to either shun conflict or crush it. Neither strategy is working. Avoidance and force only raise the level of conflict...They have become parts of the problem rather than the solution.

DeCecco and Richards, 1974

There are times when you negotiate to win. Buying a used car is an example. In **win-lose negotiations** the goal is to make an agreement more favorable to you than to the other negotiator. You go for the win when your needs and wants are important and you have a temporary, ad hoc relationship with the other person, must negotiate an agreement, and then will separate, never to interact again. The ultimate goal of negotiating in such circumstances is to gain an advantage over the other person. You go for a win.

Helpful hints in going for the win are (a) make an extreme opening offer (if you are willing to pay $1,500, offer $500), (b) compromise slowly (try to get the other person to compromise first), (c) point out everything that is wrong and unreasonable about the other person's position and (d) be ready to walk away with no agreement.

It is often a mistake, however, to assume that you will **never** be interdependent with the other person again. It is also often a mistake to assume that the conflict cannot be redefined as a mutual problem to be solved. A famous example is the dispute between Israel and Egypt. When Egypt and Israel sat down to negotiate at Camp David in October 1978, it appeared that they had before them an intractable conflict. Egypt demanded the immediate return of the entire Sinai Peninsula; Israel, which had occupied the Sinai since the 1967 Middle East war, refused to return an inch of this land. Efforts to reach agreement, including the proposal of a compromise in which each nation would retain half of the Sinai, proved completely unacceptable to both sides. As long as the dispute was defined in terms of what percentage of the land each side would control, no agreement could be reached. Once both realized that what Israel really cared about was the security that the land offered, while Egypt was primarily interested in sovereignty over it, the stalemate was broken. The two countries were then able to reach an integrative solution: Israel would return the Sinai to Egypt in exchange for assurances of a demilitarized zone and Israeli air bases in the Sinai.

There are very few times in your life when you negotiate with someone you will never work with again. The majority of the time, therefore, you will want to engage in problem-solving negotiations.

Type 2: Problem-Solving Negotiations

 *By blending the breath of the sun and the shade, true harmony comes into the world.*

Tao Te Ching

There are times when you negotiate to solve a problem. Deciding with a friend whether to go to the movies (your friend's preference) or play soccer (your preference) is an example. In **problem-solving negotiations** the goal is to discover a solution that will benefit everyone involved. You negotiate to solve the problem when you have an ongoing cooperative relationship with the other person, must negotiate an agreement to resolve the current conflict, and then will continue the cooperative efforts and the relationship. Within ongoing cooperative relationships, you share a **common fate**. You cannot succeed unless the other person succeeds and the other person cannot succeed unless you succeed. You sink or swim together. A football team shares a common fate because either all members win or all lose. In addition, in cooperative relationships, your success is **mutually caused**. Whether you succeed or fail depends both on your own efforts and the efforts of the other person. You must depend on the other person to help you succeed and he or she must depend on you to help him or her succeed. No one player can win a football game. It takes everyone's efforts on both the defensive and offensive units.

Imagine, for example, that you and another person are rowing a boat across the ocean and you cannot row the boat by yourself. You, therefore, seek food and water for the other person as well as for yourself. Otherwise, you will perish on the high seas. In a cooperative relationship, the better off, happier, and more successful the other person is, the better off, happier, and more successful you are. Because of your common fate and mutual causation, you concern yourself with both fulfilling the interests of your collaborators as well as your own and maintaining the ongoing cooperative relationship.

When dealing with friends, classmates, colleagues, fellow employees, family members, neighbors, and bosses, you negotiate to solve the problem and, therefore, you have two concerns:

1. **To negotiate in a way that gains benefits for all (as opposed to creating winners and losers).** Cooperators resolve conflicts as partners, side-by-side, not as adversaries. They are partners in a hard-headed, side-by-side search for a fair agreement advantageous to both sides. Otherwise you have to be careful when you pass dark alleys! One-sided settlements, imposed by whomever has the most power at the moment, are rarely stable or long lasting and typically damage the relationship.

2. **To negotiate in a way that improves the relationship and your ability to work together.** In long-term relationships, maintaining an effective working relationship is often more important than is meeting one's short-term needs and wants. In a marriage, for example, ensuring the survival of the marriage is almost always more important than meeting your immediate needs.

You negotiate differently with classmates, teachers, administrators, and parents than you do with strangers or acquaintances. Within ongoing relationships you are expected to show considerable concern about the other person's interests. You are, after all, striving to achieve the same goals and the productivity and quality of life of both of you are affected by how the conflict is managed. Helping students, teachers, and administrators achieve their goals is of some importance to you. How they can help you achieve your goals is of some importance to them.

Ongoing relationships are guided by a **norm of mutual responsiveness** (i.e., the rule that you should be committed to helping other people get what they want and fulfill their needs and they will do likewise). Within a work or personal relationship, there is an unspoken rule that each person is concerned about the other person's interests. A vigorous presentation of one's own interests, therefore, implies that these interests are genuinely important and the other person should agree if it is at all possible. **One-step negotiations** occur: Each person (a) assesses the strength of his or her interests, (b) assesses the strength of the other person's interests, and (c) agrees that whomever has the greatest need is given his or her way. If both people follow the norm of mutual responsiveness, each will decide that the other person's goals are more important than one's own goals about 50 percent of the time. If individuals are not equally responsive to each other's needs over time, the relationship breaks down.

Negotiable Versus Nonnegotiable Issues

Most conflicts involve issues that are negotiable. The conflict may be over:

1. Use of something (computer, book, clothes, car).

2. Agreeing on something (what movie to see, where to eat, what to do).

3. Obtaining something (money, clothes, computer games).

Sometimes you can negotiate for what you want, sometimes you can not. Not every issue is negotiable. There are times when you may need to say to others that you will not negotiate and there are times when other people will tell you that the issue is not negotiable. Whenever an issue involves something unsafe, illegal, or inappropriate, the issue is nonnegotiable. Whenever someone wants you to violate your values, the issue is nonnegotiable.

Given that an issue is negotiable (that is, does not require you to violate your values or involve something unsafe, illegal, or inappropriate), the only barrier to reaching a mutually satisfying agreement is your creativity and ability to problem-solve.

Effective Problem-Solving Negotiating

A house divided against itself cannot stand.

Abraham Lincoln

On the eve of the Revolutionary War, English political philosopher Edmund Burke eloquently asked members of the House of Commons to head off the coming conflict by negotiating with the colonials: "All government--indeed, every human benefit and enjoyment, every virtue, and every prudent act--is founded on compromise and barter." His observation is still accurate. Negotiation is woven into the daily fabric of our lives. On the interpersonal level, we buy and sell houses and cars, jointly decide where to eat dinner, and bargain over salaries. On a larger scale, unions and management negotiate contracts, and nationals arrange treaties and trade agreements. Failed negotiations may produce anything from minor inconveniences to nuclear holocaust.

Most students do not know how to negotiate effectively. Instead of negotiating, students may use such strategies to resolve their conflicts as physical violence, name calling and personal insults, and ostracizing someone until they give in. With multiple systems operating within a classroom and school, chaos can result. Life gets much easier within schools when all students are cooriented and use the same negotiation procedure to resolve their conflicts. Since effective negotiating is typically not learned in families, from television, from movies, or from books, students must be directly and purposefully taught to negotiate as part of their schooling experience.

Students do want to learn how to negotiate constructive resolutions to their conflicts. Junior high and high school students from all parts of the United States report that they prefer direct negotiations to resolve student-student and teacher-student conflicts of interests (DeCecco & Richard, 1974). But they reported that negotiations were tried in only 17 percent of the conflicts; decisions were imposed by school authorities 55 percent of the time. Thus, negotiating is not a commonly used method in most schools in the United States. And since it is the most effective method, this means that school personnel and students are not availing themselves of the most constructive procedures needed for managing conflicts.

Students not only need to know how to negotiate effectively to improve their immediate productivity as students. They need to know how to negotiate to be successful in their careers and in their future adult lives. Negotiating procedures and skills are keys to career success. A recent survey conducted for Accountemps (a large accounting, bookkeeping, and data processing temporary personnel service that is a division of Robert Half International Inc.) of vice presidents and personnel directors of 100 of the nation's 1,000 largest corporations found that the people who manage America's leading corporations spend over four working weeks a year dealing with the problems caused by employees who cannot resolve their conflicts with each other. In answer to the question, "What percent of management time is spent dealing with conflicts among employees," respondents revealed that executives spend an average of 9.2 percent of their time or, based on a 40-hour week, 4.6 weeks a year attempting to deal with employee conflicts and the difficulties and disruptions they cause. In 1976, the American Management Association sponsored a survey on conflict management (Thomas & Schmidt, 1976). The respondents included 116 chief executive officers, 76 vice-presidents, and 66 middle managers. They reported that about 24 percent of their time is spent dealing with conflict. The sources of conflicts they faced included misunderstandings, personality clashes, value and goal differ-ence, substandard performance, disagreement over methods of work, lack of cooperation, competition, and noncompliance with rules and policies. School and hospital administra-tors, mayors, and city managers report that conflict resolution commands nearly 49 percent of their attention. In addition to taking up valuable management time, employee conflicts can seriously reduce any company's productivity and its ability to compete effectively in the marketplace. Knowing how to negotiate constructive resolutions to conflicts of interests is an essential skill that will significantly affect your career success.

It is not only on the job that you negotiate. Your agreements and understandings mean the difference between success and failure in all areas of your life. Poor agreements are always breaking down. They bring nagging dissatisfaction and aggravation. **When you do not know how to negotiate with others you end up either frustrated because you do not get what you want or isolated because you alienate those closest to you.** Learning how to negotiate helps you establish a base for interacting with peers and adults in a healthy way, cope with adversity, and make sound, healthy decisions throughout your life. Good agreements help you reach and exceed your own goals while leaving others more satisfied at the same time.

Although negotiation takes place frequently every school day, and knowing how to negotiate is a key to current and future productivity and success, negotiating is not easy to do well. **There are five basic steps in negotiating a resolution to a conflict of interests:**

1. Jointly defining the conflict (what we want and how we feel).

2. Exchanging reasons and the rationale for their positions (our reasons why).

3. Reversing perspectives (my understanding of you, your understanding of me).

4. Inventing options for mutual benefit (three possible plans).

5. Reaching a wise agreement (let's shake).

An example of the steps of negotiating may be found in Table 3.1.

Step One: Agreeing On A Definition Of The Conflict

Sally Somnolent and Ms. Alert have a conflict. Sally sees it as very important that she get a good nap during geometry. Ms. Alert sees it as very important that Sally listens carefully in class to learn as much geometry as possible. "The problem is that no one understands or loves me," Sally says. "The problem is that students nowadays are rude and obnoxious," Ms. Alert says. They do not agree on what the conflict is about. Agreeing on the definition of a conflict is like putting gas in an airplane. Without it, negotiations will never get off the ground.

When two or more people act in ways that prevent, block, or interfere with each other's success, a conflict exists. Negotiations begin when you communicate to the other person that there is a conflict and you wish to resolve it. You say, "We have a conflict" and "I want to resolve it!"

Conflicts cannot be resolved unless both parties bring out into the open what they want and how they feel. Without a clear understanding of each other's interests, no constructive resolution is possible. **Everyone has a perfect right to their needs and goals and to expect that other people will treat them with respect and dignity.** Two of the major mistakes in defining a conflict is to be **aggressive** by trying to hurt the other person or to be **nonassertive** by saying nothing, giving up your interests, and keeping your feelings to yourself. You can **assert** your needs, goals, and feelings directly to another person in an honest and appropriate way that respects both yourself and the other person. Doing so enables you to act in your own best interests, to stand up for yourself without undue anxiety, to express honest feelings comfortably, and to exercise personal rights without denying the rights of others.

On the other hand, **everyone has a perfect right to refuse to meet your needs or facilitate your goal accomplishment if they see it as destructive to their own interests to do so.** No one has to act against their best self-interests just to please someone else. After asserting your needs and goals, therefore, do not expect the other person to do exactly as you wish. **Do not confuse letting others know what you want with demanding that they**

act as you think they should. Providing others with information about your interests is different from trying to force others to act in the ways you wish them to.

After expressing what you want and how you feel, and listening carefully to what the other person wants and how the other person feels, the conflict may be defined. How the conflict is defined will influence how easy the conflict is to resolve constructively.

It is not enough for a student to understand his or her position and feelings. They must be communicated and explained to the opponent. The essential element of presenting your position is communicating it without "building hills as you go," "sabotaging your chances for agreement by alienating others," or "guaranteeing closed-minded rejection." Describe, don't accuse or label.

Table 3.2 Respect For Self And Others

My Respect For Me	My Respect For You
I Have A Perfect Right To:	**You Have A Perfect Right To:**
My Needs And Wants	Your Wants And Needs
Tell You What I Want	Tell Me What You Want
Tell You How I Feel	Tell Me How You Feel
Refuse To Give You What You Want	Refuse To Give Me What I Want

We Have A Perfect Right To Negotiate With Each Other

A conflict is not defined until both you and the other person agree on a definition. Your definition of the conflict will affect how you act and feel in trying to resolve it. With a poor definition, you will feel miserable and act in ways that will make the conflict worse. With a constructive definition, you will feel confident and effective, and you will act in ways that resolve the conflict. It is important that you be able to define conflicts in a skillful way. Here are five rules that will help you do so:

1. Describe what you want.

2. Describe your feelings.

3. Listen carefully to the other person's wants and feelings.

4. Jointly define the conflict as a mutual problem.

5. Jointly define the conflict as being small and specific.

These five rules may be summarized as **TUD** (**T**ell, **U**nderstand, and **D**efine).

Rule 1: Describe What You Want (Your Interests)

If a man does not know to which port he is sailing, no wind is favorable.

Seneca

Negotiating begins when you describe what you want. Evaluating creates problems in defining the conflict. The more descriptive and less evaluative your statements, the better. Consider the following situation. Sally and Sue were working in the same cooperative group. Sally was writing part of the group's report when Sue said, "You stupid fool. It's all wrong!" Sue is frustrated because her ideas are not being used in the report. She is communicating that frustration by accusing Sally of being a fool and doing the report wrong. She is judging the report and Sally and asking Sally to agree with her. Unfortunately, the way in which she is stating her concerns tells more about her needs and her feelings than they do about Sally and the report. Judgments and generalities usually do not help communication, they just confuse and anger the receiver. Sue would have been more effective if she had described her concerns and frustrations rather than making evaluative statements.

The first step in defining a conflict is to describe what you want. This involves taking ownership of your interests by making personal statements that describe your needs and goals. To clearly communicate your needs and goals to the other person:

1. **Make personal statements** that refer to "I," "me," "my," or "mine."

2. **Be specific about your goals and needs** and establish their legitimacy.

3. **Put the problem before your answer.** Give your reasoning first and your conclusions or proposals later.

4. **Be concrete but flexible.** Know what your goals and needs are, but be open to fresh ideas.

5. **Acknowledge the other person's goals as part of the problem.** Describe how the other person's actions are blocking what you want. In doing so, separate the behavior from the person. More specifically, a **behavior description** includes:

   a. A **personal statement** that refers to "I," "me," "my," or "mine."

   b. A **behavioral description statement** that includes the specific behaviors you have observed and does **not** include any judgment or evaluation or any inferences about the person's motives, personality, or attitudes.

6. **Be hard on the problem, but soft on the other person.** Attack the problem without blaming the people. Do not label, accuse, or insult. Separate the person from the problem. Avoid personalized attacks. Keep the negotiations free of highly personal criticism, recriminations, abusive language, and especially those subtle jibes that inflict pain on the other. If you label the other person in negative ways, he or she will be defensive and hostile. Labeling creates mistrust, misunderstandings, and resentment. Support the other person while attacking the problem.

7. **Look forward, not back.** Forgive the past. Talk about where you would like to go rather than about where you have come from. Instead of arguing about the past, talk about what you want to have happen in the future. Instead of asking him or her to justify what they did yesterday, ask, "Who should do what tomorrow?"

8. **Focus on the long-term cooperative relationship.** During most conflicts of interests you will be discussing the current problems in your relationship. Negotiations within a long-term cooperative relationship include discussing how the relationship can be changed so the two of you can work together better. During such conversations, you will need to make relationship statements. A **relationship statement** describes some aspect of the way the two of you are interacting with each other. A good relationship statement indicates clear ownership (refers to I, me, my, or mine) and describes how you see the relationship. "I think we need to talk about our disagreement yesterday" is a good relationship statement.

Rule 2: Describe Your Feelings

> *Many of us in business, especially if we are very sure of our ideas, have hot tempers. My father knew he had to keep the damage from his own temper to a minimum.*
>
> Thomas Watson, Jr., Chairman Emeritus, IBM

Within negotiations you must describe how you feel for at least two reasons. **First**, the only way other people can know how you are feeling and reacting is for you to tell them. Do not expect other people to be mind readers. What other people do not know, they cannot be blamed for. There is a tendency in conflicts to hide feelings and reactions. You often do not want others to know how upset you really are. But if the conflict is to be resolved, you need to share your feelings and reactions. This helps other people understand how their actions are affecting you.

Second, unless feelings are openly recognized and expressed, the conflict will not be resolved. If individuals hide or suppress their anger, for example, they may make an agreement but they keep their resentment and hostility toward the other person. Their ability to work effectively with the other person is damaged as is their ability to resolve future conflicts constructively. And the conflict will tend to reoccur regardless of what the agreement is.

Whether the feelings are anger, sadness, hurt, resentment, frustration, or love, the feeling needs to be openly expressed in negotiating a resolution of the conflict. The feelings also have to be expressed appropriately and constructively. This takes skill.

Expressing and controlling your feelings is one of the most difficult aspects of resolving conflicts. It is also one of the most important. It is through experiencing and sharing feelings that close relationships are built and maintained. Feelings provide the cement holding relationships together as well as the means for deepening relationships and making them more effective and personal. **Feelings** are internal physiological reactions to your experiences. You begin to tremble, sweat, or have a surge of energy. Your heart may beat faster. Tears may come. Although feelings are internal reactions, they do have outward signs. Sadness is inside you, but you may frown or cry on the outside. Anger is inside you. But you may stare and shout at the person you are angry with. Feelings are always internal states, but you use overt behaviors to communicate your feelings to others.

It is often difficult to express feelings, especially within conflict situations. Whenever there is a risk of being rejected or laughed at, expressing feelings becomes very difficult. The more personal the feelings, the greater the risk you may feel. It is also difficult to hide

your feelings from other people. You may cry when you do not want to, get angry when it is best not to, or even laugh at a time that disturbs others. If you are angry and upset, typically the people you work with and the people around you will know. When you do not recognize, accept, and express your feelings a number of difficulties may arise. Relationships may deteriorate, conflicts may fester, bias may creep into your judgments, and the insecurities of your students and colleagues may increase. For many reasons it is often best to communicate your feelings directly when conflicts are building.

There are two ways of communicating feelings: verbally and nonverbally. If you want to communicate clearly, your verbal and your nonverbal expression of feelings must agree or be congruent. Many of the communication difficulties experienced in relationships spring from giving contradictory messages to others by indicating one kind of feeling with words, another with actions, and still another with nonverbal expressions.

Communicating your feelings depends on your being aware of your feelings, accepting them, and being skillful in expressing them constructively. When you are unaware or unaccepting of your feelings, or when you lack skills in expressing them, your feelings may be communicated indirectly through:

1. **Labels:** "You are rude, hostile, and self- centered" versus "When you interrupt me I get angry."

2. **Commands:** "Shut up!" versus "I'm annoyed at what you just said."

3. **Questions:** "Are you always this crazy?" versus "You are acting strangely, and I feel worried."

4. **Accusations:** "You do not care about me!" versus "When you do not pay attention to me I feel left out."

5. **Sarcasm:** "I'm glad you are early!" versus "You are late; it has delayed our work, that irritates me."

6. **Approval:** "You are wonderful!" versus "I like you."

7. **Disapproval:** "You are terrible!" versus "I do not like you."

8. **Name calling:** "You are a creep!" versus "You are embarrassing me."

Such indirect ways of expressing feelings are common. But they are ineffective because they do not give a clear message to the receiver. And the receiver often will feel rejected and "put down" by the remarks. We are taught how to describe our ideas clearly and correctly. But we are rarely taught how to describe our feelings clearly and correctly. We express our feelings, but we do not usually name and describe them. Here are **four ways you can describe a feeling.**

1. **Identify or name it**: "I feel angry." "I feel embarrassed." "I like you."

2. **Use sensory descriptions that capture how you feel**: "I feel stepped on." "I feel like I'm on cloud nine." "I feel like I've just been run over by a truck." Because we do not have enough names of labels to describe all our feelings, we make up ways to describe them.

3. **Report what kind of action the feeling urges you to do**: "I feel like hugging you." "I feel like slapping your face." "I feel like walking on your face."

4. **Use figures of speech as descriptions of feelings**: "I feel like a stepped-on toad." "I feel like a pebble on the beach."

You describe your feelings by identifying them. A description of a feeling must include:

1. **A personal statement**: Refer to "I," "me," "my," or "mine."

2. **A feeling name, simile, action urge, or figure of speech.**

A more detailed way to describe your feelings is reflected in the following format: **I _____ (feeling) when you _____ (specific behavior) because _____ (how it affects me).** An example is, "I feel angry when you break in line ahead of me because I think it isn't fair and I think you ought to wait your turn like everyone else."

Anything you say can convey feelings. Even the comment, "It's a warm day," can be said so that it expresses resentment or irritation. To build and maintain a friendship of any relationship, you must be concerned with communicating your feelings clearly and accurately, especially the feelings of warmth, affection, and caring. If you convey your feelings by commands, questions, accusations, or judgments, you will tend to confuse the person with whom you are interacting. When you want to express your feelings, your ability to describe them is essential for effective communication.

When you describe your feelings, expect at least two results. **First**, describing your feelings to another person often helps you to become more aware of what it is you actually do feel. Many times we have feelings that seem ambiguous or unclear to us. Explaining them to another person often clarifies our feelings to ourselves as well as to the other person. **Second**, describing your feelings often begins a dialogue that will improve your relationship. If other people are to respond appropriately to your feelings, they must know what the feelings are. Even if the feelings are negative, it is often worthwhile to express them. Negative feelings are signals that something may be going wrong in the relationship, and you and the other person need to examine what is going on in the relationship and figure out how it may be improved. By reporting your feelings, you provide information that is necessary if you and the other person are to understand and improve your relationship. When discussing your relationship with another person, describing your feelings conveys maximum information about what you feel in a more constructive way than giving commands, asking questions, making accusations, or offering judgments.

Besides expressing negative feelings, it is important to express positive feelings while discussing a conflict. There are positive feelings, such as liking, appreciation, and respect, that strengthen your relationship with the other person. Both positive and negative feelings have to be communicated with skill in a conflict. Some general rules to follow are:

1. When the other person expresses a feeling toward you, use the communication skills of paraphrasing and checking perceptions to show you understand how she is feeling.

2. Always describe your feelings.

3. Always describe without evaluation the actions of the other person that influenced your feelings.

4. Avoid irrational assumptions that lead to negative feelings.

5. When a person expresses a feeling toward you, always respond with a feeling. Feelings need to be answered by feelings, not by silence, uninvolved understanding, or ridicule.

6. When it can be done in a helpful way, express your feelings. Hidden feelings usually cause problems in the future.

Rule 3: Listen Carefully To Other Person's Wants And Feelings

Besides communicating clearly and descriptively your interests and feelings, you must listen carefully to the other person's interests and feelings. There is no set of skills more important for negotiating than being a good listener (see Johnson, 1990, 1991). **To listen to another person you must (a) face the person, (b) stay quiet (until your turn), (c) think about what the person is saying, and (d) show you understand.** The keystone to good listening is paraphrasing.

Paraphrasing is restating, in your own words, what the person says, feels, and means. This improves communication in several ways. **First**, it helps you avoid judging and evaluating. When you are restating, you are not passing judgment. **Second**, restating gives the sender direct feedback as to how well you understand the messages. If you do not fully understand, the sender can add messages until you do. If you are interpreting the message differently from the way he intended it, the sender can clarify. Being able to clarify and elaborate are important for making sure communication is taking place.

Third, paraphrasing communicates to the sender that you want to understand what he is saying. It shows that you care about him enough to listen carefully, that you are interested, that you take what he is saying seriously, and that you want to understand. **Finally**, paraphrasing helps you get into the sender's shoes: It helps you see the message from the sender's perspective. By restating the message as accurately and fairly as possible, you begin to see things from the sender's point of view.

Paraphrasing is often a simple restatement of what has been said. At first, it may feel dumb to restate what another person has said. It may feel awkward and unnatural until you get used to doing it. But the speaker will be grateful for a chance to clarify or add to his original statement, and he will feel grateful for being understood. Paraphrasing becomes harder when it includes feelings as well as ideas. And it is not limited to only the words the sender uses. Nonverbal cues are also important.

Often in a conflict it is helpful to follow the **paraphrasing rule**: Before you can reply to a statement, restate what the sender says, feels, and means correctly and to the sender's satisfaction. When you use paraphrasing, there is a rhythm to your statements. The rhythm is, You said...; I say.... First you say what the sender said (You said). Then you reply (I say). You will **not**, however, want to paraphrase every statement made by anyone who speaks to you. Some statements aren't important enough to bother with. When someone says hello, there is no need to paraphrase. When someone says "Look at that!" there is no need to paraphrase. Paraphrasing is for important messages, for when you are not sure what the sender means, or for when someone is being very emotional. In the middle of a conflict, when you want the sender to feel understood, or when you want to be absolutely sure what is being said before you reply, you paraphrase. Paraphrasing is essential in defining a conflict so that a constructive resolution may be negotiated.

Rule 4: Jointly Define The Conflict As A Mutual Problem

Two drivers, coming from different directions, are roaring down a one-lane road. Soon they will crash head-on. If the two drivers define the situation as a competition to see who will "chicken out," they will crash and both will die. If the two drivers define the situation as a problem to be solved, they will tend to see a solution in which they alternate giving each other the right-of-way. Even simple and small conflicts become major and difficult to resolve when they are defined in a competitive, "win-lose" way. Even major and difficult conflicts become resolvable when they are defined as problems to be solved.

One of the most destructive things you can do in a conflict is to define the conflict as a win-lose situation. Doing so will result in considerable distress. Destructive escalation of the conflict is likely to result. Whenever you are trying to prove who is right and who is wrong and who is superior and who is inferior, you are in a win-lose competition that will damage the future relationship. You may feel great at first if you win. But the person who loses will feel resentful and will dislike the winner. A win-lose definition of a conflict promotes distrust, dislike, deception, rivalry, threats, and attempts to undermine each other's work. Trying to prove you are better than the other person will only make your relationship an unpleasant experience.

One of the most constructive things you can do in a conflict is to define the conflict as a mutual problem to be solved. Doing so will increase communication, trust, liking for each other, and cooperation. No one loses when you and the other person sit down to solve a mutual problem!

Rule 5: Jointly Define The Conflict As Being Small And Specific

Fred wants to join a baseball game on the playground. "You can't play," Ralph shouts. "We already have our teams!" "You are no longer my friend," Fred shouts back. "You're selfish and mean! I'll never help you with your homework again!" In defining a conflict there is unfortunate tendency to be global and general. Fred is defining the conflict as being one of friendship and gratitude. This creates difficulty in resolving the conflict. He could just as easily have defined the conflict as being one of arriving late or finding a way to make the teams even.

In defining a conflict, the smaller and more specific it is defined, the easier it is to resolve. Think small. The more global, general, and vague the definition of the conflict, the harder the conflict is to resolve. Defining a conflict as, "She always lies," makes it more difficult to resolve than defining it as, "Her statement was not true." When it comes to resolving conflicts, small is easy, large is hard!

These five rules provide a clear, useful way of defining a conflict. The more you follow these rules, the more skillful you will be in resolving them.

Step Two: Exchanging Reasons For Positions

> *To be persuasive we must be believable; to be believable we must be credible; to be credible, we must be truthful.*
>
> Edward R. Murrow, Journalist

Once both you and the other person have expressed what you want and how you feel, listened carefully to each other, and jointly defined the conflict as a small and specific mutual problem, you must exchange the reasons for your positions. To do so, negotiators have to:

1. Express cooperative intentions.

2. Present your reasons, listen to the other person's reasons.

3. Focus on wants and needs, not positions.

4. Clarify the differences between your and the other's interests before trying to integrate them into an agreement.

5. Empower the other persons.

Express Cooperative Intentions: Enlarging The Shadow Of The Future

One of the most constructive things you can do in resolving a conflict is to highlight the long-term cooperative relationships. This is done in three ways. The **first** is to stress the dealing with the conflict in a problem-solving way. Communicate that you and the other person will strive, side by side, to solve the problem rather than fight face-to-face to determine who wins. You want to say such things as, "This situation means that we will have to work together," "Let's cooperate in reaching an agreement," "Let's try to reach an agreement that is good for both of us." The **second** is to state that you are committed to maximizing the joint outcomes. Successful negotiation requires finding out what the other person really wants and needs and showing him or her a way to get it while you get what you want. The **third** is to enlarge the shadow of the future by stating that you are committed to the continuation and success of the cooperative efforts you and the other person are involved in. In doing so, you must wish to point out (a) your long-term mutual goals and (b) the ways the two of you are interdependent and how that interdependence will continue for the foreseeable future.

The clear and unambiguous expression of cooperative intentions in negotiations results in higher quality agreements being reached in a shorter amount of time (i.e., better agreements faster). The other person becomes less defensive, more willing to change his or her position, less concerned about who is right and who is wrong, and more understanding of your views and ideas (Johnson, 1971, 1974; Johnson, McCarty, & Allen, 1976). The other person tends to see you as an understanding and trustworthy person whom he or she can confide in.

Presenting Your Reasons, Listening To Other's Reasons

To say what you want and how you feel is not enough. You must also give your reasons for wanting what you want and feeling as you do. It is not enough to say, "I want to use the computer now and I'm angry at you for not letting me have it." You must also say, "I have an important homework assignment due today and this is my only chance to get it done." Your reasons are aimed at (a) informing the other person and (b) persuading him or her to agree with you.

Many times you will have to ask the other person why he or she has taken a certain position. You may ask a friend to study with you. She may reply "no." Until you understand the reasons for the "no" you will not be able to think creatively of ways for both of you to get what you want. The statement in doing so is, "May I ask why?" If the answer is vague, you add, "Could you be more specific?, What do you mean when you say..., I'm not sure I understand." Your tone of voice is as important as the words when you ask these questions. If you sound sarcastic your attempt to understand the other person will backfire.

In listening carefully to the needs and wants of the other person, you must **stay flexible, changing your position and feelings when persuaded to do so.** Negotiating is a rational process. You are seeking a way to reach your goals and the other person is doing the same. How successful you are in reaching an agreement depends on how creatively you can think of alternatives that are good for both. This requires flexibility and a willingness to change your mind when you are persuaded that it is rational to do so.

Once both of you have explained your reasons, either of you may agree or disagree to help the other person to reach his or her goals. The decision to help the other person reach his or her goals or keep negotiating is based on two factors:

1. How important your goal is to you.

2. How important the other person's goal is to him or her (based on the reasons he or she presents).

You must listen carefully to the reasons given and decide whether they are valid or not. If you decide that the other person's goals are far more important to him or her than yours are to you, then you may wish to agree at this point. Giving up your goals to help the other person reach his or her goals only works if he or she does the same for you 50 percent of the time. This is known as the **single step solution.**

If the other person's reasons are not valid, you need to point that out so he or she may see the inadequacies of his or her proposals. If neither you nor the other person are convinced to give up your own goals in order to fulfill the goals of the other person, then the two of you must reaffirm your cooperative relationship and explore each other's reasons at a deeper level.

Focus On Wants And Needs, Not Positions

Susan is usually a compliant student in Mr. Johnson's English class. Today, however, she comes up to Mr. Johnson's desk and states, "I won't do this homework assignment. I don't care what you do to me, I'm not going to do it!" Mr. Johnson, having read this book, immediately recognized that Susan is presenting a position and he did not yet know what her needs and

wants are. He said, "May I ask why?" In order to negotiate successfully and reach an agreement that satisfies both people, you have to approach the other person on the basis of his or her needs and wants.

The classic example of the need to separate interests from positions is that of a brother and sister, each of whom wanted the only orange available. The sister wanted the peel of the orange to make a cake; the brother wanted the inner part to make orange juice. Their positions, ("I want the orange!") were opposed, but their interests were not. Often, when conflicting parties reveal their underlying interests, it is possible to find a solution that suits them both.

The heart of negotiations is meeting the goals of the other person while ensuring your goals are being met. The success of negotiations depends in finding out what the other person really wants, and showing him or her a way to get it while you get what you want. For a wise decision, therefore, reconcile wants, not positions. For every need or want, there usually exist several possible positions that could satisfy it. A common mistake is to assume that because the other person's position is opposed to yours, his or her goals must also be opposed. Behind opposed positions lie shared and compatible goals, as well as conflicting ones. To identify the other person's wants and needs ask "why," ask, "why not?" and think about his or her choice, and realize that the other person has many different needs and wants.

Differentiate Before Integrating

Conflicts cannot be resolved unless you understand what you are disagreeing about. If you do not know what you are disagreeing about, you cannot find a way to reach an agreement. You must understand the differences between your wants and needs and those of the other person. Only then will you be able to think of ways to satisfy both yourself and the other person so that the conflict can be resolved constructively. Your ability to come up with satisfactory solutions depends on your understanding of how the other person's thoughts, feelings, and needs are different from yours. The more you differentiate between your interests and those of the other person, the better you will be able to integrate them into a mutually satisfying agreement. In discussing a conflict you try to find the answers to these questions: (a) What are the differences between my wants and needs and yours, (b) where are our needs and goals the same, (c) what actions of the other person do I find unacceptable, and (d) what actions of mine does the other person find unacceptable.

Empower The Other Person

During negotiations it is important that you do not let the other person feel powerless. Shared power and wise agreements go hand in hand. **There are two ways to empower the other person.** The **first** is by being open to negotiations and flexible about the option you like the best. If he or she can negotiate with you then he or she has power and options. Willingness to negotiate is based on being open to the possibility that there may be a better option available than you now realize. Staying tentative and flexible means that you do not become overcommitted to any one position until an agreement is reached. **Second**, you provide power through choice among options. Generate a variety of possible solutions before deciding what to do. If Susan says to Mr. Johnson, "You have to agree to let me not do my homework!" he will feel powerless. If Susan said, "Let's think of three possible agreements, and then choose the one that seems the best!" both she and Mr. Johnson feel powerful.

The psychological costs of being helpless to resolve grievances include frustration, anxiety, and friction. When a person is powerless, either he or she becomes hostile and tries to tear down the system or becomes apathetic and throws in the towel. You do not want the other person to do either one. We all need to believe that we have been granted a fair hearing and that we should have the power and the right to gain justice when we have been wronged. If it becomes evident that we cannot gain justice, frustration, anger, depression, and anxiety may result.

Step Three: Understanding The Other's Perspective

The test of a first-rate intelligence is the ability to hold two opposed ideas in the mind at the same time, and still retain the ability to function.

F. Scott Fitzgerald

To reach a wise agreement, you must have a clear understanding of all sides of the issue, an accurate assessment of their validity and relative merits, and the ability to think creatively to come up with potential solutions that maximize joint outcomes and fulfill the interests of both you and the other person. All this requires that you are able to see the conflict from both your own and the other person's perspective. And you need to keep both in mind at the same time.

Betsy and Juanita work together as laboratory technicians in a large hospital. Betsy comes from a well-off upper-middle-class family. Juanita's parents had a hard struggle sending their daughter through college. Betsy and Juanita buy tickets for a state lottery in which they could win up to $5,000. When the drawing is held, they learn that they are both winners. Betsy says, "Hey, I won $5,000 in that lottery. Imagine that." Then she continues eating lunch and reading a magazine. Juanita starts jumping up and down shouting, "I won! I won! I won $5,000!" She throws her arms around her friend, crying and laughing in her excitement.

Why did Betsy and Juanita react so differently to the news that they had each won $5,000 in a state lottery?

Each person has a unique **perspective** (a way of viewing the world and his or her relation to it) that is different from the perspectives of others. Your perspective is developed as a result of the ways in which you respond to your experiences as an infant, child, youth, and adult. Other people have developed their perspectives on the basis of their responses to their life experiences.

In order to negotiate successfully with another person, you must be able to take the other person's perspective and understand how the conflict appears to the other person. **Social perspective- taking** is the ability to understand how a situation appears to another person and how that person is reacting cognitively and emotionally to the situation. The opposite of perspective-taking is **egocentrism** or being unaware that other perspectives exist and that one's own view of the conflict is incomplete and limited.

You can have different perspectives at different times. If you have been lifting 100-pound bags of cement and someone tosses you a 40- pound bag, it will seem very light. But if you have been lifting 20-pound bags, the 40-pound bag will seem very heavy. When you are hungry, you notice all the food in a room. When you are not hungry, the food does not attract your attention. As your job role, experiences, assumptions, physiological states, and values change, your perspective will change.

Different people have different perspectives. No two people will see an issue in exactly the same way. Each person will interpret identical events differently. One person will see teasing as a sign of affection while another will see it as a sign of rejection. The other person will have one perspective, you will have another. You will conclude one thing from the other person's actions while the other person will see his or her behavior entirely differently.

The same message can mean two entirely different things from two different perspectives. If you provoke your coworker, she may laugh. But if you provoke your boss, she may get angry and fire you! Different perspectives mean the message will be given different meanings. From one perspective, the same message may be interpreted as friendly teasing or as hostile insubordination. A person's perspective determines how a message will be interpreted.

Misunderstandings often occur because we assume that everyone sees things from the same perspective as we do. If we like Italian food, we assume that all our friends like Italian food. If we are interested in sports, we assume that everyone is interested in sports. If we get angry when someone laughs at our behavior, we assume that everyone will get angry when they are laughed at. If we think a teacher is stupid, we are surprised when a peer thinks the teacher is brilliant. As children, we can see things only from our perspective. As we become adults, we learn that different people have different perspectives, and we learn how to understand other people's perspectives.

Given that different people have different perspectives, that each person may have different perspectives at different times, and that misunderstandings often occur because we assume that everyone sees the world through our perspective, then an important issue for negotiations is to keep the other person's perspective in mind as well as your own, for a number of reasons (see Johnson & Johnson [1989] for a complete review of the research).

First, perspective-taking improves communication and reduces misunderstandings and distortions by influencing how messages are phrased and received. Negotiators often misunderstand and distort the positions of the others involved in the conflict due to poor communication. The better you understand the other person's perspective, the more able you are to phrase messages so the other person can easily understand them. If a person does not know what snow is, for example, you do not refer to "corn snow" or "fresh powder." In addition, understanding the other person's perspective helps you accurately understand the messages you are receiving from that person. If the other person says, "That's just great!", for example, the meaning reverses if you know the person is frustrated. You must be able to stand in the sender's shoes to understand accurately the meaning of the messages that person is sending you.

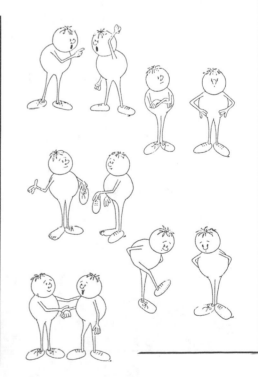

Second, perspective-taking is essential for a realistic assessment of common and opposed interests and an accurate assessment of their validity and relative merits. Often reaching an agreement requires the sacrifice of some of the opposed interests so that the common benefits, concerns, advantages, and needs may be built on. To propose workable alternative agreements you must understand how the other person sees the problem.

Third, the more able you are to take the other person's perspective, the broader the picture you get of the issue. Out of a mass of detailed information, people tend to pick out and focus on those facts that confirm their prior perceptions and to disregard or misinterpret those that call their perceptions into question. Each side in a negotiation tends to see only the merits of its case, and only the faults of the other side. It is not enough to logically understand how the other person views the problem. **If you want to influence the other person, you also need to understand empathetically the power of his/her point of view and to feel the emotional force with which he or she believes in it.**

Fourth, engaging in perspective taking tends to improve the relationship with the other person. You are more liked and respected when the other person realizes that you are seeing his or her perspective accurately and using it to create potential agreements that benefit both sides equally.

There is nothing more important to resolving conflicts constructively than understanding how the conflict appears from the other person's perspective. Overall (see Johnson & Johnson, 1989a), perspective-taking results in more information, both personal and impersonal, being disclosed; increases the capacity to phrase messages so that they are easily understood by the other; increases accurate comprehension of the other's messages; increases understanding and retention of the other's information and reasoning; facilitates the achievement of create and high- quality problem solving; and promotes more positive perceptions of negotiations, the other person, and the joint cooperative efforts. Once you can view the conflict both from your own perspective and the other person's perspective, you can find mutually beneficial solutions. You can also communicate to the other person that you really understand his or her thoughts, feelings, and needs. It is usually easier to resolve a conflict when the other person feels understood.

You ensure that you accurately see the situation from the other person's perspective by:

1. Asking for clarification or correction to make sure your understanding is accurate. This is called **perception checking**.

2. Stating your understanding of the other's wants and needs. This is often done by **paraphrasing**.

Checking Your Perception Of Another's Feelings

Before you respond to a person's feelings, you need to check to make sure you really know what the other person actually feels. Sometimes other people will clearly describe their feelings and other times they will express them in ambiguous and confusing ways. In order to respond you will have to clarify how they really feel. Feelings are internal reactions, and we can tell what people are feeling only from what they tell us and from their overt actions. Overt actions include such things as smiles, frowns, shouts, whispers, tears, and laughter. When other people describe their feelings to us, we can usually accept their feelings to be what they say they are. But if other people express their feelings indirectly (such as through sarcasm) or nonverbally (such as through a frown), we often need to clarify how they actually feel.

The best way to check whether or not you accurately understand how a person is feeling is through a perception check. A **perception check** has three parts:

1. You describe what you think the other person's feelings are.

2. You ask whether or not your perception is accurate.

3. You refrain from expressing approval or disapproval of the feelings.

"You look sad. Are you?" is an example of a perception check. It describes how you think the person is feeling, then it asks the person to agree with or correct your perception, and it does both without making a value judgment about the feeling. A perception check communicates the message, "I want to understand your feeling--is this the way you feel?" It is an invitation for other people to describe their feelings more directly. And it shows you care enough about the person to want to understand how the person feels.

Perception checking will help you avoid actions you later regret because they are based on false assumptions about what the other person is feeling. Our impressions are often biased by our own fears, expectations, and present feelings. If we are afraid of anger and expect other people to be angry, then we may think other people are about to reject us. We frequently misperceive how other people are feeling, and it is therefore essential that we check out our perceptions before taking action.

Paraphrasing

It is not enough to understand the other person's perspective. You must also let the other person know that you understand his or her perspective. One of the major ways to both clarify your understanding of the other person's perspective and communicate your understanding to him or her, is paraphrasing. **Paraphrasing** is restating, in your own words, what the person says, feels, and means. Paraphrasing helps you get into the other person's shoes and see the conflict from his or her perspective. It helps you avoid judging the other's position. It gives the other person feedback as to how well you understand his or her position. And it communicates that you want to understand the other person.

Step Four: Inventing Options For Mutual Gain

One completely overcomes only what one assimilates.

Andre Gide

The fourth step of negotiating is to identify several possible agreements. One will rarely do. People have a tendency to agree to the first reasonable solution that is proposed. But doing so shuts off consideration of even more advantageous agreements. Thus, make sure you generate at least three good alternative agreements before deciding on which one to adopt. To invent a number of potential agreements, you must avoid a number of obstacles and you must think creatively.

Avoiding Obstacles

Inventing options does not come naturally. Not inventing options is the normal state of affairs, even within the easiest negotiations. In most negotiations there are four major obstacles that inhibit the inventing of a number of options:

1. **Judging prematurely.** Nothing is so harmful to inventing options as a critical attitude waiting to pounce on the drawbacks of any new idea. Premature criticism is the first impediment to creative thinking.

2. **Searching for the single answer.** Premature closure and fixation on the first proposal formulated as the single best answer is a sure short-circuit of wise decision-making.

3. **Assuming a fixed pie.** This inhibits creative thinking. Do not assume that the less for you, the more for me. Rarely, if ever, is this assumption true. Expanding the pie is a key to flexible problem solving. Imagine you want to see one movie and your date wants to see another movie. You also know your date likes to eat at a certain restaurant. By enlarging the pie to include which restaurant you go to for dinner before going to a movie, an integrative agreement is possible (one picks the restaurant, one picks the movie).

4. **Being concerned only with your own immediate needs and goals.** In a relationship, to meet your needs you also have to meet the other person's needs. Shortsighted self-concern leads to partisan positions, partisan arguments, and one-sided solutions.

5. **Defensively sticking with the status quo to avoid the fear of the unknown inherent in change.** Changing creates anxiety about potential new and unknown problems and guilt over ineffective or inappropriate behavior in the past. Many times people try to justify their past actions by refusing to change.

Invent Creative Options

To invent creative options, you need to:

1. **Separate the act of inventing options from the act of judging them.** Invent first, judge later.

2. **Gather as much information as possible about the problem.** The more you know about the problem, the easier it is to find solutions.

3. **See the problem from different perspectives and reformulate it in a way that lets new orientations to a solution emerge.** Such a reformulation often produces a moment of insight by one or both participants. The insight is often accompanied by intense emotional experiences of illumination and excitement and leads to the reformulation of the problem so that solutions emerge.

4. **Broaden the options on the table rather than look for a single answer.** Expand the pie. The more the options, the greater the room for negotiations. One of the keys to wise decision making is selecting from a great number and variety of options.

5. **Search for mutual gains.** There always exists the possibility of joint gain. Look for solutions that will leave the other person satisfied as well. Try to maximize joint outcomes.

6. **Invent ways of making decisions easily.** Give the other person choices that are as painless as possible. If you want a horse to jump a fence, do not raise the fence! Propose "yesable" agreements.

7. **Propose possible agreements such as meeting in the middle, taking turns, sharing, letting the other person have it all, or let chance decide.** Four of the more sophisticated proposals are:

   a. **Package deals** in which several issues that are considered part of the agreement are settled. A package deal involving homework, in-class behavior, and helping another student may be easier to reach than trying to negotiate each separately.

   b. **Trade-offs** in which two different things of comparable value are exchanged.

   c. **Tie-ins** in which an issue considered extraneous by the other person is introduced and you offer to accept a certain settlement provided this extraneous issue will also be settled to one's satisfaction.

   d. **Carve-outs** in which an issue is carved out of a larger context, leaving the related issues unsettled. This is the opposite of a tie-in.

8. **Test each proposed agreement against reality.** What are its strengths and weaknesses? What does each person gain and lose? How does it maximize joint outcomes?

After inventing a number of options, you and the other person will have to agree on which one to try out first. Some realistic assessment of the alternatives then takes place. In trying to decide which alternative to try first it may help to remember Aesop's fable about the mice in trouble. The mice were saying, "It's terrible! Just terrible! We really must do something about it! But what?" The mice were talking about the cat. One by one they were falling into her claws. She would steal up softly, then spring suddenly, and there would be one mouse less. At last the mice held a meeting to decide what to do. After some discussion a young mouse jumped up. "I know what we should do! Tie a bell around the cat's neck! Then we would hear her coming and we could run away fast!" The mice clapped their little paws for joy. What a good idea! Why hadn't they thought of it before? And what a very clever little fellow this young mouse was! But now a very old mouse, who hadn't opened his mouth during the whole meeting, got up to speak. "Friends, I agree that the plan of the young mouse is very clever indeed. But I should like to ask one question. Which of us is going to tie the bell around the cat's neck?" The moral is that there is no use adopting an option that cannot be implemented by one or both persons.

In inventing alternative agreements, it often helps to describe what you are doing and neglecting to do that create and continue the conflict. Knowing how your actions help create and continue the conflict is essential for planning how to resolve it. And neglecting to do something constructive helps create and continue the conflict just as much as doing something destructive. You may want the other person to change. But the easiest thing to change is your own actions. If you wish to resolve a conflict, you must begin with deciding how to change your actions. It would be nice if everyone else changed so we would never have to. But you do not have control over the actions of others. They do. What you do have control over is your own actions. You can change your actions much more easily than you can change the other person's actions!

Step Five: Reaching A Wise Agreement

I never let the sun set on a disagreement with anybody who means a lot to me.
Thomas Watson Sr., Founder, IBM

Given that we are all separate individuals with our own unique wants and needs, whenever we interact with others, we will have some interests that are congruent and other interests that are in conflict. It takes wisdom to manage the combination of shared and opposed interests and reach an agreement. **Wise agreements** are those that are fair to all participants, are based on principles, strengthen participants' abilities to work together cooperatively, and improve participants' ability to resolve future conflicts constructively. In other words, wise agreements are those that meet the following criteria.

The first requirement for a wise agreement is that the agreement must meet the legitimate needs of all participants and be viewed as fair by everyone involved. In deciding on which option to adopt, keep in mind the importance of shared good feelings, preserving mutual interests, and preserving your shared history. Focus on the long-term relationship to ensure that the agreement is durable. Point out that your long-term survival and happiness should not be jeopardized by any agreement reached. To meet your and the other person's legitimate interests the agreement should clearly specify the responsibilities and rights of everyone involved in implementing the agreement. This includes:

1. **The ways each person will act differently in the future.** These responsibilities should be stated in a **specific** (tells who does what when, where, and how), **realistic** (each can do what he or she is agreeing to do), and **shared** (everyone agrees to do something different) way.

2. **How the agreement will be reviewed and renegotiated if it turns out to be unworkable.** This includes (a) the ways in which cooperation will be restored if one person slips and acts inappropriately and (b) the times participants will meet to discuss whether the agreement is working and what further steps can be taken to improve cooperation with each other. You cannot be sure the agreement will work until you try it out. After you have tested it for a while, it is a good idea to set aside some time to talk over how things are going. You may find that you need to make some changes or even rethink the whole problem. The idea is to keep on top of the problem so that the two of you may creatively solve it.

The second requirement for a wise agreement is that it is based on principles that can be justified on some objective criteria (Fisher & Ury, 1981). The objective criteria may be:

1. Everyone has an equal change of benefiting (such as flipping a coin, one cuts, the other chooses, or letting a third party arbitrator decide).

2. Fairness (taking turns, sharing, equal use). One way to assess fairness is to list the gains and losses for each person if the agreement is adopted and then see if they balance.

3. Scientific merit (based on theory, tested out, evidence indicates it will work).

4. Community values.

Evaluate each of the proposed options on the basis of one of these objective criteria. Think through which standards are most appropriate to evaluate the options and make a decision based on principal. The more you do so, the more likely you are to produce a final agreement that is wise and fair.

Using objective criteria to evaluate a possible agreement may result in clarifying what is "fair" and "just" from both sides of the issue. Remember King Solomon. One of the first problems the new King Solomon was presented with involved two women who both claimed the same baby. They wanted him to decide whose it was. Sitting on his throne, Solomon listened carefully. The two women lived together in the same house. Their babies had been born only three days apart. Then one of the babies died. The first woman said, "This woman's child died in the night. She then arose and took my son from beside me and placed the dead child next to me. When I woke to feed my baby, I found her dead child in my arms." "No!" the other woman cried frantically. "The living child is my son!" Solomon calmly said, "Bring me a sword and bring me the baby. Divide the living child in two and give half to the one and half to the other." Everyone was shocked. "No! Please don't!" screamed the real mother. "She can have the child. Don't kill it!" "No," the other woman said, "let the child be neither mine nor yours, but divide it." "Aha!" said Solomon. "Now I know to whom the child belongs." Then pointing to the woman who had asked that the baby's life be spared, he said, "Give her the living child. She is its mother."

The third requirement for a wise agreement is that the agreement and the process of reaching the agreement strengthens participants' ability to work together cooperatively in the future (the trust, respect, and liking among participants should be increased). All participants in the conflict must remain moral persons who are caring and just. They should see each other as being entitled to caring and justice.

The fourth requirement for a wise agreement is that the agreement and the process of reaching the agreement strengthen participants' ability to resolve future conflicts constructively. Conflicts of interests will reoccur frequently and each time one is faced and resolved the procedures and skills used should be strengthened and validated.

It is important that both you and the other person understand which actions trigger anger and resentment in the other. Criticism, put downs, sarcasm, belittling, and other actions often trigger a conflict. If the two of you understand what not to do as well as what to do, the conflict will be resolved much more easily.

Step Six: Try, Try Again

Difference of opinion leads to inquiry, and inquiry to truth.

Thomas Jefferson

The final step for negotiating in a problem-solving way is: "Keep trying. Try, try again." No matter how far apart the two sides seem, no matter how opposed your interests seem to be, keep talking. With persistent discussion a viable and wise decision will eventually become clear.

When you and the other student cannot agree, the teacher (or administrator) may send you to the **problem-solving rug** to keep negotiating until they reach agreement. The rules for the rug are:

1. Both students must sit on the rug until the conflict is resolved.

2. No touching. Verbal exchanges only.

3. Be patient. It may take them a long time.

4. When they resolve the conflict, praise them and ask what the resolution is.

Negotiating In Good Faith

You can bring your credibility down in a second. It takes a million acts to build it up, but one act can bring it down...People are suspicious because for several thousand years that suspicion was warranted...we try very hard not to do things that will create distrust.

Howard K. Sperlich, President, Chrysler Corporation

Everyone has a negotiating reputation. The promises of some people are to be believed. Other people rarely keep their commitments. You want to build a reputation of being someone who is honest, truthful, trustworthy and, therefore, fulfills your promises. You want your word to be good.

There are strategies you can use when your word has not been good in the past. They are:

1. **Pay your debts.** Whatever you have agreed to do in the past and not yet done, do it. Once you have fulfilled past promises, your current promise will be more credible.

2. **Use collateral.** The collateral should be something of value, something the other person does not expect you to give up. While being significant enough to be meaningful, the collateral should not be something so outrageous that it is not believable. Promising to give someone $1,000 if you break your word is not believable.

3. **Have a cosigner who guarantees your word.** Find someone who trusts you that the other person trusts, and have them guarantee that you will keep your word.

Refusal Skills: This Issue Is Not Negotiable

Not every issue is negotiable. Two important skills are:

1. Knowing when an issue is and is not negotiable.

2. Being able to say "no" or "I refuse to negotiate this issue."

Negotiable issues include conflicts over (a) the use of something (computer, book, car, clothes), (b) agreeing on something (what to do, what to have for dinner, what movie to see), and (c) obtaining something (money, power, fame, clothes, friends). On most issues you benefit from negotiating and reaching an agreement.

There are times, however, when you will not want to negotiate. This may be because you do not like the other person, you see the issue as being nonnegotiable, you are uncomfortable with the issue, or you cannot do what the other person wants. You always have the option of saying "no" in negotiations. And you do **not** always need a clear reason. When you think someone is trying to manipulate you instead of solving a real problem, do not negotiate and do not make an agreement.

Sometimes people find out later that they have made a bad agreement. You may have agreed to something you should not have, or you may have changed your mind, or you may have found out you cannot keep your side of the bargain. At that point, you reopen negotiations and try to find a workable resolution to the conflict.

Table 3.3 Reasons For Saying "No"

Clear	Unclear
Illegal	My intuition tells me "no"
Inappropriate	I am not sure
It will hurt other people	The right option is not there
I will not be able to keep my word	I have changed my mind

You will save considerable time and trouble by not persuading others to make agreements they do not wish to make and if you do not let others persuade you to agree to something you do not wish to do.

Coordinating Motivation To Resolve The Conflict

There are often differences in motivation to resolve a conflict. You may want to resolve a conflict but the other person could care less. The other person may be very concerned about resolving a conflict with you, but you may want to avoid the whole thing. Today you may want to resolve the conflict but the other person does not, while tomorrow the situation may be reversed. Usually, a conflict cannot be resolved until both persons are motivated to resolve it at the same time.

The motivation to resolve a conflict based on the costs and gains of continuing the conflict for each person. The **costs** of continuing a conflict may be the loss of a friendship, loss of enjoyment from work, the loss of job productivity, the loss of a friend, or the loss of respect from the other person. The **gains** for continuing the conflict may be satisfaction in expressing your anger or resentment and the protection of the status quo. By protecting the status quo, you avoid the possibility that things will get worse when the conflict is resolved. Answering the following questions may help you clarify your motivation and the motivation of the other person to resolve the conflict:

1. What do I gain from continuing the conflict?

2. What does the other person gain from continuing the conflict?

3. What do I lose from continuing the conflict?

4. What does the other person lose from continuing the conflict?

A person's motivation to resolve a conflict can be changed. By increasing the costs of continuing the conflict or by increasing the gains for resolving it, the other person's motivation to resolve it can be increased. Through changing the costs and gains, you can change both your and the other person's motivation to resolve the conflict.

When the outcomes of negotiations are presented as gains more concessions are made than when the outcomes are presented as losses. Negotiators who think in terms of losses or costs are more likely to take the risk of losing all by holding out in an attempt to force further concessions from the opponent. A negotiator should try to present information in a way that leads the opposition to see what they have to gain from a settlement.

Summary

You negotiate to resolve conflicts of interests. **Conflicts of interests** exist when your actions interfere with or block another person from achieving his or her goal. **Interests** are the potential benefits to be gained by achieving goals. Goals are based on **wants** (a desire for something) and **needs** (a necessity for survival). On the basis of our wants and needs we set goals. A **goal** is an ideal state of affairs that we value and are working to achieve. When two or more people have mutual goals they are in a cooperative relationship; when the goals of two or more people are opposed they are in a competitive relationships. Resolving conflicts of interests requires negotiation. **Negotiation** is a process by which persons who have shared and opposed interests and want to come to an agreement try to work out a settlement. There are two types of negotiations. **Win-lose negotiations** occur when participants want to make an agreement more favorable to themselves than to the other persons. It is appropriate primarily when you will never have to work with the other person in the future. When buying a used car, for example, you engage in win lose negotiations. The majority of the time, however, you negotiate within an ongoing relationship. That requires **problem-solving negotiations** where the goal is to reach an agreement that benefits everyone involved. Within ongoing relationships individuals are committed to the wellbeing of the other person as well as to their own wellbeing. In order to negotiate mutually beneficial agreements participants must state what they want and how they feel, state the reasons why they want what they do, reverse perspectives and summarize the other's position and interests, invent a series of possible agreements, and finally reach a wise decision.

Agreeing on a definition of the conflict requires that you state what you want and how you feel, listen carefully to the other person, and agree on a definition of the conflict that specifies it as a small and specific mutual problem to be solved. You tell, understand, and define (TUD). Exchanging reasons for your positions requires that you express cooperative intentions, exchange reasons, focus on interests not positions, explore how your interests are incompatible and compatible, and empower each other by giving choices. You gain understanding of the other person's perspective by paraphrasing and checking your perceptions of the other person's interests and reasons. You invent options for mutual gain by both inventing creative options and avoiding the obstacles to creative problem solving. You reach a wise agreement when the agreement meets the legitimate needs of all participants, when it is based on principles that can be justified on some objective criteria, when your ability to work cooperatively with the other person has been enhanced, and when your ability to resolve future conflicts constructively has been strengthened. Finally, you try, try again until a wise agreement is reached.

To negotiate in good faith you need to build a reputation of someone who is honest, truthful, and trustworthy. Not all issues, however, are negotiable. You must know the difference between a negotiable and a nonnegotiable issue. And you must be able to say "No, I will not negotiate on this issue" when it is appropriate to do so. One of the most problematic aspects of negotiating is to ensure that both people want to negotiate at the same time. Motivation to negotiate often must be coordinated.

Negotiations are inevitable. You negotiate every day and sooner or later you negotiate with everyone in your life. In deciding whether or not to negotiate and in ensuring that negotiations are effective and constructive, there are five basic strategies to choose from. These are discussed in the next chapter. Managing emotions, especially anger, is one of the most difficult aspects of negotiating. Managing your own anger and your responses to the anger of other individuals is covered in Chapter 5.

Creative Conflict Contract

Major Learnings	Implementation Plans

Date _____ Date of Progress Report Meeting _____

Participant's Signature _____

Signatures of Other Group Members _____ _____

_____ _____ _____

EXERCISE

MATERIALS

CHAPTER VOCABULARY

Working with a partner, learn the definitions of the following words.

1. Define each word in two ways.

   First, write down what you think the word means.

   Second, look it up in the book and write down its definition.

   Note the page on which the definition appears.

2. For each word write a sentence in which the word is used.

3. Make up a story in which all of the words are used.

4. Learn how to spell each word. They will be on your spelling test.

Dictionary

Word List

○ interests	○ conflict of interests
○ negotiation	○ mediation
○ win-lose negotiations	○ problem-solving negotiations
○ wise agreements	○ paraphrasing
○ behavior descriptions	○ carve-outs
○ common fate	○ egocentrism
○ expand the pie	○ feelings
○ goal	○ goal structure
○ joint outcome	○ manipulation
○ mutual causation	○ package deals
○ norm of mutual responsiveness	○ perception-checking
○ personal statements	○ perspective
○ relationship statements	○ single-step solution
○ social perspective-taking	○ tie-ins
○ trade-offs	

A Puzzling Problem for You!

It's time for you to do some problem-solving with the puzzle below. See if you and your partner can come up with the vocabulary words from Chapter 3 that fit into the squares. Remember that if you need a little help, simply turn the page upside-down for the word list. Some of the answers are more than one word, so check the definition in each case to see.

ACROSS

1. Negotiations which exist when each negotiator has as his or her goal the reaching of an agreement that benefits everyone involved. (3 words)
2. A person's way of viewing the world and his or her relation to it.
3. The process by which persons who have shared and opposed interests and want to come to an agreement try to work out a settlement.
4. Negotiations which exist when each negotiator has as his or her goal making an agreement more favorable to oneself than to the other negotiator. (3 words)

DOWN

5. When the actions of one person attempting to reach his or her goals prevent, block or interfere with the actions of another person attempting to reach his or her goals. (3 words)
6. An issue which involves something unsafe, illegal or inappropriate.
7. Choices.
8. Restating, in your own words, what the person says, feels and means.

Name _____   Date _____

Meet with your partner to solve this puzzle. A *CONFLICT* has taken place here. As the dust settles, you can see that some of the words in the sentences on the next page were left all scrambled up. It's your job to unscramble all the words and successfully resolve the conflict. When you read each sentence, it will give you a clue to jog your memory and help you come to a happy resolution! If you take the letters at the end of the line and shake them up a bit, you'll have the word that makes sense in the blank.

YOU CAN HELP

RESOLVE THIS CONFLICT!

3:43

To see how, turn this page over . . .

1. These two boys are having an argument about something; they
   are in _____.

   f i t c c o n l

2. In order for each of them to feel good about what's happening,
   they must go through several stages or _____

   s p e t s

   to reach a successful _____ of the conflict.

   s t o u l n i o r e

3. In the first step, each of the players should tell the other
   what he _____ to see happen.

   n t a w s

4. Then each needs to tell the other how he _____

   l s e f e

   about the problem.

5. The next step to a resolution is to give a _____

   s o a n e r

   why each feels the way he does. This will help them
   understand each other's point of view.

6. Then the two will name a few things to try and draw up
   a list of _____.

   s l a p n

7. Finally, they are going to _____ one of the plans

   h o o c c s

   that both _____ is the best for their situation.

   r e g c a

8. The sign that they have reached a successful resolution is
   when the two of them _____ _____

   k h e a s   s h a d n

   in agreement.

Conflicts Of Interests Identification Form

WHAT ARE THE CONFLICTS OF INTEREST I HAVE WITH:

1. Other Students

   a. _____

   b. _____

   c. _____

2. Teachers

   a. _____

   b. _____

   c. _____

3. Administrators

   a. _____

   b. _____

   c. _____

4. Parents

   a. _____

   b. _____

   c. _____

Which Books Do We Take?

Scientists have suddenly discovered that a large comet is going to strike the earth. All life, if not the earth itself, will be destroyed. Your group (four members) has been picked to move from Earth to a new planet. The conditions on the new planet will be harsh and difficult. You will be starting life over, trying to develop a farming and technological society at the same time. Because of the limited room in the spaceship, you can only bring three books. "Think carefully," the captain says. "You will never return to Earth. You will never be able to get more books from Earth."

1. Work by yourself. **First**, decide which book you personally want to bring. Choose the book you think will be most (a) important to save and (b) helpful to starting a new civilization. **Second**, plan how to convince the other three members of your group that the book you have chosen should be chosen by the group.

2. Meet as a group. Only three books can go. You have to decide which three. You cannot take half of one and half of another. You cannot choose by chance (such as flipping a coin). Come to an agreement as to which three books your group will take and why. Each member should present the best case for the book he or she has chosen. The group must come to an agreement as to which three books they will take to the new planet. Each member must be able to explain the reasons why the three books were chosen.

3. As a group, **first** look up **conflicts of interests** and **negotiations** in this chapter. Explain how the above situation is a conflict of interests that requires negotiation to be resolved. **Second**, decide on four pieces of advice for negotiating resolutions to conflicts of interests. Write them down. Each member of the group needs a copy.

4. Each member of the group pairs up with a member of another group. Pair members (a) present the four pieces of advice decided on by their groups, (b) listen carefully to the each other's presentation, and (c) take the best ideas from both groups and decide on four pieces of advice for negotiating resolutions of conflicts. Both members need a copy.

5. Return to your group of four. Members share their new lists. As a group, make a new list of four pieces of advice for negotiating resolutions to conflicts of interests, taking the best ideas from all members.

Conflicts of Interest

Read each conflict description and decide how you would manage the conflict if you were the teacher. Be realistic. Assume the students are in secondary school.

Form a pair with another student. Discuss each conflict and come to an agreement as to how it should be managed. Write out your plan. One member of each group will be randomly selected to share the group's solutions with the rest of the class.

Conflict Descriptions

Two students, Meg Mine and Nennah Notyours, begin to argue about who owns a pen. Both claim it. The argument leads to a small fistfight. Both students end up feeling angry and rejected.

In your class the teacher gave the assignment of making a collage on a serious social problem, such as pollution, discrimination, drugs, or crime. The idea of the project was to get the students to express themselves and their ideas in a visual manner and to increase their awareness of how art can be an impressive and persuasive tool. Sam Smartmouth raised his hand and said he did not see the importance of this sort of thing. He said he was not going to do it and asked why the teacher could not assign something more interesting and valuable.

Donna Donot and Gary Getalong are members of a cooperative group. They constantly put each other down, criticize each other, and even make fun of each other's contributions. They both want to be the group leader and spend most of their energy undermining each other's efforts to direct and control the group's activities.

Ralph Rascal rarely is prepared to take tests. One day Ms. VicTim was giving a test and Ralph tossed a lighted firecracker under her seat. After the explosion she calmly asked, "Who put that firecracker under my seat?" Several students started laughing.

Making a Profit

You are either a buyer or a seller in a wholesale market. Your ultimate goal is to maximize your profit. You will be negotiating with another person who has the same goal. This exercise will give you an opportunity to study the dynamics of negotiation between two persons with different interests. The procedure is as follows:

1. Form a group of six. Divide into two triads. One triad becomes sellers and one becomes buyers. **Task One** is to understand your profit schedule so that you will understand which possible agreements are in your best interests and which are not. The structure is cooperative. You are to make sure that all members of your triad understand the profit schedule and are ready to negotiate agreements beneficial to them. Your triad will be successful when all members understand their profit schedule. Each person will be accountable for negotiating an agreement based on their understanding of the profit schedule. In studying the schedule each member is expected to explain and ask for explanations. Remember:

   a. Each of you will negotiate, face-to-face and person-to-person, with a member of the other triad.

   b. You will not be allowed to show your profit schedule to the negotiator from the other triad.

   c. You will need to understand your profit schedule completely in order to evaluate proposals from the person you are negotiating with.

2. Each of you will be paired with a member of the other triad. You will meet face-to-face. **Task Two** is to negotiate an agreement on the price for each commodity that maximizes your profits. You have both a cooperative goal of reaching an agreement and a competitive goal of making that agreement as favorable to you as possible. How much profit you in fact make will indicate your success. You will be accountable to report the results

Making a Profit (continued)

of your negotiations to your group. It is expected that you will both make and respond to proposed agreements. **You can say anything you want to each other, but you may not show each other your profit schedule.**

3. After you have finished negotiating, write down on a sheet of paper:

   a. Which commodity was most important to the other negotiator?

   b. Which commodity was least important to the other negotiator?

4. In your group of six, discuss the following questions:

   a. What were the agreements reached by members of the group?

   b. What was the total joint outcome of each buyer-and-seller pair? The **joint outcome** is the sum of the profits of the buyer and the profits of the seller. Which pair had the highest joint outcome?

   c. What negotiation strategies were used? Were they win-lose or problem-solving strategies?

   d. How did negotiators communicate information about their profit schedules, and how did they learn about the profit schedule of the other negotiator? Were their perceptions of what commodities were most and least important to their opponent correct? Was information exchange **direct**? (Did buyer and seller accurately tell each other their profit schedules?) Or was it **indirect**? (Did they deduce each other's profit schedule by comparing each other's responses to different package offers?)

   e. Did the negotiators make package deals or did they negotiate the commodities one at a time?

   f. What conclusions can the group make about negotiations on the basis of their experience and discussion?

5. Your group will be expected to share its conclusions with the rest of the class.

Making A Profit Exercise: Buyer Profit Sheet

Oil		Gas		Coal	
Price	*Profit*	*Price*	*Profit*	*Price*	*Profit*
A	$4,000	A	$2,000	A	$1,000
B	3,500	B	1,750	B	875
C	3,000	C	1,500	C	750
D	2,500	D	1,250	D	625
E	2,000	E	1,000	E	500
F	1,500	F	750	F	375
G	1,000	G	500	G	250
H	500	H	250	H	125
I	0	I	0	I	0

The nine prices for each commodity are presented by the letters A to I. Next to each price is the profit you would make for reselling each commodity if you bought it at that price. Reach one agreement that includes all three commodiities, such as AAA, III, or BFG.

You can say anything you wish during negotiations, but you may not show this profit sheet to the seller you are negotiating with.

Making A Profit Exercise: Seller Profit Sheet

Oil		Gas		Coal	
Price	*Profit*	*Price*	*Profit*	*Price*	*Profit*
A	.0	A	0	A	0
B	125	B	250	B	500
C	250	C	500	C	1,000
D	375	D	750	D	1,500
E	500	E	1,000	E	2,000
F	625	F	1,250	F	2,500
G	750	G	1,500	G	3,000
H	875	H	1,750	H	3,500
I	$1,000	I	$2,000	I	$4,000

The nine prices for each commodity are presented by the letters A to I. Next to each price is the profit you would make for each commodity if you sold it at that price. Reach one agreement that includes all three commodiities, such as AAA, III, or BFG.

You can say anything you wish during negotiations, but you may not show this profit sheet to the buyer you are negotiating with.

Name _____ Date _____

What I Want, What You Want

Conflicts begin when two people want the same thing.

When one person says, "I want the ice cream bar" and another person says, "I want the ice cream bar," a conflict exists.

It is OK to want something. Every person has needs. Every person every minute of the day wants something. To stand up for yourself you have to let other people know what you want. **You have a perfect right to stand up for yourself.** So does the other person. You are both OK to stand up for what you want.

The **first step** of negotiating is for each person to say what he or she wants. To practice the first and the last steps of negotiating, go through the procedure of:

1. *I want . . . You want . . .*

2. *Meet me in the middle.*

   OK. Shake.

———————————————●———————————————

Divide into groups of four. Form two rows of four students each. The two rows face each other. Each person says to the person he or she is facing:

I want the cookie. No, I want the cookie.

Let's meet in the middle. Each will get half.
You cut and I'll choose.

OK. Shake.

Then move to the next person and say the same thing. Do not stop until you have practiced the sequence four times.

Why is dividing the cookie in half a good idea?

Where else can you use this procedure? Divide into pairs. Write down three places where you can use this procedure.

1. _____

2. _____

3. _____

What I Want, What You Want.
How I Feel, How You Feel.

It is not enough to say what you want. You also need to say how you feel. Sometimes you may feel angry. Sometimes you may feel frustrated. Sometimes you may feel afraid.

In conflicts, everyone has feelings. Both sides need to say how they feel. You need to say how you feel. The other person needs to say how he or she feels. To stand up for yourself you need to let other people know how you feel. To stand up for themselves, other people need to let you know how they feel. Both you and the other person have a perfect right to your feelings.

The **second step** of negotiating is for each person to say how he or she feels. To practice the first, second, and last steps of negotiating, go through the procedure of:

1. *I want . . . You want . . .*
2. *I feel . . . You feel . . .*
3. *Let's take turns. Flip a coin to see who goes first.*

OK. Shake.

Using
the
Same
Book

Divide into groups of four. Form two rows of four students each. The two rows face each other. Each person says to the person he or she is facing:

I want the book. No, I want the book.

I feel frustrated. I'm afraid you won't let me have the book.

Let's take turns. Flip a coin to see who goes first.

OK. Shake.

Then move to the next person and say the same thing. Do not stop until you have practiced the sequence four times.

Where else can you use this procedure? Divide into pairs. Write down three places where you can use this procedure.

1. _____

2. _____

3. _____

Why is flipping a coin a good idea?

What I Want, What You Want. How I Feel, How You Feel.
Why I Want It, Why You Want It.

It is not enough to say what you want. You must also say **why** you want it. You must have reasons for wanting something. And you must share your reasons with the other person. The other person needs to share his or her reasons with you.

The **third step** of negotiating is to say why you want it (the cookie or the book). To practice the first, second, third, and last steps of negotiating, go through the procedure of:

1. I want . . . You want . . .

2. I feel . . . You feel . . .

3. Why I want it. Why you want it.

4. We could do it together.

OK. Shake.

Wanting to Play

the Same Game

Divide into groups of four. Form two rows of four students each. The two rows face each other.

Each person says to the person he or she is facing:

I want to play checkers. No, I want to play checkers.

I feel frustrated. I'm angry.

I'm frustrated because you are interfering with me playing checkers. I'm angry because you won't let me play with the checkers.

We could play checkers together.
OK. Shake.

Then move to the next person and say the same thing. Do not stop until you have practiced the sequence four times.

Where else can you use this procedure? Divide into pairs. Write down three places where you can use this procedure.

1. _____

2. _____

3. _____

Why is playing checkers together a good idea?

My Understanding Of You, Your Understanding Of Me

Resolving conflicts takes more than understanding what you want and feel and why. You must also understand the other person. And you must make sure the other person knows you understand him or her.

The **fourth step** of negotiating is to summarize what the other person wants and feels and why. To practice the first, second, third, fourth, and last steps of negotiating, go through the procedure of:

Person 1	Person 2
I want . . .	I want . . .
I feel . . .	I feel . . .
My reasons are . . .	My reasons are . . .
My understanding of you is . . .	My understanding of you is . . .
You need it more that is do. You can have it.	Thanks. Shake.

Face your partner. Go through the above steps to negotiate who gets to use the computer first. Emphasize your understanding of the other person. Then repeat with a new partner.

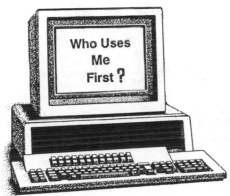

Who Uses Me First ?

Person 1	Person 2
I want to use the computer now!	*I want to use the computer now!*
I feel upset.	*I feel frustrated.*
I want to use the computer to try out a new computer game.	*I want to use the computer to do my homework.*
My understanding of you is that you will be frustrated if you do not get to do your homework on the computer now.	*My understanding of you is that you will be upset if you do not get to play your new computer game now.*
You need the computer more than I do. You can use it first.	*Thanks. Shake.*

Rules For Paraphrasing:
1. Put yourself in the other person's shoes.
2. Restate the other person's ideas and feelings in your own words. State as correctly as possible what the other person wants, feels, and why.
3. Start your remarks with, *You want...*, *You feel...*, and *You think...*
4. Show understanding and acceptance by nonverbal behaviors: tone of voice, facial expressions, gestures, eye contact, and posture.

Why is letting the other person use the computer a good idea?

Inventing Options For Mutual Gain

Resolving conflicts takes more than understanding yourself and the other person. You must also identify several possible solutions. In any conflict there are many ways to resolve it.

The **fifth step** in resolving conflicts is to think of at least three plans to solve the problem. You can practice the first four steps of negotiating by going through the procedure of:

Person 1	Person 2
I want . . .	I want . . .
I feel . . .	I feel . . .
My reasons are . . .	My reasons are . . .
My understanding of you is . . .	My understanding of you is . . .
Three plans to solve the problems are . . .	Three plans to solve the problem are . . .
Let's pick Plan B.	O.K. Shake.

He Hurt Me, I'll Hurt You

Fred's friend Sam yelled at him this morning on the playground. Fred feels sad and upset. When another friend, Ralph, says hello to him in line, Fred says, "Get out of here!" Now Ralph feels sad and upset and wants to negotiate with Fred to resolve the conflict.

Face your partner. Go through the above steps to negotiate a solution to the problem. Be sure to think of three plans before you choose one. Then repeat with a new partner.

Plan A: _____

_____

Plan B: _____

_____

Plan C: _____

_____

Negotiating: The Whole Procedure

Conflicts end when an agreement is reached. To reach an agreement, you and the other person must negotiate. The **purpose** of negotiating is to reach a **wise agreement** that is fair to everyone involved. To negotiate you must understand the procedure. The more skillful you are in using the procedure, the easier it will be to reach a wise agreement. To become skillful, practice the procedure over and over again until it becomes "automatic." The steps of negotiating are as follows.

Person 1	Person 2
I want.	I want.
I feel.	I feel.
My reasons are.	My reasons are.
My understanding of your wants & feelings is.	My understanding of your wants & feelings is.
Three plans to solve the problems are.	Three plans to solve the problem are.
We choose a plan.	O.K. Shake.

When resolving a conflict it is important to remember:

1. You both have the conflict. You must work together to solve it. Solve conflicts as friends, not enemies.

2. You both have feelings. They must be expressed in order for the conflict to be resolved constructively. Keeping frustration, angry, hurt, fear, or sadness inside only makes the conflict more difficult to resolve.

3. You both have reasons for wanting what you want and feeling like you do. Ask for each other's reasons and make sure you understand them.

4. You both have your perspective or point-of-view. In order to resolve the conflict constructively, you must see the conflict from both perspectives.

5. You both need to generate several alternative wise agreements that maximize the benefits to both of you. Wise agreements make both persons happy.

6. You both need to select the agreement that seems most wise and seal it with a handshake. Never agree on a solution that leaves one person happy and one person unhappy.

Stop Calling Me Names

Find a partner and role play the following situation:

1: *I want to you to stop calling me names.*
2: *I want to keep calling you names.*

1: *I feel hurt.*
2: *I feel fine when I call you names.*

1: *The reason I want you to stop calling me names is it upsets me so much I can't learn.*
2: *The reason I want to keep calling you names is that it makes me feel powerful to know I can hurt your feelings.*

1: *My understanding of you is that you want to call me names so you can feel powerful.*
2: *My understanding of you is that you want me to stop calling you names because it hurts your feelings and upsets you so much you can't do your schoolwork.*

1: *One way we could resolve our conflict is for one of us to give in. I could let you call me names. Or you could stop calling me names.*
2: *Another way we could resolve our conflict is for us to make a deal. I could stop calling you names. You could help me with run for student council.*

1: *A third plan would be for us to decide on a time when you could call me names and a time you could not. We could have a half-hour a day name-calling time.*
2: *Perhaps we should plan to work together on several projects so we could get to know each other better. If we got to know each other, I would not call you names.*

1: *Let's try plan four.*
2: *Shake.*

Where else can you use this procedure. Divide into pairs. Write down three places where you can use this procedure.

1. _____

2. _____

3. _____

Why is suggesting at least three optional plans a good idea?

BRIDGE TO UNDERSTANDING

Mediator _____ Date _____

	PERSON 1	PERSON 2
WANT		
FEEL		
REASONS		
UNDERSTANDING OF YOU		
THREE OPTIONS		
AGREEMENT		
SIGNATURE		

3:60

Who Owns This?

To negotiate effectively and communicate clearly you must speak for yourself. You are more easily understood if you take ownership for your thoughts, feelings, and needs. The purpose of this exercise is to give you practice in recognizing who owns the thoughts, feelings, or needs in a message. A message can be owned by the sender, no one, or someone other than the sender. The sender can be speaking for him- or herself, for no one, or for someone else.

Working in a pair, read each of the statements listed below. Put a:

> **S** for each statement where the sender is speaking for him or herself.

> **N** for statements where the sender is speaking for no one.

> **O** for statements where the sender is speaking for someone else.

Agree on each answer. Then combine with another pair and compare answers. Discuss each statement until everyone agrees.

Statements

_____ 1. Everyone loves the teacher.

_____ 2. I like you.

_____ 3. The rumor is that you are a nice person.

_____ 4. We think this song is great!

_____ 5. No one would like math.

_____ 6. Bill thinks you are strange.

_____ 7. Most people would be made if you did that to them.

_____ 8. I can tell by looking at your face that you feel terrible.

Describing Others' Behavior

To negotiate effectively and communicate clearly, you need to describe other people's behavior without passing judgment. Working with a partner, put a:

D for each statement that **describes** a person's behavior.

J for each statement that **judges** a person's behavior.

Agree on each answer. Then combine with another pair and compare answers. Discuss each statement until everyone agrees.

Statements

_____ 1. Sam interrupted Sally.

_____ 2. Mark is very sincere.

_____ 3. I do not like Sally.

_____ 4. Mark is very shy.

_____ 5. Today on the way to school, I saw three butterflies.

_____ 6. Jane is trying to make me mad.

_____ 7. Sam changed the subject.

_____ 8. Sam contributed six ideas to our discussion.

⋯❦❲ **Describing, Not Evaluating** ❳❦⋯

To define a conflict, you must tell the other person what you want. How you say what you want has positive or negative effects on how the conflict turns out.

Defining a conflict is like lacing your shoes. If you start out wrong, the whole thing gets messed up. Make the conflict over the other person's actions, not over his or her personality. If you call the other person names, insult or blame him or her, the conflict will probably turn out badly.

If you describe the conflict, then the conflict will probably turn out well. Describing needs to be caring, non-threatening, and non-judgmental. The words you use can make the other person angry at you or can make the other person want to resolve the conflict.

Using the person's name shows respect and caring.

Working as a pair, write a "**D**" by statements that describe, and write a "**E**" by statements that evaluate:

_____ 1. You are a mean person!

_____ 2. Sam. I don't like it when you call me a name. Do you want to tell me what's wrong?

_____ 3. You are a rotten bully!

_____ 4. Bob. I don't like being pushed. Please stop.

_____ 5. You're an evil witch!

_____ 6. Jane. I'm sorry when you say things about me that aren't true. Please tell me why you are angry.

Try your skill at describing, not evaluating. Working as a pair, write your answer to each of the following:

    1. A friend "snoops" into your things: _____

_____

_____.

    2. A classmate teases you: _____

_____

_____.

    3. A classmate blames you for not working hard enough: _____

_____

_____.

Your Challenge

With your partner, create a role play using one of the above situations.

"You and Me" Relationship Statements

To negotiate effectively, you must be able to make good relationship statements. Working with a partner, put a:

- **R** for each statement that describes how the speaker sees the relationship.

- **J** for a poor relationship statement that judges.

- **O** for a poor relationship statement that speaks for the other person.

- **P** for a poor relationship statement that is about a person, not a relationship.

Agree on each answer. Then combine with another pair and compare answers. Discuss each statement until everyone agrees.

Relationship Statements

_____ 1. We really enjoyed ourselves last night.

_____ 2. Our relationship is really lousy!

_____ 3. You look sick today.

_____ 4. You're angry again. You're always getting angry.

_____ 5. You have not spoken to me for two days. Is something wrong with our relationship?

_____ 6. I think we need to talk about our disagreement yesterday.

_____ 7. We are great at communicating.

_____ 8. You really make me feel appreciated and liked.

_____ 9. I think you are feeling better.

● Describing Your Feelings ●

To negotiate effectively and to communicate clearly, you must describe your feelings (as opposed to expressing them indirectly). Working with a partner, put a:

- **D** before a statement that describes the sender's feelings.
- **No** before a statement that conveys feeling without directly describing what the feeling is.

Agree on each answer. Then combine with another pair and compare answers. Discuss each statement until everyone agrees.

Statements

1. _____ a. Stop driving this fast! Slow down right now!

   _____ b. Your driving this fast frightens me.

2. _____ a. Do you have to stand on my foot?

   _____ b. You are so mean and vicious you don't care if you cripple me for life!.

   _____ c. I am annoyed at you for resting your 240-pound body on my foot.

3. _____ a. I feel ecstatic about winning the Reader's Digest Sweepstakes!

   _____ b. This is a wonderful day!.

4. _____ a. You're such a helpful person.

   _____ b. I really respect your ideas; you're so well informed.

5. _____ a. Everyone here likes to dance with you.

   _____ b. When I dance with you I feel graceful and relaxed.

   _____ c. We all feel you're a great dancer.

6. _____ a. If you don't start cleaning up after yourself, I'm moving out!

_____ b. Did you ever see such a messy kitchen in your life?

_____ c. I am afraid you will never do your share of housework.

7. _____ a. This is a very interesting book.

_____ b. I feel this is not a very helpful book.

_____ c. I get very excited when I read this book.

8. _____ a. I don't feel competent enough to contribute anything of worth to this group.

_____ b. I'm not competent enough to contribute anything worthwhile to this group.

■ Answers ■

1. a. No. Commands like these communicate strong feelings, but they do not name the feeling that underlies the commands.

   b. D. This statement both expresses and names a feeling. The person communicates the feeling by describing himself as frightened.

2. a. No. A feeling is implied through a question, but the specific feeling underlying the question is not described.

   b. No. This statement communicates considerable feeling through an accusation, but it is not clear whether the accusation is based on anger, hurt, fear, or some other feeling.

   c. D. The person describes the feeling as annoyance. Note that the speaker also "owns" the feeling by using the personal pronoun "I."

3. a. D. The speaker describes herself as feeling ecstatic.

   b. No. This statement communicates positive feelings without describing what they are. The speaker appears to be commenting on the weather when in fact the statement is

an expression of how the speaker feels. We cannot tell whether the speaker is feeling proud, happy, caring, accepted, supported, or relieved.

4. a. No. The speaker makes a value judgment communicating positive feelings about the other person, but the speaker does not describe the feelings. Does the speaker admire the other person or like the other person, or is the speaker only grateful?

   b. D. The speaker describes the positive feelings as respect.

5. a. No. This statement does name a feeling (likes) but the speaker is talking for everyone and does not make clear that the feeling is personal. A description of a feeling must contain "I," "me," "my," or "mine" to make clear that the feelings are within the speaker. Does it seem more friendly for a person to say, "I like you," or "Everybody likes you?"

   b. D. The speaker communicates clearly and specifically the feeling the speaker has when dancing with the other person.

   c. No. First, the speaker does not speak for herself, but rather hides behind the phrase "we feel." Second, "You're a great dancer" is a value judgment and does not name a feeling. Note that merely placing the word feel in front of a statement does not make the statement a description of feeling. People often say feel when they mean think or believe.

6. a. No. This statement communicates general and ambiguous negative feelings about the person's behavior. It refers to the condition of the apartment or house and the speaker's future behavior, but not to the speaker's inner feelings.

   b. No. The speaker is trying to communicate a negative feeling through a rhetorical question and a value judgment. Although it is clear the feeling is negative, the specific feeling is not described.

   c. D. The speaker describes fear as the negative feeling connected with the other person's housework.

   Note: Notice that in a and b the feelings could easily have been interpreted as anger. Many times the expression of anger results from an underlying fear. Yet when the receiver tries to respond, she may understand that the other person is angry without comprehending that the basic feeling to be responded to is a feeling of fear.

7. a. No. The speaker communicates a positive value judgment that conveys feelings, but the specific feelings are not described.

b. No. The speaker uses the words "I feel" but does not then describe or name a feeling. Instead, the speaker gives a negative value judgment. What the speaker actually meant was "I believe" or "I think" the book is not very good. People commonly use the word feel when they mean think or believe. Consider the difference between, "I feel you don't like me" and "I believe (think) you don't like me."

c. D. The speaker describes a feeling of excitement while reading this book.

Note: Many times people who say they are unaware of what they feel--or who say they don't have any feelings about something--state value judgments about recognizing that this is the way their positive or negative feelings get expressed. Many times useless arguments can be avoided if we are careful to describe our feelings instead of expressing them through value judgments. For example, if Joe says the book is interesting and Fred says it is boring, they may argue about which it "really" is. If Joe, however, says he was excited by the book and Fred says he was frustrated by it, no argument should follow. Each person's feelings are what they are. Of course, discussing what it means for Joe and Fred to feel as they do may provide helpful information about each person and about the book.

8. a. D. Speaker communicates a feeling of incompetence.

b. No. Warning! This statement is potentially hazardous to your health! Although it sounds much the same as the previous statement, it states that the speaker actually is incompetent. The speaker has passed a negative value judgment on himself and labeled himself as incompetent.

Note: Many people confuse feeling with being. A person may feel incompetent yet behave very competently or a person may feel competent and perform very incompetently. A person may feel hopeless about a situation that turns out not to be hopeless once his behavior is given an appropriate focus. A sign of emotional maturity is that a person does not confuse feelings with the reality of the situation. An emotionally mature person knows he can perform competently, even though he feels incompetent. He does not let his feelings keep him from doing his best because he knows the difference between feelings and performance and knows that the two do not always match.

Body Talk

Body langauge is another way of communicating. As you react to different situations, your body takes on certain positions.

Picture yourself at times when you feel the emotions listed below. Describe how your body looks when you feel these ways.

Embarrassment _____

_____

Nervousness _____

_____

Excitement _____

_____

Boredom _____

_____

Now draw a line from each face below to the feeling it shows.

Embarrassment

Nervousness

Excitement

Boredom

Anger

Happiness

Is This The Way You Feel?

To negotiate effectively and to communicate clearly, you need to check your perceptions of other people's feelings. Working in a pair, put a:

PC for each perception check.

J for each statement that makes a judgment about the other person.

O for each statement that speaks for the other person rather than for yourself.

Q for each question that does not include a description of your perceptions of the other person's feelings.

Agree on each answer. Then combine with another pair and compare answers. Discuss each statement until everyone agrees.

Statements

_____ 1. Are you angry with me?

_____ 2. You look as if you are upset about what Sally said. Are you?

_____ 3. Why are you mad at me?

_____ 4. You look as if you feel put down by my statement. That's stupid!

_____ 5. What is it about your teacher that makes you resent her so much?

_____ 6. Are your feelings hurt again?

_____ 7. You look unhappy. Are you?

_____ 8. Am I right that you feel irritated that nobody commended on your suggestion?

MY BEHAVIOR

Exercise

1. On a sheet of paper, list the skills that will be helpful in resolving the conflict between you and the other person.

———————————•◦•———————————

2. On a sheet of paper, list the assets you have that you can use in resolving the conflict.

———————————•◦•———————————

3. Think about the specific changes in your actions that may be helpful in resolving the conflict. Think about the skills and assets you have to help you resolve the conflict. Think about your definition of the conflict. Then list on a separate sheet of paper the specific actions you will take to resolve the conflict.

———————————•◦•———————————

4. Remember, the constructive resolution of conflict begins with your actions, your feelings, your skills and assets, your willingness to change, and your ability to define the conflict in a helpful way.

Your Actions

+

Your Feelings

+

Your Skills and Assets

+

Your Willingness to Change

+

Your Ability to Define the Conflict

Further Practice in Defining Conflicts Exercise

As a pair, identify the rule for defining a conflict being violated for each of the following statements. "My roommate is:

1. A mean, vicious, and demented person

2. Who wants my friends to like him better than me

3. Because he had a terrible childhood

4. And does not understand my feelings

5. And therefore needs to change and shape up."

Discuss the following two statements, indicating why you agree or disagree.

_____When a conflict is defined in a way that labels the other person negatively, is win-lose and general, and blames the other person for the conflict and for not understanding how you feel, considerable distress and destructive escalation of the conflict are likely to result.

_____When a conflict is defined as describing the other person's behavior, as a specific and limited problem to be solved, as including your feelings and your behaviors that contribute to the conflict, constructive resolution of the conflict is likely to result.

HMPH!

Differentiating Between Positions and Interests

For each of the following situations identify and write out each person's **position** and **interests** that caused them to take that position. Then find a partner and come to agreement on the answers. One member will be choosen randomly to give the pair's answers.

Sue wants the orange so she can use the peel to make an orange cake. Jim wants the orange so he can use the insides to make orange juice.

	Sue	Jim
Position		
Interests		

Jeremy wants the book so he can read it. Andrew wants the book so he can sit on it and see better.

	Jeremy	Andrew
Position		
Interests		

Davy wants the computer so he can write his science report. Tyler wants the computer to practice keyboarding.

	Davy	Tyler
Position		
Interests		

Jim wants the pencil so he can write with it. John wants the pencil to erase mistakes.

	Jim	John
Position		
Interests		

Betsy wants the ball so she can practice catching it. Sam wants the ball so she can practice throwing it.

	Betsy	Sam
Position		
Interests		

Whenever someone takes a position, ask them "why" in order to learn their interests.

Your Point OF View

Everyone has his or her own point of view. Some people like Chinese food. Some people do not. If you like Chinese food, you tend to assume that everyone does. If you like to be teased, you assume that everyone likes to be teased.

In resolving conflicts it is important to understand the other person's point of view. An example of the need to understand other's points of view is given below. Read the story with your partner.

The Wise Men And The Buffalo

Once upon a time, four blind men who were considered to be very wise wanted to know what a buffalo looked like. When a buffalo was brought to their town, they all went to touch it. The first wise man grabbed hold of the buffalo's tail. "The buffalo is like a rope," he yelled. The second wise man rubbed his hands over the buffalo's side. "No, No! The buffalo is like a big furry rug," he cried. The third wise man grabbed hold of the buffalo's horn. "The buffalo is like a spear!" he shouted. "You are all wrong," the fourth man exclaimed. "The buffalo is like a table!" He was holding two of the buffalo's legs. "Rope!" "Rug!" "Spear!" "Table!" The blind men yelled at each other for the rest of the day. They never did agree on what a buffalo looked like.

Your Point Of View Exercise

Working in your pair, answer the following questions. They join another pair and share your answers.

1. Which blind man was right? _____

   _____

2. What was their conflict based on? _____

   _____

3. Were they really "wise"? How do you tell if someone is wise? _____

   _____

4. How could the wise men have discovered what a buffalo really looks like? _____

   _____

5. What is the moral of the story? What does the story tell you about solving conflicts?

   _____

In your pair, rewrite the ending of the story to make it come out with a good solution to the conflict.

_____

_____

_____

_____

_____

Paraphrasing

1. Pick a real conflict that a member of the class is experiencing and identify four good alternative agreements. Number the agreements from "1" to "4" and then number the four corners of the room from "1" to "4."

2. Class members think of which option would make the best agreement. After considering the pro's and con's of each option, students write down their choice and the reasons why it is the best option on the sheet of paper.

3. All members of the class signify their choice by going to the corner of the room that represents the option they have chosen. They pair up with another student who made the same choice, compare and combine their reasons, and make a list of three reasons why their option is the best agreement. Each student needs a copy of the reasons.

4. Form groups of four (one student from each corner). Divide each group into pairs (student 1 meets with student 2, student 3 meets with student 4). One student presents his or her reasons. The other student listens carefully and then paraphrases the reasons. If the paraphrase is not accurate or complete, the student presenting corrects the paraphraser. The two students then reverse roles. Follow the rules for good paraphrasing. When both partners have paraphrased accurately and fully, switch partners (1 with 3, 2 with 4) and do present/paraphrase again. Switch partners again (1 with 4, 2 with 3) so that each student paraphrases the three other positions.

5. Students then decide if they wish to change their minds and choose a different option. The teacher asks students to go to the corner they now think would be the best option to agree to. The teacher counts how many students in each corner. The procedure may be repeated if there is time.

Rules for Paraphrasing

1. Put yourself in the other person's shoes.

2. Restate the other person's ideas and feelings in your own words. State as correctly as possible the other's reasons for believing his or her option will make the best agreement.

3. Start your remarks with, *You want...*, *You feel...*, and *You think...*

4. Show understanding and acceptance by nonverbal behaviors: tone of voice, facial expressions, gestures, eye contact, and posture.

Name _____ Date _____

DEAR ABBY 1

Below you will find a letter to Abby. Read the message and meet with your partner to write three plans to solve the problem. Both of you need to agree on the plans. Write them in the boxes below, using extra sheets if you need them.

> Dear Abby,
> One member of my group is always day-dreaming when we are supposed to be working on a group project. It really bugs me!
>
> Disgusted

Plan A

Plan B

Plan C

Name _____ Date _____

DEAR ABBY 2

Here is another letter mailed to Abby by a student. Read what "Ignored" says and then write three plans with your partner for solving his problem. Make sure that you agree on the plans. You may add extra sheets if you run out of room.

Dear Abby,

There is a person in my group who won't let me contribute. She interrupts me and refuses to listen to my ideas. How can I get her to give me a chance to talk without hurting her feelings or making her angry?

"Ignored"

Plan A

Plan B

Plan C

Name _____ Date _____

DEAR ABBY 3

"Squelched" wrote to Abby feeling put down.   Read her letter and write three plans with your partner.   The two of you should agree on each of the solutions.   If you need more room, continue the plans on extra sheets.

Dear Abby,
There is a person in our group who is always putting everyone down and pretending it is just a joke. No one wants to be in our group anymore because of all the insults we have to put up with. They are afraid to talk because this person makes fun of what they say. What can I do to get our group back together?
            "Squelched"

Plan A

Plan B

Plan C

Brainstorming Optional Agreements

Brainstorming is a procedure that encourages divergent thinking and the production of many different ideas in a short period of time. In brainstorming you first generate a list of ideas and second you evaluate them. The rules for brainstorming are:

1. Think of as many different ideas as possible. Go for quantity. Write down all ideas. The longer the list, the better.

2. Do not criticize or evaluate ideas. Accept all ideas. Encourage silly, far out ideas. Piggyback on each other's ideas.

3. Set a time limit and keep the pace quick. Review the problem frequently to keep attention focused.

Form a pair. Consider the following conflict. Then brainstorm seven potential agreements to resolve the conflict.

Davy: You keep giving me false compliments. It's embarrassing to be around you because you keep telling me how wonderful I am. I'm glad you like me, but I can't bear to be overpraised and it makes me feel you are not sincere.

Virginia: I like telling people how great they are. Whenever I see you doing something well, I'm going to tell you about it. It's a habit. I just do it.

What can Davy and Virginia do to resolve their conflict so that both get what they want and like each other better than ever. Follow the above rules for brainstorming.

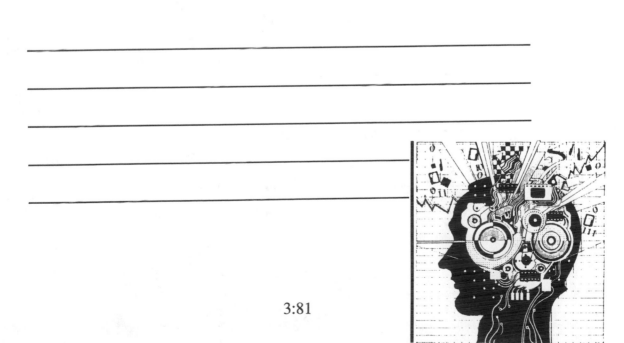

_____

_____

Put a plus or a minus to indicate what you think of each option. Then check the idea you both like the best.

With your partner pick a conflict that you or one of your friends is involve in. Brainstorm potential agreements that would solve the problem. Then evaluate each one and check the one you like the best.

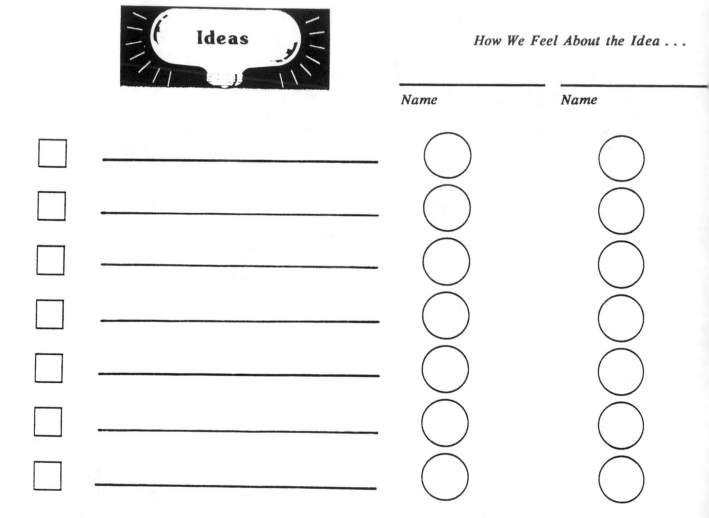

How We Feel About the Idea . . .

Name   *Name*

Using Balance Sheets to Make Wise Decisions

Roger was a coin collector; his wife, Ann, loved to raise and show championship rabbits. Their income did not leave enough money for both to practice their hobbies, and splitting the cash they did have would not have left enough for either. The conflict over whether to spend their extra money on coins or rabbits was so severe that they were thinking about getting a divorce. Think of three optional agreements that would allow them to stay married. Then use the balance sheet to decide what to do. Use the following procedure.

1. Evaluate the first alternative agreement on the basis of the gains and losses for:

   a. Person 1.

   b. Person 2.

   c. Others in the class, school, family, and/or community.

2. Once all the gains and losses have been listed for the first alternative agreement, rate each in terms of its importance on a five-point scale from 1 (no importance) to 5 (extremely important).

3. Evaluate whether (a) each person will feel proud or ashamed if this alternative is agreed to and (b) important other people think that you have made the right decision.

4. Repeat these steps for each of the other alternative agreements.

5. After a balance sheet has been completed for each alternative agreement, rank the alternatives from "most desirable" to "least desirable."

Table 3.3 Conflict Decision Balance Sheet

	Gains	Rating	Losses	Rating	Approval
Person 1					
Person 2					
Others					

Using Balance Sheets (continued)

Repeat the process with the following two conflicts. Like the one above, they actually happened.

> Edythe and Buddy shared an office but had different work habits. Edythe liked to do her work in silence while Buddy liked to socialize in the office and have the radio on. Their conflict over noise became so severe that each went to their boss and demanded that the other be moved or even fired.

> Keith loved to spend his evenings talking to people all over the world on his ham radio set. From the time he got home from work until it was time to go to bed, he would sit with his ham radio conversing with far away people. His wife, Simone, felt cheated out of the few hours of each day they could spend together. Keith did not want to give up his radio time and Simone was not willing to forego the time they had together. The conflict became so severe that Simone was thinking about getting a divorce.

Pick a conflict you are presently involved in. Complete balance sheets for your conflict. Then negotiate with the other person some more.

Each of the three conflict examples given above actually happened. Here are the **solutions** that were negotiated with the help of a counselor.

1. Roger and Ann decided to put all the first year's money into Ann's rabbits, and then after the rabbits were grown use the income from their litters and show prizes to pay for Roger's coins.

2. Edythe and Buddy decided that on Mondays and Wednesdays Buddy would help keep silence in the office. On Tuesdays and Thursdays Edythe would work in a conference room that was free, leaving Buddy alone in the office to play the radio. On Fridays the two worked together on joint projects.

3. Keith and Simone decided that four nights a week Keith would spend the evening talking with Simone. Afterwards he would stay up late and talk to his ham radio friends. On the following mornings Simone would drive Keith to work instead of having him go with a carpool, which allowed him to sleep later.

There are few problems that can not be solved with the creative thinking of two problem-solving negotiators.

Agree Or Disagree?

Read the following quotation and decide whether you agree or disagree. Give at least three reasons for doing so. Then decide whether Bach's statement accurately describes you and your classmates, teachers, administrators, and parents.

> *"What dismays me is not bloodshed per se in fighting, it is the native cowardice and abysmal crudity of the American fighting style. Most Americans will avail themselves of any sneaky excuse to avoid a fight in the first place. But if cornered they begin clobbering away at one another like dull-witted Neanderthals. They are clumsy, weak-kneed, afflicted with poor aim, rotten timing, and no notion of counterpunching. What is more, they fight dirty. Their favorite weapons are the low blow and the rock-filled glove."*

George Bach

NEGOTIABLE Versus NONNEGOTIABLE Issues

Not every issue is negotiable and you should know the difference between a negotiable and nonnegotiable issue. And you must be able to say "no" when someone tries to negotiate a nonnegotiable issue. Your **tasks** are to make a list of negotiable and nonnegotiable issues and to practice saying "no" when someone brings up a nonnegotiable issue. To prepare, read the section on **Refusal Skills** in this chapter.

1. Draw two columns on a sheet of paper. Label the first column "Negotiable" and the second column "Nonnegotiable." Under the first column write "Eat a salad for lunch." Under the second column write "shoplift." What you eat for lunch is negotiable. Breaking the law is not negotiable.

2. Working as a pair, list five issues that are negotiable and five issues that are not negotiable. Both of you need a copy.

3. Find a new partner. **Share** your list of negotiable and nonnegotiable issues. **Listen** to his or her list. **Create** a new list from the best ideas of both of you.

4. Return to your original partner. **Share** your new list. **Listen** to his or her new list. **Create** a final list from the best ideas from both of you.

5. Role play a situation in which someone is trying to get you to do something you do not want to do. Pick one of the nonnegotiable issues. Try to negotiate it with your partner. Your partner should say, to your every attempt, "No, I won't do it. That issue is nonnegotiable." Then reverse roles. Your partner tries to negotiate one of the nonnegotiable issues with you. You reply to his or her every attempt, "No, I won't do it. That issue is nonnegotiable."

Meredith	Margaret
Help me cheat on this test.	No, I won't. That issue is nonnegotiable.
It's only one test. No one will every know.	No, I won't. That issue is nonnegotiable.
If you're my friend, you'll help me cheat.	No, I won't. Cheating is nonnegotiable.

Nonnegotiable!

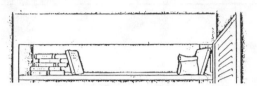

Negotiating for What You Need

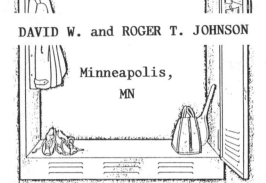

DAVID W. and ROGER T. JOHNSON

Minneapolis,
MN

Subject Area: Universal

Grade Level: Any

Lesson Summary: This lesson requires students to learn and practice negotiation skills in order to obtain the resources they need to complete the assigned task. The required resources are unequally distributed among pairs. In working on the task, students will have to (a) access the resources they need from other pairs and (b) decide how to respond to proposals from others for their pair's resources.

Instructional Objectives: Teach negotiation skills.

Time Required: Thirty to sixty minutes.

Materials:

Item	Materials Needed
Scissors, ruler, paper clips, pencils, two 4-inch squares of red paper, two 4-inch squares of white paper	One Set For Pair 1
Scissors, glue, two 8 1/2" x 11" sheets of gold paper, white paper, and blue paper	One set for Pair 2
Felt-tipped markers, two 8 1/2" x 11" sheets of green paper, white paper, and gold paper	One set for Pair 3
One 8 1/2" x 11" sheet of green, gold, blue, red, and purple paper	One set for Pair 4
Task sheet	One sheet per pair

Decisions

Cluster Size:

Eight, divided into four pairs. Groups of 12 may be used with four triads if the teacher wishes.

Assignment To Groups:

Randomly assign students to groups of eight. Within the group of eight have students count off from 1 to 4. The two 1's make a pair, the two 2's make a pair, the two 3's make a pair, and the two 4's make a pair.

Materials:

Each pair is given a packet of materials (see materials table).

The Lesson

Instructional Task:

Distribute an envelope of materials and a Task Sheet to each pair. Explain that each pair has a different set of materials, but they all have to complete the same tasks. They are to negotiate with the other pairs in their group for the materials required to complete the tasks. Pairs may negotiate only with pairs from their cluster. They may **not** negotiate with pairs who are members of another cluster. More specifically, each pair is to complete the following tasks:

1. Make a 3" x 3" square of white paper.

2. Make a 4" x 2" rectangle of gold paper.

3. Make a 3" x 5" **T** in green and white paper.

4. Make a four-link paper chain.

5. Make a 4" x 4" flag, in any three colors.

The first pair to complete all tasks is the winner. Pairs may negotiate with each other for the resources they need to complete the tasks.

Positive Interdependence:

One set of products from the pair, both members must agree on how to complete each task, and both must participate actively in the tasks and the negotiations with the other pairs.

Individual Accountability:

The teacher will observe each pair to ensure that both members are working on the tasks and negotiating with other pairs. Pairs in which both members are not engaging in the task work and in negotiations will be disqualified.

Monitoring And Processing

While the groups are working, observe to:

1. Verify that both members of each pair are working on the tasks and negotiating.

2. Determine what negotiation strategies are being used by each student.

Intervene to energize any lagging pairs and keep pairs aware of the time limits.

After all pairs have completed the tasks, have each cluster discuss how resources were negotiated, which pair had the most power and why, and what effects the competition had on the negotiations. Each student should receive feedback on the strategies they used in negotiations.

Negotiating Task Sheet

Each group is to complete the following tasks:

1. Make a 3" x 3" square of white paper.

2. Make a 4" x 2" rectangle of gold paper.

3. Make a 3" x 5" **T** in green and white paper.

4. Make a four-link paper chain.

5. Make a 4" x 4" flag, in any three colors.

The first pair to complete all tasks is the winner. Pairs may negotiate with each other for the resources they need to complete the tasks.

The tasks are to be completed cooperatively: One set of products from the pair, both members must agree on how to complete each task, and both must participate actively in the tasks and the negotiations with the other pairs.

We'll trade you some of our red paper for some of your blue.

4 Conflict Strategies

Basic Concerns Of Negotiators

> *I hold it be a proof of great prudence for men to abstain from threats and insulting words toward anyone, for neither . . . diminishes the strength of the enemy; but the one makes him more cautious, and the other increases his hatred of you and makes him more persevering in his efforts to injure you.*
>
> Niccolo Machiavelli, an adviser to 16th Century Florentine princes

When you become engaged in a conflict, two major concerns you have to take into account are:

1. **Reaching an agreement that satisfies one's needs and meets one's goals.** This is why one negotiates. Each person has personal goals that he or she wishes to achieve. You are in conflict because you have a goal or interests that conflict with another person's goal or interests. Your goal may be placed on a continuum between being of little importance to you to being highly important.

2. **Maintaining an appropriate relationship with the other person.** Some relationships are temporary while some are permanent. Some people you interact with infrequently while others you interact with several times a day. Within career and family settings you need to maintain caring and committed relationships so you can work together effectively to achieve mutual goals. With a store clerk you see only once, a pleasant but more impersonal interaction may be appropriate. Your relationship with the other person may be placed on a continuum between being of little importance to you to being highly important.

Within an ongoing relationship the shadow of the future is ever present. There are immediate problems to be solved and there are ongoing future joint efforts that should not be jeopardized. A long-term perspective must be maintained while dealing with immediate issues. Potential short-term gains must be weighed against potential long-term losses. **The shadow of the future looms largest when interactions among individuals are frequent and durable.** **Durability** ensures that individuals will not easily forget how they have treated, and been treated by, each other in the future. **Frequency** promotes stability by making the consequences of today's actions more salient for tomorrow's dealings. When individuals realize they will work with each other frequently and for a long period of time making the consequences of today's actions more salient for tomorrow's dealings. When individuals realize they will work with each other frequently and for a long period of time (such as a year or more), they see the need to be supportive and cooperative in current dealings with each other. Usually, the future outweighs the present so that the quality of the ongoing relationship is more important than the outcome of any particular negotiation. The long-term benefits of cooperation outweigh the short-term benefits of taking advantage of the other person. But when problems arise, the goals of each person and the commitment to the ongoing relationship are in conflict.

Deciding How To Manage A Conflict

Dealing with a conflict of interests is like going swimming in a cold lake. Some people like to test the water, stick their foot in, and enter slowly. Such people want to get used to the cold gradually. Other people like to take a running start and leap in. They want to get the cold shock over quickly. Different people use different strategies for managing conflicts. These strategies are learned, usually in childhood, and they seem to function automatically on a "preconscious" level. We just do whatever seems to come naturally. But we do have a personal strategy and, because it was learned, we can always change it by learning new and more effective ways of managing conflicts. How important your personal goals are to you and how important the relationship is perceived to be affect how you act in a conflict. Given these two concerns within a relationship, there are five basic strategies that may be used to manage conflicts:

1. **Withdrawal**. This involves giving up both your goals and the relationship and, therefore, you avoid the other person and the issue. When the goal is not important and you do not need to keep a relationship with the other person, you may want to act like a turtle and withdraw. Avoiding a hostile stranger may be the best thing to do. Or you may wish to withdraw from a conflict until you and the other person have calmed down and are in control of your feelings.

2. **Forcing**. This involves meeting your goals at all costs, demanding that the other person let you have your way, no matter how much it hurts the relationship. When the goal is very important but the relationship is not, such as when you are buying a used car, you may want to act like a shark and force. Never use forcing with someone you will have to relate to again soon.

3. **Smoothing**. This involves giving up your goals in order to maintain the relationship at the highest level possible. When the goal is of no importance to you but the relationship

High
Importance

RELATIONSHIPS

Smoothing

Confronting

Compromising

Withdrawing

Forcing

GOALS

Low
Importance

© 1975 by David W. Johnson

High
Importance

4 : 3

is of high importance, you may want to act like a teddy bear and smooth. When a colleague feels strongly about something, and you could care less, smoothing is a good idea. When you are smoothing, do so with good humor. Be pleasant about it. At times, to smooth you may need to apologize. Saying "I'm sorry" does not mean "I'm wrong." "I'm sorry" lets the other person know that you are sorry about the situation. When you think the other person's interests are much stronger or important than yours, smooth and give the other person their way.

4. **Compromising**. This involves giving up part of your goals and sacrificing part of the relationship in order to reach an agreement. When both the goal and the relationship are moderately important to you and it appears that both you and the other person cannot get what you want, you may want to negotiate like a fox. When there is a limited amount of money, and both you and a fellow employee want a large raise, for example, negotiating a compromise may be the best way to resolve the conflict. You can meet in the middle, each taking half, or flip a coin and let chance decide who will get their way.

5. **Confronting**. This involves initiating negotiations aimed at ensuring that you and the other person both fully meet your goals and maintain the relationship at the highest level possible. An agreement is sought that satisfies both you and the other person and resolves any tensions and negative feelings between the two of you. When both the goal and the relationship are highly important to you, you may want to act like an owl. Face the conflict. Negotiate to solve the problem. Think of solutions that will give both you and the other person what you want and will keep the relationship positive.

Each conflict strategy has its place. **You do not want to be an overspecialized dinosaur who can deal with conflict in only one way.** You need to be able to use any one of the five, depending on your goals and the relationship. In one conflict, you may wish to use one strategy, while in another conflict you may wish to use a different strategy. To be effective in resolving conflicts, you have to vary your actions according to what will work best in the situation. You need to be able to switch actions according to what will work best.

Within an ongoing relationship, there are six basic rules to follow in dealing with conflicts of interests.

Rule 1: Do Not Withdraw From Or Ignore Conflict

In headaches and in worry
Vaguely life leaks away.

W. H. Auden

When the goal is not important and you do not need to keep a relationship with the other person, you may wish to withdraw from a conflict. Avoiding a hostile stranger in the lunchroom may be the best thing to do. Withdrawal involves giving up your personal goals and the relationship. You stay away from the conflict issue and from the person you are in conflict with. There are a number of reasons why you may want to withdraw from a conflict. **First,** you may not know the other person and may not care about the issue. **Second,** from past experience with the person you may believe that it is hopeless to try to resolve the conflict or you may feel helpless to do so. **Third,** you may be inhibited to express anger, resentment, or envy toward another member of your classroom or school because you consider it bad manners or immature to do so. **Fourth,** you may believe that it is easier to physically and/or psychologically withdraw from a conflict than to face it. **Fifth,** you may fear that if you express your anger or resentment you will be disliked, be rejected, be attacked, or be seen as a complainer. **Finally,** you may recognize the risk that dealing with the conflict directly might create a residue of interpersonal antagonisms and hurt your career. There are many reasons why you may want to ignore a conflict.

Ignoring a problem, however, keeps emotional energy tied up in fear, resentment, and hostility. It takes emotional energy to suppress your anger and resentment, but it may take even more emotional energy to confront the other person. Conflicts are often played out in some indirect way because it takes less energy in the short run. **Indirectly dealt-with conflicts, however, have the longest life expectancy and have the most costs** (often seemingly unrelated to the original conflict). If feelings such as anger, resentment, and envy are not expressed directly, they usually will be expressed indirectly, often in ways that create still new conflicts and incur other costs. Indirect expressions of anger include sulkiness, uncooperativeness, sarcasm, or talking behind the other person's back. Repressing anger can lead eventually to angry explosions that end in fights and other destructive outbursts.

There may be times when temporarily withdrawing from and ignoring a conflict may be constructive in order to confront the other person at a more advantageous time or deal with the conflict when more information is available. Ignoring a problem, however, does not make it disappear. It keeps plaguing you and the other person until it is faced and solved. In the long run, it is never easier to withdraw (physically and psychologically) from a conflict than to face it. When dealing with the other person be sure to face your conflicts and openly negotiate them.

The **procedure** for withdrawing is to walk away and avoid the other person and your needs and goals related to the conflict. Refuse to identify and talk about the issue. Leave if the other person insists on doing so.

Rule 2: Do Not Engage In "Win-Lose" Negotiations

I know I am among civilized men because they are fighting so savagely.

Voltaire

When the goal is very important to you but the relationship is not, you may wish to engage in forcing. **Forcing** involves overpowering opponents by requiring them to accept your solution to the conflict. You seek to achieve your goals at all costs and without concern with the needs of others. You do not care whether others like or accept you. You assume that conflicts are settled when one person "wins" and the other person "loses," and you want to be the winner. When you force you try to win by attacking, overpowering, overwhelming, and intimidating others. Buying a used car or trying to get into a crowded restaurant are two instances where forcing may be appropriate. When two people each attempt to force the other to accept an agreement favorable to oneself, "hard" negotiations follow and the basic strategy is to take an extreme opening position and refuse to compromise or reconsider until you are forced to do so.

Forcing usually has negative efforts on the other person and reduces the likelihood of working together effectively in the future. Forcing creates resistance and resentment. The more you force, the more the other person resists and the more angry the other person gets. When forcing is successful winning may result in a sense of pride and achievement. When it is unsuccessful, it may result in depression, guilt, shame, and failure.

Forcing can develop inadvertently. In negotiations, each person takes a position, argues for it, and makes concessions to reach a compromise or searches for a mutually beneficial solution. This involves successively taking, and then giving up, a sequence of positions. The danger in this procedure is that individuals tend to lock themselves into the positions they are taking. The more you clarify your position and defend it against attack, the more committed you become to it. The more you try to convince the other person of the impossibility of changing your position, the more difficult it becomes for you to do so. Your ego becomes identified with your position. You may become more interested in "saving face" than in seeking a wise agreement. In defending your position, and trying to "win," less attention is devoted to meeting the underlying concerns of the other person. Agreement becomes less likely.

The **procedure** for forcing is to bring up the issue, take an extreme opening position, and refuse to compromise or reconsider until you absolutely have to. Forcing, however, is inappropriate within long-term relationships. While avoiding trying to force the other person to adopt a position that lets you "win," you may wish to assess the situation for possible "smoothing."

Rule 3: Assess For Smoothing

A soft answer turneth away wrath.

Holy Bible

When you attach little importance to the goal, but you care about the relationship, you may wish to smooth. Smoothing involves letting the other person have his or her way. **Inappropriate smoothing** is based on wanting to be liked and accepted by others. The conflict is avoided in favor of harmony. People may fear they cannot discuss the conflict without damaging the relationship. They may be afraid that if the conflict continues, someone will get hurt, and that would ruin the relationship. They, therefore, may approach conflicts with the attitude, "I will give up my goals and let you have what you want, in order for you to like me."

You negotiate differently within long-term relationships than you do short-term ad hoc relationships. Within long-term relationships you have considerable concern about the other person's interests. You are, after all, striving to achieve the same goals, the quality of the work life of both of you is affected by how the conflict is managed, and the group's success is largely determined by how members manage their conflicts. Within negotiations, therefore, your true wants and needs have to be clearly presented at the beginning so that they may be weighed against the true wants and needs of the other person. By weighing the true interests of each person against each other, the agreement can be determined. **Appropriate smoothing** occurs when two people share mutual goals, each determines whose interests are stronger or more important, and one person gives up his or her interests to help the other. This is known as **one- step negotiating**.

Smoothing only works if it is reciprocal. Ongoing relationships are guided by a **norm of mutual responsiveness** that says you should be committed to fulfilling each other's goals and concerned about each other's interests. If both people follow this norm, over time each will have his or her major needs satisfied by the other.

The **procedure** for appropriate smoothing may be summarized as follows:

1. You relax and make sure your emotions are under control. You engage the other person directly by looking at him or her.

2. You bring up the issue to be discussed, describe what you want and how you feel, and listen to the other person describe what he or she wants and feels.

3. You ask the other person to describe the reasons underlying his or her position and you describe your reasons. You separate interests from positions.

4. You show considerable concern about the other person's interests and you expect the other person to do likewise.

5. If the issue is of little importance to you, or if you determine that the other person's interests are much stronger than yours, you smooth by agreeing to his or her proposal.

Rule 4: Compromise When Time Is Short

When both the goal and the relationship seem of moderate importance to you and it appears that both you and the other person cannot get what you want, you may want to agree to a compromise. Half a loaf is better than none! When you seek a **compromise**, you give up part of your goal and try to persuade the other person to do the same. You seek a solution in which both sides gain something and settle on an agreement that is the middle ground between your two opening positions. You are willing to sacrifice part of your goals and part of the relationship in order to find a quick agreement. For example, when there is a limited amount of computer time and both you and your classmate want to use the computer, negotiating a compromise may be the best way to resolve the conflict.

The **procedure** for appropriately compromising may be summarized as follows:

1. You relax and make sure your emotions are under control. You engage the other person directly by looking at him or her.

2. You bring up the issue to be discussed, describe what you want and how you feel, and listen to the other person describe what he or she wants and feels.

3. You ask the other person to describe the reasons underlying his or her position and you describe your reasons. You separate interests from positions.

4. You show considerable concern about the other person's interests and you expect the other person to do likewise.

5. You propose a compromise (usually requiring each person to give up 50 percent of what he or she wants so the two of you meet in the middle) when:

   a. You believe your goals are so important that they cannot be given up.

   b. The other person believes the same thing.

   c. There is not enough time to discuss the issue until a mutually acceptable solution is found.

The problem with compromising is that any agreement that is reached may reflect a mechanical splitting of the difference between positions rather than a solution carefully crafted to meet the legitimate interests of each person. The result is frequently an agreement less satisfactory to each person than it could have been. Sometimes, though, you should be satisfied with less. Remember the story of the boy and the nuts. A boy who was very fond of nuts was told one day that he could have a handful. "As big a handful as I like?" he asked. "As big a handful as you can take," his mother replied. The boy at once put his hand into the pitcher of nuts and grasped all his fist would hold. But when he tried to get his hand out, he found he could not because the neck of the pitcher was too narrow. He tried and tried to squeeze his hand through. At last he burst into tears. There he stood crying, yet unwilling to let a single nut go. "The fault is not with the pitcher," his mother said. "It is your greed that makes you cry. Be satisfied with half as many nuts and you will be able to get your hand out."

Within an ongoing relationship most issues do not have to be settled immediately. People can find the time necessary to explore their differences and search for optional agreements that will allow both to get what they need.

Rule 5: Confront To Begin Negotiations

He that wrestles with us strengthens our nerves, and sharpens our skill. Our antagonist is our helper.

Edmund Burke, **Reflection of the Revolution in France**

When both your goals and the relationship are of high importance to you, you confront the other person in order to begin problem-solving negotiations. A **confrontation** occurs when you directly express your view of the conflict and your feelings about it while inviting the other person to do the same. Confrontations are aimed at clarifying and exploring (a) the issues, (b) the nature and strength of the underlying interests of the participants, and (c) participants' current feelings. It is a deliberate attempt to begin a direct and problem-solving discussion about the conflict with the other person. A number of studies have found that the use of confrontations was related to the constructive resolution of conflicts (Burke, 1969, 1970; Lawrence & Lorsch, 1967).

If a resolution to a conflict is to be negotiated, the individuals involved must discuss it. If they do not discuss the conflict, solutions cannot be negotiated. But, just any old discussion will not do. To derive benefits from the conflict, it must be discussed with some skill. **How the discussion of the conflict is initiated largely determines how beneficial or harmful the discussion of the conflict will turn out to be.** You confront to initiate negotiations to solve a mutual problem. The **procedure** for confronting may be described as follows:

1. You relax and make sure your emotions are under control. You engage the other person directly by looking at him or her.

2. You bring up the issue to be discussed, describe what you want and how you feel, and listen to the other person describe what he or she wants and feels.

3. You ask the other person to describe the reasons underlying his or her position and you describe your reasons. You separate interests from positions.

4. You show considerable concern about the other person's interests and expect him or her to do likewise.

5. You continue negotiations by reversing perspectives, developing a number of optional agreements, and reaching a wise agreement.

6. You keep trying until a wise agreement is reached.

Confronting another person is **not** aimed at identifying and punishing offenders. Confrontation is the first step in initiating problem-solving negotiations. You and the other person want to solve the mutual problem as partners in a hard-headed side-by-side search for a fair agreement advantageous to both. The purpose is to bring up problems for discussion so individuals can resolve their differences and improve their relationship. When you confront another person, remember (a) what the other person is doing should directly affect you and (b) it should be something that the other person can change. Do not wait too long to confront. Small conflicts are much easier to resolve than are large ones. Confront when issues are immediate, small, and concrete.

Within confrontations the most troublesome feelings to deal with are anger and fear. You cannot confront effectively if your anger is out of control and you want to punish and hurt the other person. You cannot confront effectively if you are afraid that the other person will lose his or her temper and harm you psychologically or physically. Managing anger is perhaps the most complex and difficult aspect of confronting another person and, therefore, it is dealt with at length in the next chapter.

To Talk Or To Button Your Lips: Confrontation Or Silence

Within classrooms, it is inevitable that students will engage in conflicts. It is impossible to interact day after day without irritations and conflicts arising. When students are working together, sharing ideas, information, resources, and materials, they are bound to encounter problems. Some students may be unwilling to contribute, may stray off topic, may attempt to dominate their learning groups, or may struggle over who is going to be the leader. Two students may want the same book, compete for the same friend, strive for the same position on an athletic team, want to be the best speller in the class, or even want to date the same person. Many times the actions of one student will offend or hurt the feelings of another student.

An open discussion of a conflict is not always a helpful thing to have. It is a mistake to assume that you can always be open and discuss a conflict with another person. It is also a mistake to assume that you can never openly and directly discuss a conflict with another person. Whether you decide to open your mouth or button your lips depends on the other person and on the situation.

When you are trying to decide whether or not to begin a discussion about the conflict with the other person, you should ask yourself two questions:

1. What is your relationship with the other person like? How open is it? How strong is the relationship? Generally, the stronger the relationship, the more direct and open your discussion can be.

2. How able is the other person to discuss the conflict? The other person may not be able to discuss the conflict in a problem-solving way if his or her (a) anxiety or distress level is too high, (b) ability to change is too low, (c) conflict-resolution skills are too low, or (d) ego-strength or self-esteem are too low.

If you do not think the relationship is strong enough, do not confront the other person. If you do not think the other person is able to discuss the conflict in a problem-solving, helpful way, do not initiate negotiations.

Making A Date: Do Not Hit And Run!

Confronting another person and beginning a discussion of the conflict does not mean that the conflict will be quickly resolved. It is a start, not the end. Be prepared for some time to be spent in negotiations before the conflict is fully resolved. You need to time your discussion so that you do not simply hit-and-run. A **hit-and-run** occurs when you start a conversation about the conflict, give your definition and feelings, and then disappear before the other person has a chance to respond. Hit-and-runs tend to be harmful. They create resentment and anger rather than a constructive discussion of the conflict.

One of the most important aspects of confronting another person is timing. Destructive discussions often begin because the initiator confronts a person who is not ready. There are many times when the other person will not be in the right frame of mind to face a conflict,

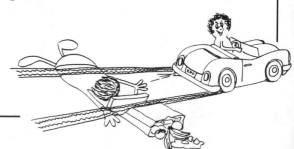

perhaps owing to fatigue, being in too much of a hurry to take the necessary time, being upset over another problem, or feeling physically sick. Confronting a person when there is not enough time to at least define the conflict is a sure way of making the discussion destructive. At times it is unfair to confront a person without notice and expect to get his or her full attention to the conflict. Instead, approach the other person with a request to discuss the conflict. Say, for example, "Something has been bothering me. Can we talk about it?" If the answer is "yes," then you are ready to go further and confront. If the answer is "no," find a time that is agreeable to both of you.

Focus On The Problem, Not The Person

When negotiating it is imperative that you separate the person from the problem. Fight over issues, not personalities. Avoid personalized attacks. Keep the negotiations free of highly personal criticism, topics, recriminations, abusive language, and especially those subtle jibes that inflict pain on the other. You may do so by:

1. Making it clear it is ideas or actions you disagree with, not the other individual as a person.

2. Separating the other person's criticism of your actions and ideas from rejection of you as a person. Accept criticism of your ideas and actions without feeling rejected as a person.

3. Keeping your sense of humor.

4. Keeping all "weapons" out of reach. Do not let one of you hurt the other.

5. Recognizing that people have egos. Protect the other's ego. One way to do this is to provide visible, acceptable reasons for him or her to switch to your viewpoint.

Take Easy Conflicts First

Learning how to confront effectively follows the pattern of all skill learning. When individuals learn new skills they first perform them awkwardly, progress to a phony/role-playing enactment of the skills and then to a mechanical performance, and finally integrate the skills into their behavioral repertoire by learning them at a routine-use level. Confrontation skills are no exception. **A common error many individuals make in learning confrontation skills is not to practice them sufficiently to reach the routine- use level**

of mastery before a serious conflict arises. When a conflict is serious, and individuals are upset and angry, an awkward, phony, or mechanical use of confrontation skills will be limited in their effectiveness. You will want to have the confrontation skills mastered at a routine-use level before you face a serious conflict and attempt to use them. Look for any opportunity, no matter how small, to practice the skills with students and colleagues so that you will perfect the skills and they will understand the procedures before serious conflicts arise. Practice, practice, practice on small conflicts to ensure that the procedures and skills are in place to manage the big ones.

In confronting others, take the easiest problems first. Learn to walk before you run. First use your negotiating procedures and skills on the easy problems and then use them on the harder issues. If it is not possible to identify a small issue, you may wish to choose a large one and then fractionate the conflict. Break the big issue into smaller parts. A number of small agreements can then be pieced together into sizable packages.

Rule 6: Use Your Sense Of Humor

Humor is one of the most important aspects of keeping conflicts constructive. Keep your sense of humor during negotiations. Help the other person to do the same. Do not make the same mistake that David and Linda did. David and Linda both worked as copy writers for different advertising firms. Their daily job was to think up funny and humorous lines to go into commercials. One of the things they most enjoyed about each other was their sense of humor. Yet when they began to talk about a conflict, all humor was buried. They would yell, scream, demand, force, withdraw, pout, and try to hurt each other. Their creativity was locked away by their anger. Their relationship dramatically improved when they learned to stop yelling and deliberately wrote three humorous lines about the nature of the conflict to share with each other.

If laughter is not the best medicine, it is surely one of the best. Laughter can help keep you healthy, not only psychologically but physically. Laughter is a reflex, a series of involuntary spasms of the diaphragm. This movement forces the breathing muscles to contract and relax in quick succession, increasing the size of the chest cavity--which allows the lungs to take in more oxygen and expel more carbon dioxide than normal. As a result, laughter exercises the lungs, increases the blood's oxygen level, increases circulation and metabolism, and gently tones the entire cardiovascular system--"internal jogging." Muscles of the chest, abdomen, and face get a gentle workout and, if the joke is a real winner, so do the arms and legs. Following the laugh, these muscles relax and the pulse rate and blood pressure temporarily decline. Since muscle relaxation and anxiety cannot exist at the same time, the effect is that a good, hearty laugh may buy you up to 45 minutes of relaxation. Laughter also releases endorphins, the body's natural painkiller.

Conclusions

Within any conflict you will have two concerns: to achieve your goals and to maintain effective working relationships. Those two concerns result in five possible strategies for managing conflicts: withdrawal, forcing, smoothing, compromise, and confrontation. In deciding which of the five strategies to use within any one conflict, there are six rules to consider:

1. Do not withdraw from or ignore the conflict.

2. Do not engage in "win-lose" negotiations.

3. Assess for smoothing.

4. Compromise when time is short.

5. Confront to begin problem-solving negotiations.

6. Use your sense of humor.

In following those rules there are a number of guidelines to keep in mind. First, **competent individuals use all five strategies, depending on the situation.** You need to practice all five strategies until they are thoroughly mastered. Although smoothing, confrontation, and compromise should dominate conflicts within the classroom and school, there are times when forcing and withdrawal may prove useful. Second, **the most competent business executives, managers, and supervisors tend to use confrontation and smoothing as their dominant conflict strategies.** They tend to be highly relationship oriented, confronting when the goals and needs involved in the conflict are important to them and smoothing when they are not. Incompetent business executives, managers, and supervisors tend to use forcing and withdrawal most frequently. **Within schools, teachers and administrators typically use forcing and withdrawal as their most frequent strategies.** When faced with misbehaving students teachers often first try to force the student to behave and then to expel the student from the classroom or school (which is a form of withdrawal). Thus, you will want to learn how to use all five strategies appropriately, especially confrontation and smoothing. Being able to choose how you wish to manage your conflicts empowers you considerably.

In some ways the five strategies present a simplified view of how most conflicts are managed. The complexities of the interaction between two individuals far exceed their initial approaches to the conflict. Conflicts can deteriorate. You need to be aware of your backup strategies as well as your dominate one. **Of most importance is the second most frequently used strategy, as that is the one you will tend to use when you are highly anxious and upset.** Within most conflicts there are initial strategies followed by backup strategies followed by other strategies that are based on what the other person is doing. You may wish to confront but when faced with a colleague who is forcing, you may force back.

The use of certain strategies may increase the probability that other strategies will appear. Withdrawal, for example, often deteriorates into forcing. When individuals cannot withdraw any more, when they feel backed into a corner and have to deal with the conflict, they are likely to strike out and try to force the other person into letting him or her have their way. When a person attempts to smooth, and the other person responds with forcing and anger, withdrawal may follow. That, in turn, may be followed by forcing if the other person continues to be angry and competitive. Forcing creates counter-forcing. Even confrontation may deteriorate into forcing when (a) the timing is wrong and the other person does not respond constructively or (b) the person confronting lacks the skills necessary to keep the management of the conflict constructive. When time is short, confrontation sometimes deteriorates into compromise. **The best time to confront is when the issue is small, concrete, and immediate.** This way issues are dealt with when they are most easily resolved.

Most of the time, you will want to act like either an owl and confront or like a teddy bear and smooth. In most conflicts, these are the two strategies that work best. When the goal is important to you, confront. When it is not, smooth. Because you almost always need to maintain good relationships, you will rarely want to force or withdraw. Compromising is usually only helpful if confronting has failed or when there is not enough time to resolve the conflict. Ideally, however, you will be able to use any of the five conflict strategies, depending on the situation. It is important that you can use each strategy skillfully.

One of the most difficult aspects of confronting another person and initiating problem-solving negotiations is managing emotions. Managing anger is especially problematic. If you try to hide it, very likely the problem will not be correctly identified and a wise agreement will not be reached. But if you express your anger destructively, the relationship may be severely damaged if not ruined. Anger is the focus of the next chapter.

❧❦ Creative Conflict Contract ❧❦

Major Learnings	Implementation Plans

Date _____ Date of Progress Report Meeting _____

Participant's Signature _____

Signatures of Other Group Members _____ _____

_____ _____ _____

EXERCISE

MATERIALS

CHAPTER VOCABULARY

Working with a partner, learn the definitions of the following words.

1. Define each word in two ways.

     First, write down what you think the word means.

     Second, look it up in the book and write down its definition.

     Note the page on which the definition appears.

2. For each word write a sentence in which the word is used.

3. Make up a story in which all of the words are used.

4. Learn how to spell each word. They will be on your spelling test.

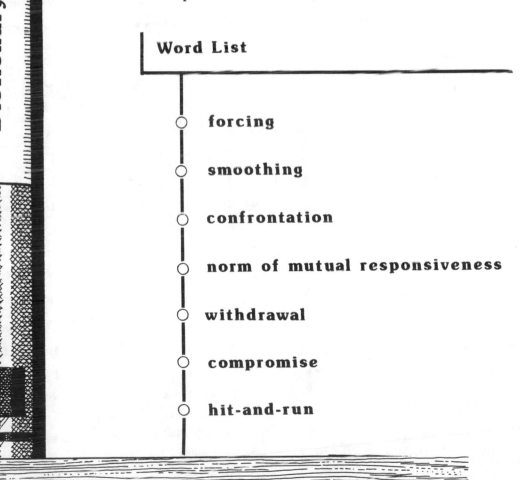

Word List

- forcing
- smoothing
- confrontation
- norm of mutual responsiveness
- withdrawal
- compromise
- hit-and-run

HIDDEN RESOLUTIONS

Recently we discussed methods of resolving conflicts. For this puzzle, you and your partner will be asked to think back to those different ways to resolve conflicts. Hidden in the box below are several terms for you to find having to do with conflict resolution. The words run across (left to right) or down (top to bottom). Circle each one when you locate it. Use the clues below to help you figure out which words you're looking for. GOOD LUCK!

1. Another term for **methods** or **ways** to solve conflicts is s___t___ies.

2. The type of strategy where you take turns or pick the highest card is called _____.

3. The strategy you should **never** use with someone you see often is _____.

4. If you decide to face the conflict and use negotiation to resolve it, you c__fr____ the problem.

5. You also might w__hd____ from the conflict. That means you put off discussing it until both of you are ready.

6. There are several ways to s_____ in a conflict. You can simply let the other person have it, you can apologize, or you can give in with a laugh.

```
D H F A R K E P W O T S A M T
E T O V E B B E D Y P I L T R
S T R A T E G I E S Y P O W U
C O C T I W H I R Z W I E A Q
O R E S S Y F V C A I L L G Z
D O E C O N F R O N T I N C E
P R O G H A P W M I H T T Y O
B S M O O T H U P I D Y L L O
S T E W N G E A R Y R I D D O
I L D P R O X T O L A Q U I M
R A I W T H E C M O W S S Y L
M I A T R H M E I Q U K E E B
G L T O U J C T S E E T H Y M
L O O T H R I X E F F I L T R
A T R O M M G Y I C S T O U M
```

7. If you have tried several ways to solve the conflict yourself with no success, you will seek help from a _____.

How I Act In Conflicts

Instructions

Different people learn different ways of managing conflicts. The strategies you use to manage conflicts may be quite different from those used by your classmates, teachers, and administrators. The following tasks give you an opportunity to increase your awareness of what conflict strategies you use and how they compare with the strategies used by others.

Task 1: Common Conflicts

1. Review the definition of conflicts of interests. List the most frequent and most difficult conflicts you have with other students, teachers, administrators, and parents. The conflicts need to be interpersonal and of some importance.

2. Meet in a group of four. Each member shares his or her conflicts. The most common conflicts of interests members have are listed.

Task 2: Your Conflict Behavior

Working individualistically, by yourself, complete the conflict strategies questionnaire, **How I Act In Conflicts**.

Task 3: Case Studies

1. Working individualistically, read the first case study carefully and rank order the alternative resolutions for "most effective" to "least effective" and for "most likely" to "least likely."

2. Do the same two rankings in your group of four. **Work cooperatively.** One group member should observe using the attached observation sheet. The other three members should do the ranking. All three active members of the group need to agree on the rankings and be able to explain the reasoning behind the two rankings. Each member of the group should:

   a. Listen carefully.

   b. Argue his or her point of view.

c. Not change his or her mind unless he or she is logically persuaded.

d. Express his or her feelings.

After finishing the first case study the group should go on to the second and then the third, repeating the same procedure of first ranking individually and then cooperatively as a group.

Task 4: Understanding The Conflict Strategies

1.   Divide the group into pairs. Each pair reads this chapter, using the pair-reading procedure given below, to ensure that both members understand what the five conflict strategies are and when they may be used appropriately. The pair-reading procedure is:

   a. Read all of the section headings to get an overview.

   b. Both persons silently read the first paragraph.

   c. The **summarizer** summarizes the content of the paragraph in his or her own words.

   d. The **accuracy checker** listens carefully, checks the summary for accuracy and completeness, adds anything that is left out, and relates the content of the paragraph to something learned previously.

   d. The two persons then silently read the next paragraph. The roles of summarizer and accuracy checker are rotated. The procedure is repeated. The two continue until they have read and discussed all the paragraphs in the chapter.

2.   Write the name of each group member on separate slips of paper. Then write the conflict strategy that best fits the actions of the person named. Give the slips of paper to the person named. Each member should end up with three slips of paper describing how the other members perceive his or her strategy in managing conflicts.

Task 5: Processing How The Group Manages Conflicts

There are four sources of information about conflict behavior of group members:

1. The responses on the questionnaire:

   a. Score your questionnaire using the table provided. Rank the five conflict strategies from the one you use the most to the one you use the least. This will give you an indication of how you see your own conflict strategy. The second most frequently used strategy is your backup strategy, that is, the one you use if your first strategy fails.

   b. Determine the average rankings for the group on the "group summary sheet."

2. The results of the discussions of the case studies. Each of the alternatives listed in the case studies represents one of the strategies discussed in this chapter. Match the alternatives to the strategies they represent. Determine which order you would have used the strategies and which order the group would have used the strategies.

3. The data collected by the observer. The observers total the rows and columns of their observation sheets. Group members analyzed the data collected by the observer. Note how you behaved during the discussion of the case studies. The categories on the observation sheet do **not** match the five strategies measured in the questionnaire. You can, however, make some conclusions as to whether your behavior matched the way you see yourself behaving in conflict situations.

4. Your own impressions as to how group members interacted with each other. Think carefully about the interaction among group members during the discussion of the case studies. What strategies were used when members disagreed with each other. Share your impressions as to how conflict was managed in the group discussion of the case studies.

In your group discuss:

1. What is your group's "most" likely strategies?

2. What is your group's "least" likely strategies?

3. What are 5 conclusions about managing conflicts constructively in your group?

4. What positive behaviors were demonstrated by each member of the group?

This is a cooperative task. One set of conclusions should be derived from the whole group and everyone should receive feedback on his or her behavior. All members are expected to participate, give their impressions and information about the way in which members manage conflicts, ensure that all members receive some positive feedback, and summarize the group's conclusions.

How I Act in Conflict
Questionnaire

The proverbs listed below can be thought of as descriptions of some of the different strategies for resolving conflicts. Proverbs state traditional wisdom, and these proverbs reflect traditional wisdom for resolving conflicts. Read each of the proverbs carefully. Using the following scale, indicate how typical each proverb is of your actions in a conflict.

5 = *very often the way I act in a conflict*

4 = *frequently the way I act in a conflict*

3 = *sometimes the way I act in a conflict*

2 = *seldom the way I act in a conflict*

1 = *never the way I act in a conflict*

_____ 1. It is easier to refrain than to retreat from a quarrel.

_____ 2. If you cannot make a person think as you do, make him or her do as you think.

_____ 3. Soft words win hard hearts.

_____ 4. You scratch my back, I'll scratch yours.

_____ 5. Come now and let us reason together.

_____ 6. When two quarrel, the person who keeps silent first is the most praiseworthy.

_____ 7. Might overcomes right.

_____ 8. Smooth words make smooth ways.

_____ 9. Better half a loaf than no bread at all.

_____ 10. Truth lies in knowledge, not in majority opinion.

_____ 11. He who fights and runs away lives to fight another day.

_____ 12. He hath conquered well that hath made his enemies flee.

_____ 13. Kill your enemies with kindness.

_____ 14. A fair exchange brings no quarrel.

_____ 15. No person has the final answer but every person has a piece to contribute.

Taken from: Reaching Out: Interpersonal Effectiveness and Self Actualization
(4th ed.)(1990) by David W. Johnson. Englewood Cliffs, NJ: Prentice-Hall.

How I Act in Conflict (continued)

_____ 16. Stay away from people who disagree with you.

_____ 17. Fields are won by those who believe in winning.

_____ 18. Kind words are worth much and cost little.

_____ 19. Tit for tat is fair play.

_____ 20. Only the person who is willing to give up his or her monopoly on truth can ever profit from the truths that others hold.

_____ 21. Avoid quarrelsome people as they will only make your life miserable.

_____ 22. A person who will not flee will make others flee.

_____ 23. Soft words ensure harmony.

_____ 24. One gift for another makes good friends.

_____ 25. Bring your conflicts into the open and face them directly; only then will the best solution be discovered.

_____ 26. The best way of handling conflicts is to avoid them.

_____ 27. Put your foot down where you mean to stand.

_____ 28. Gentleness will triumph over anger.

_____ 29. Getting part of what you want is better than not getting anything at all.

_____ 30. Frankness, honesty, and trust will move mountains.

_____ 31. There is nothing so important that you have to fight for it.

_____ 32. There are two kinds of people in the world, the winners and the losers.

_____ 33. When one hits you with a stone, hit him or her with a piece of cotton.

_____ 34. When both people give in half-way, a fair settlement is achieved.

_____ 35. By digging and digging, the truth is discovered.

How How I Act in Conflict:
Scoring

Withdrawal	Forcing	Smoothing	Compromise	Confrontation
____ 1	____ 2	____ 3	____ 4	____ 5
____ 6	____ 7	____ 8	____ 9	____ 10
____ 11	____ 12	____ 13	____ 14	____ 15
____ 16	____ 17	____ 18	____ 19	____ 20
____ 21	____ 22	____ 23	____ 24	____ 25
____ 26	____ 27	____ 28	____ 29	____ 30
____ 31	____ 32	____ 33	____ 34	____ 35
____ Total	____ Total	____ Total	____ Total	____ Total

The higher the total score for each conflict strategy, the more frequently you tend to use that strategy. The lower the total score for each conflict strategy, the less frequently you tend to use that strategy.

A discussion of the five conflict strategies and exercises to help develop competency in managing conflicts can be found in:

Johnson, D. W. (1990). **Reaching Out: Interpersonal Effectiveness and Self-Actualization (**4th ed.). Englewood Cliffs, NJ: Prentice-Hall.

Johnson, D. W. (1991). **Human Relations and Your Career** (3rd ed.). Englewood Cliffs, NJ: Prentice-Hall.

Johnson, D. W., & Johnson, F. (1991). **Joining Together: Group Theory and Group Skills** (3rd ed.). Englewood Cliffs, NJ: Prentice-Hall.

	1	2	3	4	5	Total
CONFRONTATION						
SMOOTHING						
COMPROMISING						
FORCING						
WITHDRAWAL						

Individual Conflict Profile

Name _____   Date _____

Questionnaire	Case Study	Observation
1. _____	1. _____	_____
2. _____	2. _____	_____
3. _____	3. _____	_____
4. _____	4. _____	_____
5. _____	5. _____	_____

How I Would Describe My Approach to Conflict:

_____

_____

_____

_____

_____

Conflict Observation Form

Actions					Total
Contributes Ideas/Opinions					
Encourages Others Participation					
Emphasizes Mutual Goals					
Asks For Proof, Facts, Rationale					
Paraphrases, Summarizes					
Criticizes Others' Ideas / Disagrees					
Differentiates Positions					
Integrates Members' Ideas					
Total					

Insert the name of each group member above the columns. Record the frequency with which each member engages in each action. Total the rows and columns. Give the team feedback about its overall performance and the actions of each member.

❧ Jimmy Anderson ❧

You have a classmate, Jimmy Anderson, who is very active, easily bored, and seeks attention. He often disrupts your work and the work of your classmates by being a nuisance and by being aggressive. He often does not stay with one task long enough to finish. He seems to prefer to bother others rather than do his own work. Today, as you are reading a book, he sits down next to you and starts squirming, pokes you with a pencil, puts his hand over the page you are reading, and generally bothers you. This has happened several times before and you are fed up with Jimmy's behavior.

This conflict could be resolved several ways. Five are described below. Read them carefully and rank them from:

1. Most effective in resolving the conflict (1), next most effective (2)...least effective (5).

2. Most likely to be used to resolve the conflict (1), next most likely (2)...least likely (5).

Effective		**Likely**
	I lay it on the line. I tell Jimmy that I am fed up with his actions. I state that the interrupting and annoying actions had better stop because I will not stand for it. Whether he likes it or not, he is going to stop bothering me or else.	
	I ignore what he is doing and keep my feelings to myself. I try to be extra nice to him. I want to win him over to be a friend. I engage him in friendly conversation, find out about his interests, and smooth over any disagreements between us.	
	I ignore Jimmy and continue working. I plan to avoid any contact with him in the future. I can sit across the room from him. I hope that he will stop as he sees me less and less. .	
	I turn around and try to bargain with him. If he will stop bothering me and interrupting my work I will help him with his schoolwork. .	
	I turn around and confront him. I state that I want him to stop interrupting my reading. I share that his actions are frustrating me and making me angry at him. I ask him to state how he sees the conflict and how he feels. I suggest that we follow the negotiation procedure to solve our problem.	

Donna Jones

You have a classmate, Donna Jones, who seems to dislike you and everything about school. When you work on group projects with her you can feel the resentment. She never seems to do anything overtly, but classmates have reported incidences of Donna making faces behind your back and making rude remarks about you outside of class. Today Donna is sitting next to you. Out of the corner of your eye you see her making faces and gestures at you. Several of your classmates are smiling. You decide enough is enough.

This conflict could be resolved several ways. Five are described below. Read them carefully and rank them from:

1. Most effective in resolving the conflict (1), next most effective (2)...least effective (5).

2. Most likely to be used to resolve the conflict (1), next most likely (2)...least likely (5).

Effective   **Likely**

	I turn around and "nail her" in the act. I tell Donna that I am fed up with her actions. I state that the rude remarks, faces, and gestures had better stop because I will not stand for it. Whether she likes it or not, she is going to keep her mouth shut about me or else.	
	I ignore what she is doing and keep my feelings to myself. I try to be extra nice to her. I want to win her over to be a friend. I engage her in friendly conversation to find out about her interests.	
	I ignore Donna and continue working. I plan to avoid any contact with her in the future. I can sit across the room from her. I hope that she will stop as she sees me less and l e s s .	
	I turn around and try to bargain with her. If she will stop making rude remarks, faces, and gestures I will help her with math (which is a hard subject for her).	
	I turn around and confront her. I state that I want her to stop making rude remarks and gestures. I share that her actions hurt my feelings and make me angry. I ask her to state how she sees the conflict and how she feels. I suggest we use the negotiation procedure to solve our problem.	

The Book That Both Wanted

Form pairs. Read the case study. Answer each question as a pair. If you cannot answer the question, seek help from a nearby pair. Probe your partner's ideas by asking such questions as, "Yes, that might happen, what else do you think might happen?"

Donald and David usually have lots of fun together. One day, however, they have trouble. Donald is using a book that David wants to read. David wants the book right now. So does Donald. What can David do so he can read the book? David can think of five ways.

1. Rank the five alternatives from the best thing to do to resolve the conflict (1) to the worst thing to do (5). Why is Number 1 the best thing to do?

2. Rank the five from the one you would do first to resolve the conflict (1) to the one you would do last (5). Why would you do Number 1 first?

Best	Alternative	Me
	Force Donald to let him have the book now. David grabs the book and says "Give me the book or else you'll be sorry."	
	Give up wanting the book and give up on Donald as a friend. "I don't want the book anymore and I don't like you anymore," David says.	
	Let Donald use the book as long as he wants to keep Donald as a friend. "You can have the book. I really didn't want it," says David.	
	Make a deal by trading for it or alternating reading the book. "If you let me use the book I will let you have my turn at the computer," David says.	
	Negotiate a way that both can use the book together. "Let's negotiate and think of several ways we both can use the book," David says.	

Discuss the following three alternative endings to the story. How does each person feel in each ending and what will happen next?

First, David decides to force Donald to let him have the book. He says, "Give me the book now or else you'll be sorry!" Then he grabs the book and tries to keep it away from Donald, who jumps up and tries to grab it back.

How does David feel?

How does Donald feel?

What do you think will happen next?

Second, David decides to make a deal. "Is there anything else you want to do right now besides read the book?" David asks. "I would like to use the computer," Donald replies. "If I give you my turn on the computer will you give me the book now?" David asks.

How does David feel?

How does Donald feel?

What do you think will happen next?

Third, David decides to negotiate for the book. "We have a problem," David says. "Both of us want to read the book now. Maybe we can think of several options as to how we both could use the book." "I don't see how, but I'm willing to try," Donald replies. "We both want the book," David said. "Let's say how we feel and give our reasons for wanting the book now. Then we can show our understanding and think of options as to how we can both get to read the book." "OK," Donald said.

How does David feel?

How does Donald feel?

What do you think will happen next?

What are three ways for the two of them to use the book together?

1.

2.

3.

Which Option

Sounds Best?

Which Strategy Would You Use?

① Pick a real conflict that a member of the class is involved in. Write out five different ways of managing the conflict (forcing, withdrawal, smoothing, compromise, confrontation). Number the strategies from "1" to "5" and then number five spots in the room from "1" to "5."

② Class members think of which strategy they would use. After considering the pro's and con's of each option, students write down their choice and the reasons why it is the best option on the sheet of paper.

③ All members of the class signify their choice by going to the spot in the room that represents the option they have chosen. They pair up with another student who made the same choice, compare and combine their reasons, and make a list of three reasons why their choice is the best strategy. Each student needs a copy of the reasons.

④ Form groups of up to five members (one student for each strategy). Each student presents the reasons for using the strategy they picked. The other students listen carefully and then paraphrase the reasons. If the paraphrase is not accurate or complete, the student presenting corrects the paraphraser. Follow the rules for good paraphrasing.

⑤ Students decide if they wish to change their minds and choose a different strategy. The teacher asks students to go to the spot they now think would be the best strategy to use. The teacher counts how many students in each spot. The procedure may be repeated if there is time.

Paraphrasing Rules

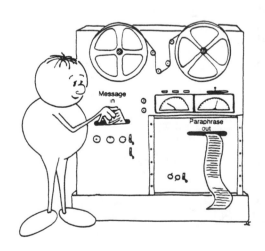

- Put yourself in the other person's shoes.

- Restate the other person's ideas and feelings in your own words. State as correctly as possible the other's reasons for believing his or her option will make the best agreement.

- Start your remarks with, *You want...*, *You feel...*, and *You think...*

- Show understanding and acceptance by nonverbal behaviors: tone of voice, facial expressions, gestures, eye contact, and posture.

● Using the Conflict Strategies ●

First, with a partner, write a story about two students who have a conflict. **Second**, write out five different endings for the story, one for each of the strategies (Forcing, Withdrawal, Smoothing, Compromise, Confrontation). For each strategy, what would you do and what would you say?

Table 4.2 Using Conflict Strategies

	Actions And Behaviors	Phrases
Withdrawal		
Forcing		
Smoothing		
Compromising		
Confronting		

You need to be competent in applying all five strategies. The most important, however, is confrontation. Working with a partner, write out what happens in each of the instances when two individuals use different strategies:

Confronter against a withdrawer.

Smoother against a forcer.

Compromiser against a forcer.

Confronter against a smoother.

Strategy Game

Form groups of three. Each member rolls a dice to select a strategy. The member then acts the stra'egy out. Continue until each group member has acted out all the strategies.

Compromise

Take a chance,
such as flipping a coin.
Let luck decide who wins.

Compromise **Meet in the middle!**

Compromise

Take turns!

Confront

Face the conflict.
Negotiate. Think
of solutions that
give both of you
what you want and
keep your relation-
ship positive.

Smooth

Decide who needs it the most.
Let that person have it.

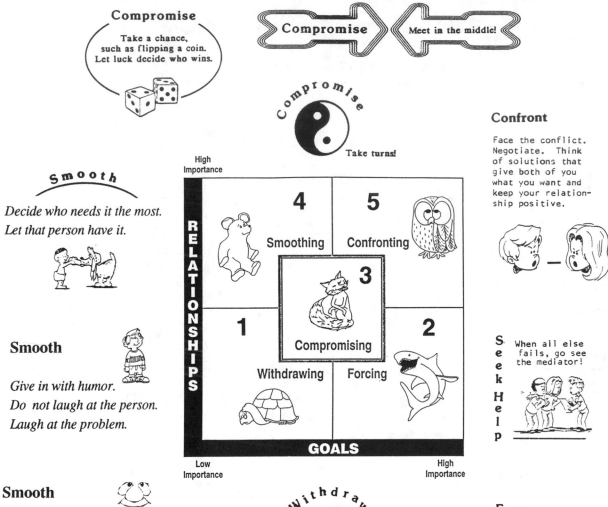

High
Importance

RELATIONSHIPS		
4 Smoothing	**5** Confronting
1 Withdrawing	**3** Compromising	**2** Forcing

GOALS

Low
Importance

High
Importance

Smooth

Give in with humor.
Do not laugh at the person.
Laugh at the problem.

Seek Help

When all else
fails, go see
the mediator!

Smooth

Apologize. When you do not want
to engage in the conflict, saying
"I'm sorry" will help you find an exit.

Withdraw

Postpone.
Put off discussing the
conflict until you both
want to resolve it and are
in control of your emotions.

Force

Never
use force
with someone
you'll see
soon!

5 Managing Anger

The Nature And Value Of Anger

If you are patient in one moment of anger,
you will escape a hundred days of sorrow.

Chinese Proverb

Jim and Sam have been in the same classes for two years. Repeatedly Sam pushes Jim, teases him, takes his pencils, and generally bothers him. Today Jim has had enough. When Sam grabs his pencil, Jim loses his temper, jumps up, and tries to grab his pencil back. The teacher quickly intercedes, but Jim keeps yelling at Sam to leave him alone.

Emotions are always involved in conflicts, and one of the most common is anger. **Anger** is a defensive emotion reaction that occurs when we are frustrated, thwarted, or attacked. You get angry when other people obstruct your goal accomplishment, frustrate your attempts to accomplish something, interfere with your plans, make you feel belittled and rejected, or indicate that you are of no value or importance. When you get angry at other people the results can be either destructive or constructive. **Anger tends to be destructive** when (a) you express anger in a way that creates dislike, hatred, frustration, and a desire for revenge on the part of the other person or (b) it is repressed and held inside (which tends to create irritability, depression, insomnia, and physiological problems such as headaches and ulcers). **Anger tends to be constructive** when you feel more energy, motivation, challenge, and excitement, and the other person feels friendship, gratitude, goodwill, and concern. In this chapter we shall examine the nature of anger and how it can be managed in constructive rather than destructive ways.

Anger both causes and accompanies distress. Anger can result in tight muscles, teeth grinding, piercing stares, headaches, heart attacks, loud voices, projectiles, and smashed furniture. When we are angry our blood boils, we are fit to be tied, we have reached the end of our rope, and what happened is the last straw. Anger is an emotion that occurs regularly in the life of every person, more often and with greater intensity at some times than at others. Failure to manage anger constructively can lead to alienation of loved ones, disrupted work performance, and even cardiovascular disorder. Proper recognition, understanding, acceptance, and channeling of anger can make life more comfortable, productive, and exciting. In order for anger to be managed constructively, its components must be identified, and its major functions must be understood. The useful and constructive aspects of anger must be promoted while the destructive and useless aspects of anger are quelled. Rules for constructive anger management must be followed.

The main components involved in most human anger are as follows:

1. Anger is usually a defense against something.

2. Anger occurs when we are not getting something we want or would like. We get angry when we are frustrated, thwarted, or attacked.

3. Anger has in it a sense of righteousness and a belief that one's personal rights have been violated. When we are angry, we usually believe that we are rightfully angry because the other person has acted unjustly or irrationally.

4. There is a narrowing of perceptual focus and priorities when we are angry. All our attention is focused on the person and behavior we are angry with.

5. There is a demand aspect of anger. It makes us demand that we get our way.

6. There is considerable physiological arousal that demands expression in physical action. We not only are ready to "fight" or "flee," there is a demand that we actually do so.

When we plan how to manage our anger constructively, we need to keep in mind that **anger** is a righteous but defensive reaction to frustration and aggression based on an unidimensional perceptual focus, a physical demand to take action, and a belief that we must get our way.

There are at least eight major functions of anger. Each is described briefly below.

1. **Anger gives us energy and increases the strength with which we act.** Anger mobilizes us for action and thereby provides considerable physical energy to apply toward achieving our goals.

2. **Anger disrupts ongoing behavior by making us agitated and impulsive as well as interfering with our ability to process information and attend to what is taking**

place. Anger disrupts behavior. It causes people to focus continually on the injustice that has been done to them or on the attack they are defending against. Someone who is angry has trouble attending to the tasks at hand and has difficulty comprehending new information. Anger often results in impulsive actions aimed at correcting the situation.

3. **Anger makes it easier to express negative feelings and give negative feedback, which might not be expressed if we were not angry.** Expressing negative feelings often provides information needed for accurately defining problems. Anger is a sign that something is going on that needs to be changed. Expressing anger constructively can increase trust by showing that the relationship is strong enough to handle strains. Healthy relationships depend on the ability of both partners to give accurate but negative feedback to each other, and anger helps them to do so. But the potential negative aspect of such forthrightness is that the strength of the negative feelings or feedback may be inappropriate to the provocation, may be overstated, or may be stated in such an offensive and threatening way that the conflict is escalated and the other person becomes fearful and angry.

4. **Anger is defense against being vulnerable.** Anger changes internal anxiety to external conflict. Anger can overcome anxiety and fear and encourage us to take actions we would never take otherwise. A small child may strike out in anger against a much bigger peer. A subordinate may confront a boss she is afraid of. A very shy person when angry may introduce himself to strangers.

5. **Anger makes us more aggressive and antagonistic.** Feeling angry can be a signal that aggressive actions are called for. Many times we become aggressive through habit when faced with a provocation and strike out verbally or physically at the other people in the situation.

6. **Anger can be a signal that an event is a provocation or that something frustrating or unpleasant is taking place.** Discovering that we are angry can help clarify what is taking place within a situation.

7. **Anger helps us maintain a sense of virtue and righteousness in the face of opposition.** Anger helps us maintain a belief that we are right, justified, and superior.

8. **Anger can intimidate other people and is therefore a source of interpersonal power and influence.** When we want to overpower another person, get our way, or dominate a situation, being angry can often help us to do so.

Being angry at another person can be an unpleasant experience. We can make the other person resentful and hostile when we express anger. We can become anxious after we have expressed anger as we anticipate rejection, counter-anger, and escalation of the conflict. Yet anger can have many positive effects on our problem solving if we learn to manage it constructively.

Rules for Managing Anger Constructively

Aesop tells of a bear roaming through the woods in search of berries who happened on a fallen tree in which a swarm of bees had stored their honey. The bear began to nose around the log very carefully to find out if the bees were at home. Just then one of the swarm came home from the clover field with a load of pollen. Guessing what the bear was after, the bee flew at him, stung him sharply, and then disappeared into the hollow log. The bear immediately lost his temper and sprang on the log tooth and claw to destroy the nest. But this only brought out the whole swarm. The poor bear had to take to his heels, and he was able to save himself only by diving into a pool of water. Sometimes it is wiser to bear a single hurt in silence than to provoke a thousand injuries by flying into a rage.

In managing your anger constructively, there is a set of rules to follow. **The first rule in managing anger is to recognize and acknowledge the fact that you are angry.** Anger is a natural, healthy, normal human feeling. Everyone feels it. You need not fear or reject your anger. For one thing, repressed, denied anger does not vanish but often erupts suddenly in verbal and physical assaults on people and property as well as overreactions to minor provocations. In addition, repression and denial of your anger can create headaches, ulcers, muscle pains, and other physiological ailments. Remember that anger and aggression are not the same thing. You can express anger without being aggressive.

The second rule is to decide whether or not you wish to express your anger. This involves at least two steps--clarifying the intent of the other person and deciding how to respond. **First,** you ask for clarification to make sure the other person has done something aggressive or provocative in nature. Do not assume that aggression was intended without checking it out. It may be a misunderstanding. If it was not a misunderstanding, you proceed to the second step. **Second,** you decide whether to express your anger directly or keep it hidden. There are a number of considerations to keep in mind. Remember that anger makes you impulsive. Impulsive, antagonistic acts can escalate conflict and get you into trouble. Remember that your information-processing capacity will decrease as your anger increases, making your decision about how to respond somewhat suspect. Remember to beware of the righteousness of your anger. In most situations it is not a matter of punishing people you think have acted in an unjust way. It is a matter of ensuring that a constructive outcome results from the situation. Do not attempt to prove you were right or that you are morally superior. Think of how to solve the problem. Remember to face your anger and respond while the provocation is small. Do not disregard small irritations and little frustrations. Small feelings, if they are kept inside and allowed to build up, become big feelings. Finally, remember it is often helpful to delay taking action and talk the situation over with a friend before deciding how to respond. There are times when you should avoid expressing anger. When letting the other person know you are angry will be ineffective or destructive, you need to be able to switch to a more productive and suitable pattern of behavior. Whenever it is possible, however, express your anger. Keep your life clear. Deal with issues and provocations when they arise and when you feel angry, not after days or weeks of letting resentment and hostility build up.

The third rule is to express your anger directly and descriptively when it is appropriate to do so. The specific procedures and skills for expressing anger are discussed later in this chapter. To preview that discussion, five points may be mentioned. First, express your anger to the appropriate person and make it to the point. Do not generalize. Be specific about the provocation. Make the statement of your anger descriptive, accurate, and to the point, and express it to the appropriate person. Second, take responsibility for your anger (the other person did not make you become angry, your anger resulted from your interpretation of the causes of the other person's behavior). Third, make your anger part of a confrontation aimed to beginning negotiations. You must be willing to become more involved with the other person and the situation when you express your anger. Fourth, use both verbal and nonverbal messages skillfully. Nonverbal messages are more powerful in expressing feelings than are words, but they are also more difficult to understand. To communicate your anger clearly, you need to be skilled in both verbal and nonverbal communication. You need to be able to make your words and nonverbal messages congruent with each other. Finally, make the expression of anger cathartic. **Catharsis** is the release of pent-up emotion either by talking about feelings or engaging in active emotional release by crying, laughing, or shouting. Anger needs to be expressed in a way that

terminates it and gets it over and done with. Anger is not a feeling to hold on to. Once you have expressed your anger constructively, let it go.

The fourth rule of managing your anger constructively is to express it indirectly or react in an alternative way when direct expression is not appropriate. If it is not appropriate to express your anger directly, free yourself from the anger before discussing the conflict with the other person. Feelings do need to be expressed. The stronger the feeling, the stronger the need for expression. In privacy you can swear at your boss, hit a punching bag, or swim hard while imagining what you would like to say to a certain acquaintance. There may be many times when you cannot express your anger directly to the people provoking you. Yet it is important to express your anger in a way that ends it. You do not want to stay angry forever. The sooner you get rid of the feelings, the happier your life will be. Expressing and terminating anger indirectly usually involves the following:

1. **Physical Exercise:** There is a general maxim that when one is angry and wants to feel better tomorrow, then one should exercise today. Vigorous exercise like jogging, swimming, tennis, or volleyball provides physical release of energy that is important in releasing anger.

2. **Private Physical Expression:** Strongly express the feeling in private by shouting, swearing, crying, moaning, throwing pottery, pillow fights, and even hitting a pillow against a wall while yelling. This will provide a physical release of energy and anger.

3. **Psychological Detachment:** Resolve the situation in your mind or resign yourself to it. Tell yourself things that can help. Give up thoughts of revenge and getting back at other people. You want to resolve the problem. You can put up with an unfair teacher. An obnoxious peer is not really that bad. Let the negative feelings go, do not hang on to them. They will only make your life unpleasant. Another alternative is to change the way you view the provocation, thereby changing your feeling of anger. Through modifying your interpretations of what the other person's behavior means, you can control your feelings, responding with amusement or indifference rather than with anger. This skill is discussed at length later in this chapter.

4. **Relaxation:** Learn to relax when you wish so that you can relax yourself when your anger has been triggered. As you learn to relax more easily, your ability to regulate your anger will improve.

By learning alternative ways of reacting to provocations and indirect ways of expressing anger, you will be able to choose the most effective response. Such freedom gives you an advantage in situations in which other people are trying to provoke you, as the best way to take charge of such a situation is not to get angry when most people would expect or even want you to do so.

The fifth rule is to stay task oriented. You can control and contain your anger and usually be far more effective in managing the situation by staying focused on the goal to be achieved, not on what the other person is saying and doing. When the other person is angry, do not get distracted into his or her anger. Rather, stay focused on the task. Do not let yourself get sidetracked or baited into a quarrel. Taking insults personally distracts you from your task and involves you in unnecessary conflict. Recognize what the other person is doing, but do not be provoked by it; rather, stay task-oriented and focused on the issue. There is evidence that anger directed toward a person will be far more destructive than will anger directed toward an issue. Viewing an incident as a personal affront is likely to result in disruptive and defensive anger, while viewing an incident as a problem to be solved is likely to result in discriminative, expressive, and energizing anger.

The sixth rule is to analyze, understand, and reflect upon your anger. Get to know yourself so that you recognize (a) the events and behaviors that trigger your anger and (b) the internal signs of arousal that signal you are becoming angry. You **can** control your anger. You can find your own buttons so that you know when someone else is pushing them. It is important for you to understand the regularities of your anger patterns--when, in what circumstances, and with whom you become angry. You can then plan how to avoid frustrating, anger-provoking situations. And you can explicitly decide what you want and plan in detail how to manage situations to obtain it without getting angry. As you become more and more sharply tuned to the signs of tension and upset inside you, you will achieve greater ability to short- circuit the anger process. You can train yourself to use the initial flash of irritation as a signal that anger is on the way and that you may therefore need to switch to a more productive and suitable behavior pattern. Signs of internal arousal can be alerting signals that you are becoming upset and that effective action is called for if a positive outcome is to result. Thus you can learn to stop anger before it develops.

Anger often results from your believing that things are not going the way you want them to go or that you are powerless in a situation in which you want to be able to influence other people. Remember, you gain power and influence when you keep calm and refuse to get angry. Since anger is sometimes due to doubting yourself or letting yourself feel threatened by someone else, it is important to remember that you are a worthwhile person and that you have many strengths and competencies. This can keep you from feeling angry. And you should always beware of the righteousness of your anger. It can be blind.

The seventh rule is to congratulate yourself when you have succeeded in managing your anger constructively. Feel good about your success. Don't focus on your mistakes and failings or on the nastiness of other people. Focus on your ability to manage your anger constructively.

The eighth rule is to express emotions other than anger. Besides expressing negative feelings, it is important to express positive feelings while discussing a conflict. There are positive feelings, such as liking, appreciation, and respect, that strengthen your relationship with the other person. Both positive and negative feelings have to be communicated with skill in a conflict.

Expressing Anger Constructively

I was angry with my friend:
I told my wrath, my wrath did end.
I was angry with my foe:
I told it not, my wrath did grow.

William Blake

Expressing anger constructively can be one of the most difficult aspects of resolving conflicts. There is a risk in expressing feelings such as anger. When you express anger, you have to worry about alienating the other person. Expressing anger could lead to losing the relationship or even losing your job. And you have to worry whether the other person will also get angry at you. Being exposed to the anger of others is painful. To express anger constructively you must first be aware that you are angry, accept anger as natural and normal, and decide to express it.

Keeping anger buried is usually harmful, causing a number of problems. First, it adds to your frustrations. This is not sensible. Getting angry over a frustration does not usually remove the frustration and always adds to your discomfort. **Second**, anger prevents you from solving problems. Being hateful simply fills your thoughts with delicious ways of getting even with others, not with how to get others to behave differently toward you. The net result is that things get worse and worse as you become angrier and angrier. **Third**, concealed anger is often displaced onto other persons. Not expressing anger at a student or colleague can lead to displacing anger at your friends, family, or some stranger. Hidden anger does not vanish, but often suddenly erupts in physical violence and assaults on both people and property. **Fourth**, anger can make you physically sick. Headaches, high blood pressure, and physical pains are not helpful when you are trying to resolve a conflict. **Fifth**, repeated failure to express anger in words sometimes produces the appearance of apathy. If you repeatedly fail to express anger in words, you may give the impression that you don't care. In the long run, keeping anger to yourself will only hurt you and your relationships.

There are several advantages to expressing anger directly in a conflict. Anger conveys to other people what your commitments are and which commitments must be respected or changed. Expressing anger can clear the air so that positive feelings can once again be felt and expressed. Problems that are being ignored are brought to the surface and highlighted through the expression of anger. Anger can override fear and feelings of vulnerability and lead you to act more competently in troublesome situations.

Directly Expressing Anger

I never let the sun set on a disagreement with anybody who means a lot to me.
Thomas Watson, Sr., Founder, IBM

Many of us in business, especially if we are very sure of our ideas, have hot tempers. My father knew he had to keep the damage from his own temper to a minimum.
Thomas Watson, Jr., Chairman Emeritus, IBM

Ralph has been caught taking other students' things all year. Today Jim brought a special rock he found on his vacation to Canada last summer to school and suddenly it was missing. The teacher finds it in Ralph's desk, but Ralph denies all knowledge of how it got there and claims he did not take it. Jim is fed up. He believes Ralph is dishonest. Jim accuses Ralph of stealing his rock. Ralph stubbornly claims he is innocent, Jim gets more and more angry.

To express your anger constructively, you describe the other person's behavior, you describe your feelings, and you make your nonverbal messages congruent with your words. The purpose of asserting your anger is to create a shared understanding of the relationship so it may be improved or so you may be more effective in achieving your goals. You want the other person to know how you perceive and feel about his or her actions, and you wish to end up knowing how the other person perceives and feels about your actions. You want to discuss the situation until you and the other person have a common perspective or frame of reference in viewing the relationship and your interactions with each other.

Behavioral Descriptions

A **behavioral description** is a combination of describing the other person's actions and a personal statement to take ownership of your observations. In describing the other person's provocative actions, you need to be skillful in observing what actually occurred and in letting the other person know what behavior you are responding to by describing it clearly and specifically. To do this, you must describe visible evidence, behavior that is open to anyone's observation. Restrict yourself to talking about the actions of the other person. Using personal statements is also a good idea so that it is clear that you are taking ownership for your observations. An example of a good behavior description is, "Jim, by my count, you have just interrupted me for the third time." (Not, "Jim, you are really being rude," which is negative labeling or, "Jim, you always want to be the center of attention," which imputes an unworthy motive.)

Descriptions of Your Own Feelings

You describe your feelings by using personal statements (referring to "I," "me," or "my") and specifying the feeling by name or by action-urge, simile, or some other figure of speech. Your description will be more helpful and effective if it is specific rather than general ("You bumped my arm" rather than "You never watch where you are going"), tentative rather than absolute ("You seem unconcerned about completing our project" rather than "You don't care about the project and you never will"), and informing rather than demanding ("I haven't finished yet" rather than "Stop interrupting me"). This latter point needs reemphasizing because of its importance; the description of your anger should be noncoercive and should not be a demand that the other person change. Avoid judgments of the other person ("You are egocentric"), name calling or trait labeling ("You're a phony"), accusations and imputing undesirable motives to the other person ("You always have to be the center of attention"), commands, demands, and orders ("Stop talking and listen!"), and sarcasm ("You're really considerate, aren't you?" when the opposite is meant). By describing your feelings about the other person's actions, your feelings are seen as temporary and capable of change rather than as permanent. It is better to say, "At this point, I am very annoyed with you" than "I dislike you and I always will."

Making Nonverbal Messages Congruent

In describing your feelings you need to make your nonverbal messages similar to your verbal ones. When you express anger verbally, your facial expression should be serious, your tone of voice neutral to cold, your eye contact direct, and your posture rather stiff. Contradictory verbal and nonverbal messages may indicate to the other person that you are untrustworthy and often make the other person anxious.

Listening Skills

While discussing your anger with another person it is important to use good listening skills. Use perception checks to make sure that you are not making false assumptions about the other person's feelings and intentions ("My impression is that you are not interested in trying to understand my ideas. Am I wrong?" "Did my last statement bother you?"). And when negotiating the meaning of the other person's actions and in clarifying both your feelings and the feelings of the other person, use paraphrasing to make sure you accurately understand the other person and that the other person feels understood and listened to.

Assess Impact On Other

Take into account the impact your anger will have on the other person. While you will usually feel better after expressing anger constructively and directly to another person, the other person may feel alienated and resentful. After expressing anger directly, it is important to make sure that the other person has a chance to respond and clarify his or her feelings before the interaction is ended.

Summary

To express anger constructively, first describe the other person's provocative behavior and then describe your anger verbally while making your nonverbal messages congruent with your words. An example would be, "Jim, by my count you have just interrupted me for the third time in the past half hour, and I am both frustrated and angry as a result" (while maintaining a serious facial expression, a neutral to cold tone of voice, direct eye contact, and a rather stiff posture). You should then be ready to negotiate on the meaning of Jim's actions and on whether or not anger is the appropriate feeling to have.

In expressing anger your attitude should not be, "Who's right and who's wrong?" but rather, "What can each of us learn from this discussion that will make our relationship more productive and satisfying?" As a result of the discussion, each of you will act with fuller awareness of the effect of your actions on the other person as well as with more understanding of the other person's intentions. One, both, or neither of you may act differently in the future because of this increased awareness. Any change in future behavior needs to be self-chosen rather than compelled by a desire to please or a need to submit to the other person.

Finally, make sure the timing of the expression of your anger is appropriate. Generally, express your anger when there is time enough to discuss the situation and the provocation. The closer in time your reaction is expressed to the provocation, the more constructive the discussion will be.

Assertiveness and Aggressiveness

All people have a perfect right to express their thoughts, feelings, opinions, and preferences and to expect that other people will treat them with respect and dignity. In interpersonal situations involving stress and anger, you may behave nonassertively, aggressively, or assertively. When you behave **nonassertively**, you say nothing in response to a provocation, keeping your feelings to yourself, hiding feeling from others, and perhaps even hiding your feelings from yourself. Nonassertive behavior is often dishonest and involves letting other people violate your personal right to be treated with respect and dignity.

Aggressive behavior is an attempt to hurt someone or destroy something. It infringes on the rights of others and involves expressing your feelings indirectly through insults, sarcasm, labels, put-downs, and hostile statements and actions. Aggressive behavior involves expressing thoughts, feelings, and opinions in a way that violates others' rights to be treated with respect and dignity.

Assertive behavior involves describing your feelings, thoughts, opinions, and preferences directly to another person in an honest and appropriate way that respects both yourself and the other person. It enables you to act in your own best interests, to stand up for yourself without undue anxiety, to express honest feelings comfortably, and to exercise personal rights without denying the rights of others. Assertive behavior is direct, honest, self-enhancing self-expression that is not hurtful to others and is appropriate for the receiver and the situation.

In general, it is a good idea to raise your restraints and inhibitions against aggressive and nonassertive behavior and to lower any inhibitions, restraints, or anxieties you have about being assertive.

Irrational Beliefs Underlying Anger And Blaming

Long-term anger is based on two irrational beliefs. The **first** is that you must have your way and that it is awful not to get everything you want. This is known as **catastrophizing**. The **second** is that people are bad and should be severely dealt with if they have behaved wrongly. If you see the cause of your frustration as being wicked people who deserve to be punished for their evil acts, you are stuck in a blame orientation. A blame orientation distracts you from finding a solution to your frustration.

A blame orientation is especially destructive when it is applied to yourself. **Self-blame** exists when you say "bad me" to yourself or when you judge your basic self-worth on the basis of your inadequate or rotten behavior. Self-blame is in effect being angry at yourself. Self-blame involves a double attack: one against your actions and the other against yourself as a person. If you spill coffee on your desk you can see your behavior as being uncoordinated, or you can see your behavior as clumsy and yourself as rotten and no good. Self-blame is similar to giving yourself a grade on the basis of a behavior you do not like. When you blame yourself you believe it is catastrophic that you are not getting what you want, that it is your fault, and therefore you are a bad person who should be severely punished. When you blame yourself (or others) you have to carry the anger around inside you, subjecting yourself to a great deal of stress and even making yourself sick. Perhaps most important, blaming yourself distracts you from finding a solution to your problems. All the punishment in the world does not promote creative insight into how a situation may be more constructively managed.

You should never blame yourself (or others) for:

1. **Not having the intelligence to do as well as you would like.** If the intellectual ability is not there, you cannot blame yourself. Either it is in your genes or it is not.

2. **Being ignorant.** Ignorance means that you have not yet learned a skill. You cannot blame yourself if you did not know better.

3. **Having behaved badly.** You should separate your behavior and your self-worth. You are not your actions. Engaging in a bad behavior does not make you a bad person.

4. **Not being perfect.** In perfectionism, you attempt to be all things rather than who you are. A perfectionist never has developed an internal sense of how much is good enough. Only when you can stop trying to be perfect do you ever become free to be who you are.

5. **Being psychologically disturbed at the time.** Everyone at times enters psychological states such as anger, depression, grief, fear, and even extreme tiredness that result in behaving in ways destructive to the best interests of ourselves or others. Psychological problems do not result from being possessed by demons. Being psychologically disturbed does not make you an evil person.

To combat a blame orientation you must **first** change your basic assumptions that (a) it is a catastrophe when you do not get what you want and (b) whoever is the blame must be severely punished. **Second**, you must engage in an internal debate to replace your old assumptions with the new, more constructive, ones. Never blame anyone (including yourself). Always separate the person from his actions. **Third**, you must forgive yourself (and others) for everything. The sooner you forgive yourself the better. Sooner or later you forgive yourself and those you disagree with. Since you will eventually forgive, the sooner you do so the better for you. **Finally**, you must be problem oriented. Focus on the problem to be solved, not on the failure of you or others to live up to your expectations. Remember that when you blame others they become much more hostile and angry with you, escalating the conflict into destructive directions.

Managing Your Feelings

I have known a great many troubles,
but most of them never happened.

Mark Twain

There are times when your relationships may result in great happiness, satisfaction, growth, and joy. There are other times when your relationships may result in depression, sadness, anger, worry, frustration, or guilt. You will be depressed occasionally about a relationship or angry at the way in which other people are treating you. If the feelings are dealt with constructively, they will not last very long. But if you have destructive patterns of interpreting what is happening in your life, you can be depressed and upset all the time. You can turn small events into tragedies. You could, for example, react as if a colleague's not liking you were as serious as finding out you have incurable cancer. There are people who are talented at taking an occasional small event and creating major feelings of depression or anger that stay with them for several days or weeks. Don't be one of them.

How you feel is important for your enjoyment of life and for your ability to relate effectively to other people. If you are depressed, angry, worried, and anxious about your relationships, then you need to take some sort of action. You need to get rid of negative feelings and to promote positive feelings, such as happiness, contentment, pride, and satisfaction.

To change negative or destructive feelings, you have two choices. You can choose to try to change things outside of yourself. You can change jobs, friends, location, and careers. **Or you could choose to change things within yourself.** You can change your interpretations of what is happening in your life. Changing your interpretations will change your feelings. In choosing whether to try to change something outside of yourself or inside yourself, it is important to remember that **the easiest thing to change in your life is yourself.**

Let's take an example. Sam believes his boss is always picking on him. He thinks that his boss gives him the dirtiest jobs to do. Sam thinks that his colleagues are not made to work as hard as he is. The principal always seems to be criticizing Sam but not his colleagues. All this makes Sam angry, depressed, worried, and frustrated. Sam also feels that the situation is hopeless. "What can I do?" asks Sam. "My boss has all the power. He can fire me, but I can't do anything to him."

5 : 15

Sam has two choices. He can try to change his boss. Or he can try to change his feelings. Psychologists would tell Sam it is easier to change his feelings than to change his boss. What do you think?

Disposable Feelings: Like It or Dump It

Habits can not be thrown out the upstairs window. They have to be coaxed down the stairs one step at a time.

Mark Twain

The five aspects of expressing feelings discussed are:

1. Gather information through your five senses.

2. Interpret the information.

3. Experience the feelings appropriate to your interpretations.

4. Decide how you intend to express your feelings.

5. Express your feelings.

It is your interpretations that cause your feelings, not the events in your life. **Feelings are not caused by events and people around you; they are caused by the ways in which you interpret your experiences.** Your classmates or teachers cannot upset you; only the interpretations you make about their behavior can upset you. Your friends cannot upset you; only the interpretations you make about your friends' behavior can upset you. This means that you can control your feelings. You can decide which feelings you would like to keep and expand. You can decide which feelings you would like to dump and get rid of. Your feelings are disposable!

Depending on your interpretations, you can feel satisfaction, pride, enjoyment, fun, contentment, and challenge about your relationships. Or you can feel depressed, anxious, worried, angry, sad, hopeless, and helpless about your relationships. When your interpretations result in feelings that contribute to a painful and troubled life, you are managing your feelings destructively. When you have feelings of depression and anxiety, your work suffers, the people around you suffer, and you are just no fun to be around. Maintaining relationships means that you are able to manage your interpretations so that you are not overly depressed, anxious, angry, or upset.

Your interpretations are heavily influenced by the assumptions you make about what is good or bad, what you do or do not need, and what causes what in the world. Sometimes people have assumptions that cause them to be depressed or upset most of the time. You can assume, for example, that your teachers have to like you more than any other student. Since there is always somebody your teachers will like better than you, such an assumption will keep you unhappy. You will be depressed because your teachers do not like you best! Assumptions such as this one are irrational. **An irrational assumption** is a belief that makes you depressed, anxious, or upset most of the time. The belief (such as, the teacher has to like me best or else my life is ruined) is accepted as true without any proof. If you believe that you have to be perfect or else you are absolutely worthless, you have an irrational assumption. If you believe that everyone in the world has to think you are absolutely marvelous or else you will be miserable, you have an irrational assumption. If you think you are unemployable because you can't immediately find a job, you have an irrational assumption. Irrational assumptions can only make you feel miserable because they lead to depressing interpretations. **All you have to do to ruin your life is to make a few irrational assumptions and refuse to change them no matter how much pain they cause!**

It takes energy to have destructive feelings. It takes energy to hold on to irrational assumptions. It takes energy to make interpretations that lead to miserable feelings. It takes energy to try to ignore, deny, and hide these miserable feelings. The fewer irrational assumptions you have the more energy you will have for enjoying yourself and your relationships! The more quickly you get rid of your irrational assumptions and the destructive feelings they cause, the more energy you will have for enjoying yourself and your relationships!

To maintain constructive relationships you need to:

1. Be aware of your assumptions.

2. Know how they affect your interpretation of the information gathered by your senses.

3. Be able to tell how rational or irrational your assumptions are.

4. Dump your irrational assumptions by replacing them with rational ones.

You can change your irrational assumptions. The easiest way is to: (1) become highly aware of when you are making an irrational assumption; (2) think of a rational assumption that is much more constructive; and (3) argue with yourself until you have replaced your irrational assumption with a rational one.

Irrational assumptions are learned. Usually they are learned in early childhood. They were taught to you by people in your past. Irrational assumptions are bad habits just like smoking or alcoholism. What was learned as a child can be unlearned as an adult. If you keep arguing against your irrational assumptions, you will soon develop rational ones! Do not let yourself feel bad just because you have developed bad thinking habits in the past!

How To Deal With Another Person's Anger

David is a senior who never does his homework. The teacher assigned a major project that counts for a major part of your grade. If all members do their part of the project, each group member will receive 10 bonus points. You were assigned to a cooperative learning group that included David. Today the first efforts of all group members were due and David has done nothing. You calmly tell him that you need the bonus points to ensure an "A" in the course and that he should do his part of the project. David becomes furious at you. The intensity of his anger is frightening, even though normally he is not a particularly aggressive person.

Everybody gets angry. You do, and so do your classmates and teachers. But figuring out what to do when another person is angry at you is tough. Letting your anger or another student's anger get out of hand is disastrous. But so is hiding it. Hidden anger only smolders until it explodes later "for no good reason." Here are some suggestions for dealing with an angry classmate.

1. **Give others the "right" to feel angry.** Remember that anger is a natural human feeling. Other students have a "right" to feel and express anger as well as happiness, joy, sadness, grief, and pain. So do you. Remember that anger is different from aggression. Aggression is an attempt to hurt someone or destroy something. It infringes on the rights of others. Anger is a feeling indicating that the person feels frustrated or thwarted. This distinction may help you to react appropriately to the

many kinds of upsetting things an angry classmate may do. Also, remember that it is better for the anger to be expressed and dealt with than hidden. When feelings are repressed, denied, or ignored, they will come out later in one way or another, usually in ways that are more difficult to deal with.

2. **Do not get angry back.** When another student gets angry at you, the first step is for you to control your own feelings. Losing your temper will only escalate the conflict and make things worse.

3. **Recognize the temptation to use aggression is a sign that the person is feeling weak and helpless.** The other person is probably at his or her wit's end and does not know what to do. Help him or her back off, cool down, and try something else. Remind them that being hurtful escalates the situation.

4. **Focus attention on the task, not on the other person's anger.** Focus both your and the other person's attention on the task to be completed. Losing your temper will not help to identify and solve the problem. Do not let yourself get sidetracked or baited into a quarrel when the other person is angry. Recognize what the other person is doing, but do not be provoked by it. Rather, stay focused on the task. Keep refocusing the other person's attention on the task.

5. **Explain the situation.** Understanding a situation can help the other person understand the cause of his or her anger, and begin to calm down. Your explanation can include telling how you feel, and asking for consideration. An example is, "Your yelling usually does not bother me, but today I have a headache; could you please keep your voice volume down?"

6. **Talk to yourself.** Prepare yourself for the experience by saying such things to yourself as, "I'm good at managing other peoples' anger," ignore the anger by saying such things to yourself as, "His anger is a minor annoyance, not a major catastrophe," cope with your arousal and agitation by saying such things to yourself as, "Breath deep, relax, slow your pulse down," and reward yourself for coping successfully by saying such things to yourself as, "You were terrific; you were calm during the whole conversation!"

7. **Use affection.** Sometimes a sudden show of affection will help an angry classmate regain control.

8. **Teach the person to express anger in words.** Talking is an acceptable steam valve, and helps the student to avoid "blowing up." Teach your fellow students to put angry feelings into words instead of fists.

9. **Be a good model.** Model expressing anger constructively.

10. **When you can not handle a situation, seek help.** Do not hesitate to seek help from others when you need to. The help could be to physically restrain a violent person. Or it could be a person to talk through a situation with in order to think more creatively about how to handle a person who is emotionally upset at the time.

Anger And Negotiations

Negotiating is an ever present activity. Negotiations within the ongoing relationships are different from negotiations between strangers and adversaries. If you must live, work, and interact with each other after an agreement is reached, the long-term relationship becomes more important than the settlement of any one issue. This means that negotiations are aimed at solving a problem, not at "winning." Most negotiations occur informally. When negotiating must be done in a more careful and complete way, they are initiated through confrontation.

In confronting another person and beginning negotiations, individuals must express their feelings constructively and respond to the emotional expressions of the other in a constructive way. Perhaps the most difficult emotion to manage constructively within conflict situations is anger. Individuals may refuse to negotiate out of anger, they may engage in forcing out of anger, and they may avoid smoothing out of anger. At any time in negotiations participants may become angry at each other and express it. Both your own anger towards the other person and the other person's anger toward you must be managed constructively. If you perfect your skills in managing your anger and in responding to the anger of others constructively, you will tend to be a highly competent negotiator even under the most difficult conditions.

Summary

Emotions are always involved in conflicts, and one of the most common is anger. **Anger** is a defensive emotion reaction that occurs when we are frustrated, thwarted, or attacked.

You get angry when other people obstruct your goal accomplishment, frustrate your attempts to accomplish something, interfere with your plans, make you feel belittled and rejected, or indicate that you are of no value or importance. When you get angry at other people the results can be either destructive or constructive. **Anger tends to be destructive** when (a) you express anger in a way that creates dislike, hatred, frustration, and a desire for revenge on the part of the other person or (b) it is repressed and held inside (which tends to create irritability, depression, insomnia, and physiological problems such as headaches and ulcers). **Anger tends to be constructive** when you feel more energy, motivation, challenge, and excitement, and the other person feels friendship, gratitude, goodwill, and concern.

To manage anger constructively you should recognize and acknowledge that you are angry. The then decide whether or not you wish to express your anger. You express your anger directly and descriptively when it is appropriate to do so. You express it indirectly or react in an alternative way when direct expression of anger is not appropriate. During it all, you stay task oriented. You analyze, understand, and reflect on your anger. You congratulate yourself on managing your anger constructively and you express any other emotions (such as respect or appreciation) you are feeling directly and descriptively. To express anger constructively your describe the other's actions, you describe your angry feelings verbally while making your nonverbal messages congruent with your words. You listen carefully to what the other person is saying, and you assess the impact of the anger on the other person. And you let your anger go.

Long-term anger is based on two irrational beliefs--that you must get your way and the other person must be punished. To ensure that you do not keep anger long-term, you must manage your feelings in ways that let you dispose of anger. You begin by deciding to change yourself (rather than the other person) because you can control yourself while you cannot control external events. You dispose of your anger through controlling how you interpret the information you receive through your senses. Your interpretations are based on the assumptions you make about what is good or bad, what you do or do not need, and what causes what in the world. Finally, in a conflict you must control your reactions to other people's anger toward you as well as your anger toward them. You give them the "right" to feel angry, you try not to get angry back, you focus on your attention on the task. You describe the situation, and talk to yourself to keep yourself calm.

Once you have mastered establishing a cooperative context, negotiating to solve a mutual problem, confronting constructively to initiate negotiations, and managing your own and other people's anger, you are ready to help classmates manage their conflicts. You do this by being a mediator. The next chapter spells out how to be a mediator.

⟨ Creative Conflict Contract ⟩

Major Learnings	Implementation Plans

Date _____ Date of Progress Report Meeting _____

Participant's Signature _____

Signatures of Other Group Members _____ _____

_____ _____ _____

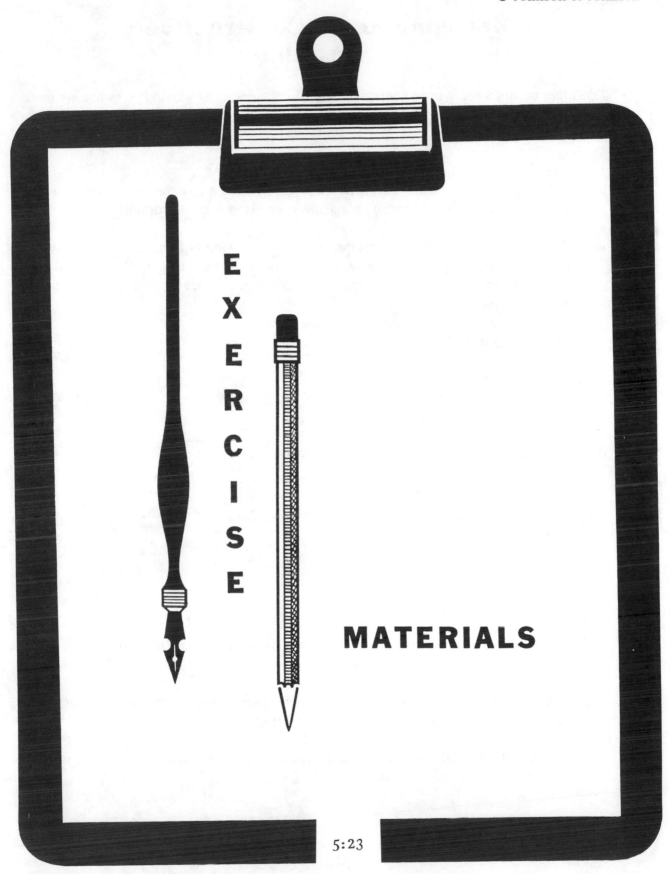

EXERCISE

MATERIALS

Managing Anger Constructively
A Checklist

▷ 1. Anger occurs when we are not getting something we want or would like (when we feel frustrated, thwarted, attacked, belittled, devalued).

▷ 2. Anger can:

✓ a. Add to your frustrations. This is not sensible. Getting angry over a frustration does not usually remove the frustration and always adds to your discomfort.

✓ b. Prevent you from solving problems. Being hateful simply fills your thoughts with delicious ways of getting even with others, not with how to get others to behave differently toward you. The net result is that things get worse and worse as you become angrier and angrier.

✓ c. Make you physically sick.

▷ 3. Beware of angers:

✓ a. Narrowing of perceptual focus and priorities.

✓ b. Righteousness, blame orientation, and desire to punish.

✓ c. Demand that you get your way.

✓ d. Physiological arousal.

▷ 4. Rules for managing anger:

✓ a. Recognize and acknowledge your anger.

✓ b. Decide whether you wish to express it. Know how to detach and let it go if you decide not to.

✓ c. When it is appropriate to do so, express anger directly and descriptively. Once you have expressed your anger constructively, let it go.

✓ d. Express it indirectly or react in an alternative way when direct expression is not appropriate. Indirect ways include:

- 1. Physical exercise.

- 2. Private physical expression.

- 3. Psychological detachment.

- 4. Relaxation.

✓ e. When the other person is angry, stay focused on the task/issue. Do not get distracted into his or her anger.

✓ f. Analyze, understand, and reflect upon your anger.

▷ 5. Anger is based on two irrational beliefs:

✓ a. You must have your way. It is awful not to get everything you want.

✓ b. People are bad and should be severely dealt with if they have behaved wrongly. They are wicked for frustrating you and deserve to be punished.

▷ 6. Express your anger constructively by:

✓ a. Describing the other person's behavior.

✓ b. Describing your anger.

✓ c. Making your verbal and nonverbal messages congruent.

✓ d. Checking your perceptions of the other person's behavior and the assumptions you are making about the meaning of the behavior.

✓ e. Paraphrasing the other person's replies.

▷ 7. Respond to other people's anger constructively by:

✓ a. Giving others the "right" to feel angry.

✓ b. Not getting angry back.

Managing Anger Constructively

✓ c. Recognize that the temptation to use aggression as a sign that the person is feeling weak and helpless.

✓ d. Focus attention on the task, not on the other person's anger.

✓ e. Explain the situation.

✓ f. Talk to yourself to manage provocations.

CHAPTER VOCABULARY

Working with a partner, learn the definitions of the following words.

1. Define each word in two ways.

   First, write down what you think the word means.

   Second, look it up in the book and write down its definition.

   Note the page on which the definition appears.

2. For each word write a sentence in which the word is used.

3. Make up a story in which all of the words are used.

4. Learn how to spell each word. They will be on your spelling test.

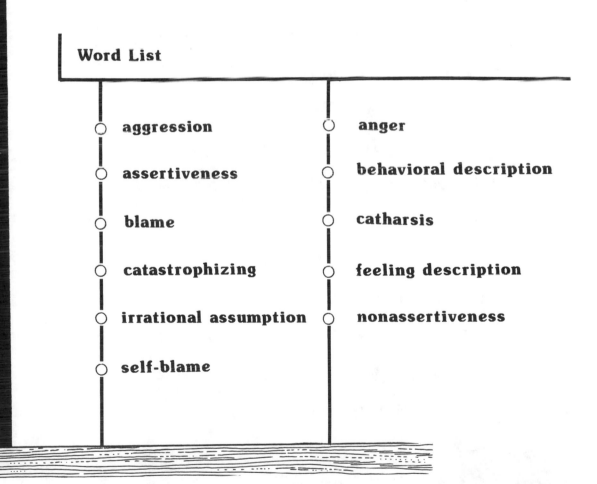

Word List

○ **aggression**	○ **anger**
○ **assertiveness**	○ **behavioral description**
○ **blame**	○ **catharsis**
○ **catastrophizing**	○ **feeling description**
○ **irrational assumption**	○ **nonassertiveness**
○ **self-blame**	

Understanding My Anger EXERCISE

Being aware of our feelings is an important and somewhat difficult task. Many of us were taught to hide our feelings. We learned to pretend we did not have them. This is especially true of feelings we consider negative, such as anger. We often keep our anger inside and act as if it were not there. We deny to ourselves that we are angry. In order to be aware of our anger and express it appropriately, we must understand what makes us angry.

Working by yourself, complete the following statements. Be specific. Try to think of times when you were angry or someone was angry at you.

1. I feel angry when my friends...

2. When I'm angry at my friends, I usually...

3. After expressing my anger, I feel...

4. The way I express anger usually makes my friends...

5. When my friends express anger toward me, I feel...

6. When I feel that way, I usually...

7. After reacting to my friends' anger, I feel...

8. My reaction to my friends' anger usually results in...

9. I feel angry when my teacher...

10. When I'm angry at my teacher, I usually...

11. The way I act when I'm angry at my teacher makes me feel...

12. The way I act when I'm angry at my teacher usually results in my teacher...

13. When my teacher expresses anger at me, I feel...

14. When I feel that way I usually...

15. After reacting to my teacher's anger, I feel...

16. My reactions to my teacher's anger usually result in my teacher...

In a group of two share your answers and listen carefully to your partner's answers. Write down:

a. Five major things that make you and your partner angry.

b. Five major ways in which you and your partner express anger.

c. Five major conclusions you and your partner have come to about what happens when anger is expressed.

Find a new partner. **Share** answers, **listen** to his or her's, and utilize the best ideas of both to **create** a new list of conclusions about what happens when anger is expressed.

How Would You Feel If . . .?

Different people feel differently about the same thing. Some people get angry when they are teased, others do not. You are going to play a game about feelings. For each of the situations given below, write down how you would feel. Then meet with a partner and share your answers. If the two of you would feel differently, discuss why until you both understand each other's reactions. How would you feel if:

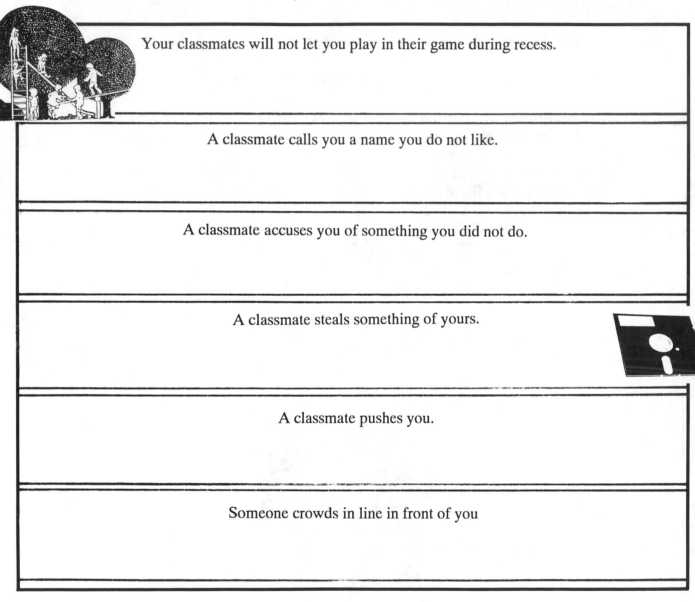

Your classmates will not let you play in their game during recess.

A classmate calls you a name you do not like.

A classmate accuses you of something you did not do.

A classmate steals something of yours.

A classmate pushes you.

Someone crowds in line in front of you

Does your partner feel differently than you in these situations? Explain why different people feel differently about the same experience. Explain why you may feel differently at two different times about the same experience.

ℰ Talking to Yourself to Manage Provocations ℥

Any meeting to discuss a conflict can be divided into four states:

1. Preparing emotionally for the meeting.

2. Listening to the other person's angry statements.

3. Coping with the arousal and agitation resulting.

4. Congratulating yourself for coping successfully.

For each stage, there are a number of statements you should make to yourself to help you manage the provocation successfully. The assumption is that through controlling what you say to yourself before, during, and following a provocation, you can change your conflict behavior and instruct yourself in more constructive behavioral patterns. The purpose of this exercise is to give you some practice in differentiating among the self- statements for each stage and applying them to a conflict situation you have recently been involved in. The procedure is:

1. Form triads and classify the self-statements on the following page according to the four stages of managing a provocation constructively.

2. Have each member of the triad identify a conflict situation that usually creates anger and distress in him or her.

3. Working as a triad, take each conflict situation and work out a series of self-statements that can be used during each stage of managing the provocation constructively. Each member of the triad should develop a set of self-statements that will help him or her manage the conflict situation more constructively next time it appears.

Managing Provocations by Talking to Yourself

Given below are statements you could say to yourself to help yourself manage a conflict situation constructively. Working as a triad, classify each statement given below as belonging in one of the four stages of managing a provocation constructively (1 = Preparing, 2 = Listening, 3 = Coping, 4 = Congratulating).

Stage **What I Say to Myself**

1. _____ Dealing with her anger is only a minor annoyance.
2. _____ Listen carefully for the issue, not the feelings.
3. _____ Getting upset will not work. Stay relaxed.
4. _____ I did that well!
5. _____ I got through that without getting angry. Way to go!
6. _____ What does she want?
7. _____ It is not worth getting upset over.
8. _____ Listening to her anger will be easy.
9. _____ I will be able to manage the situation.
10. _____ He is trying to get me angry. I am not going to.
11. _____ I did not take anything personally. Good job!
12. _____ What is the issue? Do not get distracted into a quarrel.
13. _____ I am excellent at managing provocations.
14. _____ So he is insulting me. So what? The issue is more important.
15. _____ Calm down. I can't expect people to act the way I want them to.
16. _____ Take a few deep breaths and relax before we start.
17. _____ Good for me!
18. _____ It will be easy.
19. _____ What does she want?
20. _____ Relax.

Were You Talking About Me?

One of your classmates, John, has asked to talk with you after school. He has heard that you were talking about him in the cafeteria during lunch. He is hurt, angry, and upset. You did mention several good points and a couple of bad points about John in a general discussion of who were the most and least popular students. Although you mention far more positive than negative points about John, he has heard only that you were criticizing him behind his back. In preparing for the meeting, what are the statements you can make to yourself to:

1. Prepare emotionally for the meeting.

2. Prepare to listen to the John's angry statements.

3. Cope with your arousal and agitation during the meeting.

4. Congratulate yourself for coping successfully with his anger.

I Didn't Do It!

Sally is a student in your class who continually bothers everyone. She pushes, nudges, hits, and trips people regularly. Jane came to you crying with a cut lip and a bruised knee, complaining that Sally hit her and then pushed her down. You ask Sally if the two of you can talk about it during your joint study hall. Sally is extremely angry, saying that she did not touch Jane and Jane is lying. Sally sees you as being very unfair. You know that once study hall starts and you start to talk to Sally, she will start yelling and calling you names. In preparing for the meeting, what are statements you can make to yourself to:

1. Prepare emotionally for the meeting.

2. Prepare to listen to the Sally's angry statements.

3. Cope with your arousal and agitation during the meeting.

4. Congratulate yourself for coping successfully with her anger.

Assumptions, Assumptions, What Are My Assumptions?

What are common irrational assumptions? How do you know if your assumptions are rational or irrational? One way is to compare them with the following list of rational and irrational assumptions taken from the writings of Albert Ellis (1962). Do you make any of these assumptions? Do you have any of the irrational assumptions listed below? Do you make any of the rational assumptions listed below? Can you tell the difference between the rational and the irrational ones?

Read each of the statements listed below. Write *yes* for any assumption that describes how you think. Write *no* for any assumption that does not describe how you think. Then reread each statement. Write *R* for the rational assumptions. Write *I* for the irrational assumptions. Keep your answers. You will use them in a later lesson.

Common Assumptions

_____ 1. I must be loved, liked, and approved of by everyone all the time or I will be absolutely miserable and will feel totally worthless.

_____ 2. It would be nice if I were liked by everyone, but I can survive very well without the approval of most people. It is only the liking and approval of close friends and people with actual power over me (such as my boss) that I have to be concerned with.

_____ 3. I have to be absolutely 100 percent perfect and competent in all respects if I am to consider myself worthwhile.

_____ 4. My personal value does not rest on how perfect or competent I am. Although I'm trying to be as competent as I can, I am a valuable person regardless of how well I do things.

_____ 5. People who are bad, including myself, must be blamed and punished to prevent them from being wicked in the future.

_____ 6. What is important is not making the same mistakes in the future. I do not have to blame and punish myself or other people for what has happened in the past.

Taken from: Reaching Out: Interpersonal Effectiveness and Self-Actualization (4th ed.) by David W. Johnson. Englewood Cliffs, NJ: Prentice Hall, 1990.

_____ 7. It is a total catastrophe and so terrible that I can't stand it if things are not the way I would like them to be.

_____ 8. There is no reason the world should be the way I want it to be. What is important is dealing with what is. I do not have to bemoan the fact that things are not fair or just the way I think they should be.

_____ 9. If something terrible could happen, I will keep thinking about it *as if* it is actually going to take place.

_____10. I will try my best to avoid future unpleasantness. Then I will not worry about it. I refuse to go around keeping myself afraid by saying, "What if this happened?" "What if that happened?"

_____11. It is easier to avoid difficulties and responsibilities than to face them.

_____12. Facing difficulties and meeting responsibilities is easier in the long run than avoiding them.

_____13. I need someone stronger than myself to rely on.

_____14. I am strong enough to rely on myself.

_____15. Since I was this way when I was a child, I will be this way all my life.

_____16. I can change myself at any time in my life, whenever I decide it is helpful for me to do so.

_____17. I must become upset and depressed about other people's problems.

_____18. Having empathy with other people's problems and trying to help them does not mean getting upset and depressed about their problems. Overconcern does not lead to problem solving. How can I be of help if I am as depressed as others are?

_____19. It is terrible and unbearable to have to do things I don't want and don't like to do.

_____20. What I can't change I won't let upset me.

INTERPRETATIONS

The assumptions we make greatly influence our interpretations of the meaning of events in our life. These interpretations determine our feelings. The same event can be depressing or amusing, depending on the assumptions and interpretations we make. The purpose of this exercise is to focus a group discussion on the ways in which assumptions affect our interpretations and how we feel.

1. Form groups of four. Take the ten episodes below and discuss the following questions:
    a. What irrational assumption is the person making?
    b. How does this assumption cause the person to feel the way she does?
    c. What rational assumption does the person need in order to change her feelings into more positive feelings?
2. In your group, discuss assumptions each of you have that influence your feelings of depression, anger, frustration, distress, and worry. When you are experiencing each of these feelings, what assumptions are causing you to feel that way? How can you change these assumptions to make your life happier?

Episodes

1. Sally likes to have her coworkers place their work neatly in a pile on her desk so that she can add her work to the pile, staple it all together, and give it to their supervisor. Her coworkers, however, throw their work into the supervisor's basket in a very disorderly and messy fashion. Sally then becomes very worried and upset. "I can't stand it," Sally says to herself. "It's terrible what they are doing. And it isn't fair to me or our supervisor!"

2. Jill has been given responsibility for planning next year's budget for her department. This amount of responsibility scares her. For several weeks she has done nothing on the budget. "I'll do it next week," she keeps thinking.

3. John went to the office one morning and passed a person he had never met in the hallway. He said, "Hello," and the person just looked at him and then walked on without saying a word. John became depressed. "I'm really not a very attractive person," he thought to himself. "No one seems to like me."

Taken from: Reaching Out: Interpersonal Effectiveness and Self-Actualization
(4th ed.) by David W. Johnson. Englewood Cliffs, NJ: Prentice Hall,
1990.

Interpretations (continued)

4. Dan is an intensive-care paramedic technician and is constantly depressed and worried about whether he can do his job competently. For every decision that has to be made, he asks his supervisor what he should do. One day he came into work and found that his supervisor had quit. "What will I do now?" he thought. "I can't handle this job without her."

5. Jane went to her desk and found a note from her supervisor that she had made an error in the report she worked on the day before. The note told her to correct the error and continue working on the report. Jane became depressed. "Why am I so dumb and stupid?" she thought to herself. "I can't seem to do anything right. That supervisor must think I'm terrible at my job."

6. Heidi has a knack for insulting people. She insults her coworkers, her boss, customers, and even passersby who ask for directions. Her boss has repeatedly told Heidi that if she doesn't change she will be fired. This depresses Heidi and makes her very angry at her boss. "How can I change?" Heidi says. "I've been this way ever since I could talk. It's too late for me to change now."

7. Tim was checking the repairs another technician had made on a television set. He found a mistake and became very angry. "I have to punish him," he thought. "He made a mistake and he has to suffer the consequences for it."

8. Bonnie doesn't like to fill out forms. She gets furious every day because her job as legal secretary requires her to fill out form after form after form. "Every time I see a form my stomach ties itself into knots," she says. "I hate forms! I know they have to be done in order for the work to be filed with the courts, but I still hate them!"

9. Bob is very anxious about keeping his job. "What if the company goes out of business?" he thinks. "What if my boss gets angry at me?" "What if the secretary I yelled at is the boss's daughter?" All day he worries about whether he will have a job tomorrow.

10. Jack is a very friendly person who listens quite well. All his coworkers tell their problems to Jack. He listens sympathetically. Then he goes home deeply depressed. "Life is so terrible for the people I work with," he thinks. "They have such severe problems and such sad lives."

CHANGING YOUR FEELINGS

Now that you have discussed how people can make their assumptions more constructive, you may want to apply your own advice to yourself. The purpose of this exercise is to give you a chance to discuss your own negative feelings and see what assumptions are causing them. The procedure is:

1. Form groups of four. Draw straws to see who goes first in your group. Then go around the group in a clockwise direction. Each member completes the following statements:
    a. What depresses me about school or work is . . .
    b. When I get depressed about school or work I . . .
    c. The assumptions I am making that cause me to be depressed are . . .
    d. Constructive assumptions I can adopt to change my depression to more positive feelings are . . .
    Listen carefully to what each group member says. If he is not sure of his assumptions, help him clarify them. Give support for making his assumptions more constructive.
2. Now go around the group again and discuss how each member completes these statements:
    a. The things I worry about are . . .
    b. What I do when I get worried is . . .
    c. The assumptions I am making that cause me to be worried are . . .
    d. Constructive assumptions I can adopt to change my worry to more positive feelings are . . .
3. Now try anger:
    a. The things I get angry about are . . .
    b. What I do when I get angry is . . .
    c. The assumptions I am making that cause me to be angry are . . .
    d. Constructive assumptions I can adopt to change my anger to more positive feelings are . . .
4. Let's see how you feel about your career!
    a. The negative feelings I have when I think about my career are . . .
    b. The things I do when I have those feelings are . . .
    c. The assumptions I am making that cause the feelings are . . .
    d. Constructive attitudes I can adopt to change these feelings to more positive ones are . . .
5. Discuss in your group what the members learned about themselves and the ways in which they manage their feelings.

- - - - -

Taken from: Reaching Out: Interpersonal Effectiveness and Self-Actualization
(4th ed.) by David W. Johnson. Englewood Cliffs, NJ: Prentice Hall, 1990.

HOW DO I MANAGE MY FEELINGS ?

There are five questions below. Each question has two parts. Check *a* if your way of managing feelings is best described by the *a* part of the question. Check a *b* if your way of managing feelings is best described by the *b* part of the question. Think about each question carefully. Be honest. No one will see your answers. The results are simply for your own self-awareness.

1. ____ **a.** I am fully aware of what I am sensing in a given situation.
   ____ **b.** I ignore what I am sensing by thinking about the past or the future.

2. ____ **a.** I understand the interpretations I usually make about other people's actions. I investigate my feeling by asking what interpretation is causing it. I work to be aware of interpretations I am making.
   ____ **b.** I deny that I make any interpretations about what I sense. I ignore my interpretations. I insist that I do not interpret someone's behavior as being mean. The person *is* mean.

3. ____ **a.** I accept my feeling as being part of me. I turn my full awareness on it. I try to feel it fully. I take a good look at it so I can identify it and tell how strong it is. I keep asking myself, "What am I feeling now?"
   ____ **b.** I reject my feeling. I ignore it by telling myself I'm not angry, upset, sad, or even happy. I deny my feeling by telling myself and others, "But I'm not feeling anything at all." I avoid people and situations that might make me more aware of my feelings. I pretend I'm not really feeling the way I am.

4. ____ **a.** I decide how I want to express my feeling. I think of what I want to result from the expression of my feeling. I think of what is an appropriate way to express the feeling in the current situation. In my mind, I review the sending skills.
   ____ **b.** Since I've never admitted to having a feeling, I don't need to decide how to express it! I don't think through what might happen after I express my feelings. I never think about what is appropriate in a situation. When my feelings burst I am too emotional to remember good sending skills.

- - - - - - -

Taken from: Reaching Out: Interpersonal Effectiveness and Self-Actualization (4th ed.) by David W. Johnson. Englewood Cliffs, NJ: Prentice Hall, 1990.

How Do I Manage My Feelings? (continued)

5.　___ **a.** I express my feelings appropriately and clearly. Usually, this means describing my feeling directly. It also means using nonverbal messages to back up my words. My words and my nonverbal messages communicate the same feeling.

　___ **b.** I express my feelings inappropriately and in confusing ways. Usually, this means I express them indirectly through commands, accusations, put-downs, and evaluations. I may express feelings physically in destructive ways. My nonverbal messages express my feelings. I shout at people, push or hit them, avoid people, refuse to look at them, or don't speak to them. I may hug them, put my arm around them, give them gifts, or try to do favors for them. My words and my nonverbal messages often contradict each other. I sometimes smile and act friendly toward people I'm angry at. Or I may avoid people I care a great deal for.

Being Positive About Yourself While Trying Again

Critical Thoughts	Encouraging Thoughts
Circle the self put-down that you might use when you make a mistake.	**Circle the comments you like best for handling a mistake.**
You stupid idiot. Why can't you do something right!	That didn't work. What shall I try next?
I'll never get it.	Everyone makes mistakes. Just try it again.
.
I really blew it this time.
.	I'll see if I can do better next time. .
I hate myself.	I only did one thing poorly. Look at everything I did right!
Why am I such a loser?	I'm learning from my mistakes and that makes me a winner!

1. Form a group of three.

2. Each member writes out a failure or two they have experienced recently. The failures are placed in a hat (or bag).

3. Each member draws a failure out of the hat. The member then:

   a. Makes a series of negative self-statements about the failure.

   b. Makes a series of positive self-statements about the failure.

4. This procedure is repeated until every member has gone through the sequence at least twice.

5. List three reasons why it is hard to change negative self-statements to positive ones. Then list three reasons why it is important to learn how to change negative self- statements to positive ones.

Predicting:
Short-Term and Long-Range Thinking

Form a group of three. Discuss and agree on the meaning of short-term and long-range.
Then discuss the following situations.

1. Roger took something of yours. What could you do?

    a. What might be the short-term effect of your action?

    b. What might be the long-range effect of your action?

2. Edythe pushed you in the hallway and you fell down. What could you do?

    a. What might be the short-term effect of your action?

    b. What might be the long-range effect of your action?

3. Helen is telling lies about you. What could you do?

    a. What might be the short-term effect of your action?

    b. What might be the long-range effect of your action?

4. Frank is calling you names. What could you do?

    a. What might be the short-term effect of your action?

    b. What might be the long-range effect of your action?

5. Sally and Jane have asked Rosita not to play with you. What could you do?

    a. What might be the short-term effect of your action?

    b. What might be the long-range effect of your action?

Childhood Messages

Usually we act out of habit, automatically, without conscious decision-making and planning. Habitual ways of responding to a conflict situation are based on messages we learned about conflict as we were growing up.

1. Your **task** is to identify key messages about conflict that you have learned while you were growing up from parents, teachers, peers, religious leaders, and so forth.

2. Work **cooperatively** in a pair. List six messages the two of you were taught. Each member must make a copy of the list.

3. Form a new pair. **Share** your list with your new partner. **Listen** carefully to his or her list. **Create** a new list out of the best ideas from the two of you.

4. Return to your original partner. **Share** your modified list. **Listen** to his or her modified list. **Create** a final list based on the best thinking of the two of you. Be ready to share your list with the whole class.

5. With your partner write down three conclusions about how these messages affect your actions in conflict situations today. Pick one of the people who taught you the messages and role play a scene in which the message is being taught to you.

Examples Of Childhood Messages About Conflict

Don't hit below the belt.	Fighting never solved anything.
Girls don't fight.	Don't pick a fight, but if you're in one, win!
Turn the other cheek.	Never hit a girl.
Bite your tongue.	An eye for an eye, a tooth for a tooth.
If you haven't anything nice to say, don't say anything at all.	If you finish second, no one will know your name.

Handling Put-Downs

Everyone gets put down. Often put-downs are presented as humor and sometimes they are funny. Other times they just hurt. Everyone needs to learn how to manage put-downs so that the behavior of those who attack the person are not reinforced and so that the person's self-esteem is not damaged. Two basic approaches are to determine whether the put-down is valid or invalid. If it is invalid then it is the other person's mistake and shortcoming to make an invalid accusation. If the put-down is valid, then there is no reason to feel overwhelmed because no one is expected to be perfect. When someone puts you down things you could do include the following:

1. **The very best thing to do when you get a put-down is to ignore it and the person making it.** Most times people make put-downs to get attention. Being ignored is the thing that attackers dislike most.

2. **But, if you must say something to the person who put you down, do not respond with a put-down.** Insulting back only escalates the situation and results in more put-downs.

3. **Much better is to cut the person off by giving a quick comeback that is not nasty and shows that you are unaffected by the put-down.**

    "I don't agree."

    "Big deal."

    "So what?"

    "Really? I didn't know that."

    "Who cares?"

4. **You could also agree with the person.**

   "How did you know?"

   "Who told you?"

   "You know, you're right."

5. **Finally, you could make a joke of it.**

   "Would you put that in writing?"

   "Watch it or I'll call my lawyer."

   "That was supposed to be a secret."

   "Are you sure you are talking to the right person?"

Protecting Yourself From Put-Downs

When you are "put down" you can (a) feel hurt, rejected, and ashamed, (b) become angry at the other person, and/or (c) avoid both through the images you think of and the things you say to yourself. Practice the following:

1. Imagine yourself protected from put-downs by:

   a. A suit of armor.
   b. An invisible cape.
   c. A bullet-proof vest.

2. Imagine the put-down is something you can side step:

   a. A breeze that sails by without touching you.
   b. An arrow or bullet that speeds by and misses you.

3. Instead of thinking of what the other person says to you, say things to yourself that are true:

   a. About the other person:

      1. "Something must be bugging him."
      2. "Someone who puts others down usually feels bad about him- or herself."
      3. "Poor person. She must not like herself."
      4. "She is trying to impress others. She must need friends."

   b. About yourself:

      1. "No matter what they say, I'm still an O.K. person."
      2. "I know it isn't true."
      3. "I won't let this bother me. I know I'm a good person."
      4. "Sticks and stones will break my bones, but words will never hurt me."
      5. "If they really knew me,
         they wouldn't say that."

Just Joking

Sometimes we say things that hurt other people's feelings. Put- downs are common in most schools. Making cutting remarks that attack schoolmates self-esteem may be seen as "cool."

1. With a partner, write out how each person feels in the following situations.

2. Rewrite each of the situations, changing the rejecting behavior to accepting behavior.

Just Joking!

Sam, a new student, is assigned to a coooperative learning group. Jim says, "Does he have to be in our group?"

Sam:

_____

_____

Jim:

_____

_____

_____

Jane walks by a group in the hallway. Sally says, "She is having a bad hair day."

Jane:

_____

_____

_____

Sally:

_____

_____

_____

Just Joking!

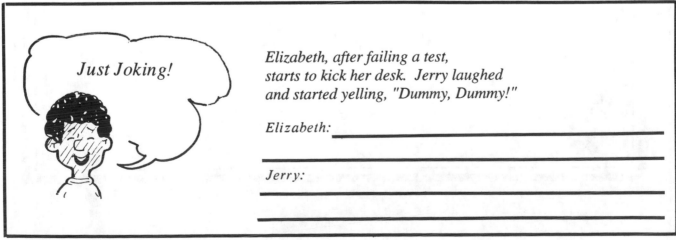

Just Joking!

Elizabeth, after failing a test, starts to kick her desk. Jerry laughed and started yelling, "Dummy, Dummy!"

Elizabeth: _____

_____

Jerry: _____

_____

The "I'm Bugged" Board

1. What has "bugged" you recently (that is, made you annoyed or angry)?

2. Draw a picture of something that "bugs" you. Label what it is. The teacher will write the label if you cannot.

3. Show your picture to three other students and look at theirs. Discuss what "bugs" the four of you. Put your pictures on the bulletin board.

4. Pick some of the situations to use with the problem puppets.

5. As a class discuss:

   a. What do you do when someone or something bugs you?

   b. What else could you do?

   c. Do two or more of you get bugged by the same thing?

I'M BUGGED

6 Mediating Conflicts Among Students

The Choice

Jane and Ann have always been good friends. Today, during lunch, they suddenly started yelling at each other in the cafeteria. Far too angry to negotiate with each other, they seek the help of a peer mediator. You, their mediator, are concerned because you thought they were good friends. You ask Jane what is bothering her. Jane says, "I am never going to talk to Ann again. I told her I liked Frank and she went and blabbed it to everyone! I can't believe I ever liked her! I tried to tell her about it in the cafeteria and she started to yell at me!" You then ask Ann what happened. She says, "I only told one person that Jane liked Frank. It was Frank's friend, Bob. I thought it would be a help to Jane if Frank knew. How was I supposed to know that Bob would tell the whole school and Frank would get steamed. You'll never see me trying to help anyone again!"

A **mediator** is a neutral person who helps two or more people resolve their conflict. A mediator stands in the middle and assists two people go through each step of negotiating so that an agreement is reached that both believe is fair, just, and workable. The mediator keeps everything fair. A mediator can not "decide" the case like a judge. A mediator does not tell classmates what to do, decide who is right and who is wrong, or talk about what he or she would do in such a situation. The mediator can not command someone to do something and expect obedience. The mediator can not enforce rules. A mediator has no authority to make a decision that is binding on the disputants. The disputants do not have to agree with anything the mediator says.

Mediation exists, therefore, when a neutral and impartial third party assists two or more people in negotiating a constructive resolution to their conflict. The participants in the conflict who seek mediation are called **disputants**. When mediation has been successful:

1. The conflict will be resolved so that all disputants have benefited.

2. The relationship between the students will be as good as or even better than ever.

3. Students' negotiating skills and self-confidence in using them will be increased. An important purpose of the mediator is to teach negotiation procedures and skills so that the individuals can manage their conflicts on their own in the future.

Mediation is an extension of the negotiation process and is a collection of strategies to promote more efficient and effective negotiations. The main difference between negotiating and mediating is that a neutral third party, the mediator, ensures that both persons engage in each step of the negotiation process.

Value Of Peer Mediation

Meg and Sarah both want to take the class rabbit home for the vacation. Both of their parents have said it is all right. They cannot agree on who brings the rabbit home. "It's my turn," insists Meg. "And besides, you don't even like the rabbit." "This is the first time my parents have agreed to bring a pet home from school," exclaims Sarah. "It's my only chance!" "Let's go find the class mediator," Meg suggests.

When students have a conflict their alternatives are:

1. Fight destructively, forcing against forcing, to see who will win.
2. Withdraw and avoid each other and have their energies tied up in hostility and resentment toward each other.

3. Smooth by giving in to make the other person happy and helping the other person meet his or her needs and goals.

4. Directly confront each other and either negotiate a mutually beneficial resolution to the conflict or a livable compromise.

5. Ask a mediator to assist in making their negotiations more effective and constructive.

6. Ask a higher authority to arbitrate the conflict and then live with the decision gracefully.

Ideally, students would first try to negotiate a mutually beneficial solution to their problem. If they cannot, they should seek out a mediator.

Evidence That Peer Mediation Works

Peer mediation is being used in a growing number of high, middle, and elementary schools throughout the United States. Conflicts among students are resolved neither by teachers nor by principals but rather by the disputants themselves with the help of a trained peer mediator. A number of positive outcomes of such programs have been documented. **First**, peer mediation programs tend to create more stable and lasting solutions to conflicts among students than does adult arbitration. Traditional disciplinary procedures such as detention and suspension often only avoid or defer conflicts. Mediation helps solve the underlying problems so students do not sit and "fester" with resentment. At Gilmore Middle School in Racine, Wisconsin, for example, 189 disputes involving 415 students were mediated by 21 different student mediators in the first six months of the program. Of these, all but three of the mediated resolutions "held." In two other instances, the students could not come to an agreement but did agree to a "cease fire" and did not end up fighting.

Second, peer mediation programs tend to decrease discipline problems such as violence, vandalism, and truancy. As a result of peer mediation programs, appropriate student behavior increased, suspensions were reduced, some of the school's "toughest" problem students were reformed, and, consequently, teachers' and principals' disciplinarian duties were decreased. One evaluator reported that after one year of operation a peer mediation program reduced the number of suspensions by 70 percent in a school where suspension rates have traditionally been high.

Third, peer mediation programs tend to improve student and faculty morale and overall school climate. **Fourth**, peer mediation programs tend to teach conflict resolution skills that are transferred to the home. Students used the mediation strategies at home with parents and/or siblings.

Two carefully conducted evaluations of a peer mediation program were recently completed (Johnson, Johnson, & Dudley, 1991a, 1991b). Both studies were conducted in midwestern, sub-urban elementary school. Students from first through sixth grades were involved. They received 30 minutes of training per day for six weeks. The training focused on the negotiation and mediation procedures and skills presented in this book. Measures were given (a) before and

after the training program and (b) to students who did and who did not receive the training.

Prior to the mediation training, the conflicts reported by students and teachers were (in terms of frequency) put-downs and teasing, playground conflicts, access or possession conflicts, physical aggression and fights, academic work conflicts, and turn taking. Most students were involved in these conflicts daily.

Untrained students were characterized by:

1. Referring the majority of conflicts to the teacher. Conflicts were primarily brought to the teacher for arbitration. Students seemed conditioned to look to the teacher for a solution to their conflicts. One of the teachers, in her log, stated that before training the students seemed to view conflict as fights that always resulted in a winner and a loser. To avoid such an unpleasant situation, students typically placed the responsibility for resolving conflicts on the teacher.

2. Using destructive strategies that tended to escalate the conflict rather than resolve it. When untrained students did not refer the conflict to the teacher, they tended to use destructive strategies (such as repeating their request and trying to force the other person to give in) that escalated the conflict and increased the likelihood that the teacher would have to intervene. Trained students never used these strategies. Few untrained students wanted to discuss the conflicts with their classmates or were willing to smooth by allowing the other person to get their way.

3. Lacking knowledge of how to negotiate. Not once did untrained students negotiate a solution to their conflicts. When videotaped in a simulated conflict situation, untrained students took longer to resolve the conflict and the majority participated in some type of nonproductive behavior (physical or destructive actions) before even the first step of negotiation was undertaken. Almost half of the untrained students did not state what they wanted. Even when the 54 percent of the students who at least established a position to be negotiated were considered, they did not engage in the steps of expressing feelings, reversing perspectives, and suggesting multiple possible agreements.

The training program was successful. Students did learn how to negotiate. Their negotiation skills were measured immediately following training and six months after the training program ended. In both cases, trained students knew and were able to use the negotiation procedures and skills.

After the negotiation and mediation training, the student-student conflicts that did occur were by and large managed by the students themselves without the involvement of adults. The frequency of student-student conflicts teachers had to manage dropped 80 percent after the training and the number of conflicts referred to the principal was reduced to zero. Such a dramatic reduction of referrals of conflicts to adult authorities changed the discipline program from arbitrating conflicts to maintaining and supporting the peer mediation process.

Finally, students generalized their conflict training and spontaneously applied the negotiation and mediation procedures and skills to situations outside of the class. Among the trained students, one third-grade student wrote two stories about the mediation process and at the end-of-the-year variety show a mediation scene was included by 5th-grade students. Many of the students reported using the negotiation and mediation skills at home with their siblings. A number of parents volunteered to teachers that students used the negotiation and mediation procedures and skills with their brothers and sisters, neighborhood friends, grandparents, and even their pets.

Perhaps the most interesting evidence that the conflict training program worked was that (a) many parents whose children were not part of the project requested that their children receive the training next year, and (b) a number of parents requested that they receive the training so that they could use the methods to improve the conflict management within the family.

In summary, there are a number of conclusions that may be tentatively made from the results of this study. **First**, conflicts among students do occur frequently. **Second**, many students do not seem to have been taught how to manage conflicts constructively in their homes or in the community at large. **Third**, conflict training can be successful in teaching students how to negotiate and mediate. This success is reflected in the reduction of the number of student-student conflicts referred to teachers and principals, the students' retention of the negotiation and mediation procedures and skills, and the frequency with which students applied their ability to negotiate and mediate in settings other than the classroom. The most difficult parts of the negotiation procedure for students to master were expressing feelings and reversing perspectives.

How Mediating Benefits Students

Every student needs to be trained in how to mediate classmates' conflicts. And each student needs to take a turn at being class mediator. Perhaps the best way to learn how to negotiate resolutions of your own conflicts is to help classmates do so. Given the need for students to learn how to manage conflicts constructively, and the benefits received from knowing how to negotiate and assisting others by being their mediator, all students should both be taught how to mediate and be given experience actually mediating. The ways students benefit from being peer mediators include the following.

1. Being a peer mediator teaches students the negotiation procedure and increases their commitment to gaining negotiation skills and using the negotiation procedure when they are involved in a conflict of interests.

2. Being a peer mediator requires both **interpersonal skills** such as communication, trust-building, and decision-making skills, and **academic skills** such as critical thinking, divergent thinking, oral and written expression, note taking, and creative problem solving. These skills can contribute to increased academic achievement and make the school environment more conductive to learning.

3. Mediation encourages communication and cooperation and provides the entire school community with a forum for constructive dialogue and problem solving to resolve conflicts.

4. Student maturity and responsibility is encouraged, which results in an improved school climate.

5. High-risk students, after being trained as mediators, discover a positive and exciting way to contribute to their schools. Their interest in and commitment to education can increase as a result.

6. Students develop skills they can generalize to their interaction with others in their classroom, school, family, and community. The attitudes required to behave responsibly and be law-abiding citizens are enhanced. **Mediating conflicts among their peers prepares students to be citizens in a complex and conflict-filled world.**

7. Mediation frees teachers, administrators, and support staff to concentrate more on teaching and academic issues. Fewer students become involved with school disciplinary processes and thereby reduce discipline demands on the staff.

Establishing A Classroom Peer Mediation Program

Within the classroom it is traditionally the teacher to whom students bring their conflicts and ask for assistance when conflicts occur. Teachers have a great many responsibilities. While teachers are responsible for ensuring that conflicts among students are managed constructively, they do not have to mediate each one personally. They are only responsible for ensuring that a competent mediator is available. The mediator may be another student. More specifically, **teachers are responsible for:**

1. **Building a cooperative context within which conflicts may be resolved constructively.** This involves using cooperative learning the majority of the time. Teachers carefully structure cooperation within and among learning groups so that the entire classroom is a learning community made up of collaborators.

2. **Structuring academic controversies so that students challenge each other's reasoning.** This involves teaching students how to plan, present, and advocate positions; how to view an issue from a number of perspectives; and how to arrive at the best possible solution based on a synthesis of the best evidence from all points of view (see Johnson & Johnson, 1987).

3. **Teaching all students how to negotiate.** By teaching the negotiation procedure and skills, teachers ensure that all students are co-oriented and use the same procedures for resolving conflicts of interests.

4. **Teaching all students how to mediate.** By teaching the mediation procedure and skills, teachers ensure that all students help classmates work through the negotiation sequence and gain negotiation skills. Knowing that in the future they will be class mediators helps ensure that students are open to the process of mediation and the suggestions of a mediator.

5. **Implementing a peer mediation process.** Each day two students are selected to be the class mediators. They help classmates negotiate resolutions to their conflicts. The role of class mediator is rotated throughout the class so that each student serves as class mediator an equal amount of time. Students need to know how to arrange for a mediator when they need one.

6. **Being a skilled mediator who can mediate conflicts among students when the peer mediator is unable to do so.**

7. **Being willing to arbitrate a conflict among students when mediation fails.**

8. **Being willing to send the students to the principal when both mediation and arbitration have failed.** The principal first tries to mediate the conflict and, if that fails, arbitrates.

If a teacher does a thorough and competent job of the first five steps, the last three will be rarely used.

How To Mediate

Stephanie was standing by her locker before her first hour class when Brian, her ex-boyfriend, walked up and started teasing her. She ignored Brian, pretending he was not there, but he continued to tease her. Finally, Stephanie took her purse by its strap and swung it at Brian, trying to hit him. He grabbed her purse, pulled it out of her hand, and ran down the hall with it. Later in the day, Stephanie and Brian had a class together. Before the class started Brian said that he would give Stephanie her purse back if she would start dating him again. She screamed "No!" and went to her seat as the bell rang. After class Brian slammed the purse down on Stephanie's desk and said that he still wanted to go out with her. Stephanie found that the strap on her purse was ripped and discovered that the $32 she had in her purse was missing. She found Brian in the hallway and told him she wanted her money back and he had to buy her a new purse. Brian said he had not taken any money and that the strap had torn when she had tried to hit him with the purse. They started yelling at each other. They need the help of a mediator.

Most students would rather have a student mediator handle their disputes than a teacher, counselor, or principal. Their reasons include, "It's easier to talk to someone your own age," "Another student understands," "Other students have had similar problems," and "Students don't 'bust' you!" Staff members like it because it works. No escalation. No teacher intervention. No fight. No injury. No cheering onlookers. No detention. No suspension. Most types of student conflicts can be resolved through mediation, although serious disputes involving weapons, drugs, or criminal behavior are excluded.

The mediator's job is to assist classmates to negotiate agreements about what they will and will not do in order to resolve their conflict. Being a mediator is very satisfying. Peer mediators help classmates and schoolmates with real problems. Mediators often learn something new about others and/or about themselves. For numerous reasons students sometimes dislike the mediator. Being liked, however, is not important. What is important is being an effective mediator. Helping others, furthermore, does not mean that the mediator will not need similar help in the future. Students are not mediators because they are better persons than their classmates. They are mediators because they have been trained in the procedures and skills required and it is their turn to fulfill the mediator role. Some day they too will need help in resolving a conflict.

It is not enough for a student to want to help classmates solve their problems. Students must be skilled in using mediation procedures. Being a mediator is fun. It provides meaning and satisfaction to life. But it takes a lot of hard work and practice to be a good mediator. Mediation is not magic and it is far more than using "common sense." Mediators must know exactly what they are doing and why they are doing it. The **procedure for mediation** consists of a series of steps:

1. **End hostilities**: Break up fights and cool down students.

2. **Ensure both people are committed to the mediation process**: To ensure that both persons are committed to the mediation process and are ready to negotiate in good faith, the mediator introduces the process of mediation, sets the ground rules, and introduces him- or herself.

3. **Help the two people negotiate with each other successfully**: This includes taking the two persons through the negotiation sequence of:

   a. Jointly defining the conflict by both persons stating what they want and how they feel.

   b. Exchanging reasons.

   c. Reversing perspectives so that each person is able to present the other's position and feelings to the other's satisfaction.

   d. Inventing at least three options for mutual benefit.

   e. Reaching a wise agreement and shaking hands.

4. **Formalize the agreement**: The agreement is solidified into a contract. Disputants must agree to abide by their final decision and in many ways the mediator becomes "the keeper of the contract."

Step 1: End Hostilities

Mediation begins with ending the hostilities among students and cooling them down enough so that constructive negotiating may take place.

Breaking Up Hostilities

Peer mediators are helpers, not police officers. If there is physical fighting, peer mediators do not get involved. They find an adult to separate the fighters. Then they may help to implement one of the procedures the teacher trained students to use to break up hostilities:

1. **Find a teacher.** The mere presence of a teacher is enough to stop many hostilities. If a teacher is going to separate two students who are physically fighting, the teacher:

   a. Should be sure he or she is bigger than are the students.

   b. Should have a clear procedure in mind.

   c. Never restrains one student without restraining the other. Restraining one person may open him or her to the attack of the other, which will not win the teacher any points as a peacemaker.

   d. In a real emergency, grabs the students by their hair. This will usually stop a fight right away. But taking violent action against a student opens the teacher to counter-violence.

   e. Uses one of the restraint methods taught in mental hospitals.

2. **Divert the physical and emotional energy being expressed in the hostilities** (if a teacher is not available):

   a. Breaking eye contact between participants will often stop a fight.

   b. Distracting students' attention: "Hey, who lost this ten dollar bill?"

   c. Getting very close and shouting loudly.

3. **Using spectators to end hostilities.** The teacher should train your class in "fight drills" the same way they are trained in "fire drills." Students should practice:

   a. Everyone leaves.

   b. Chanting, "Stop fighting, stop fighting."

   c. Singing some happy song such as "Ring around the Rosy" to create a situation in which fighting is incongruous.

Cooling Off Hostile Persons

It is often helpful to help students dissipate their emotions by separating them for a period of time. The teacher may have the class practice cool down procedures. Some procedures for cooling disputants down are:

1. **Cool-off corners** where hostile individuals are sent not to be punished but to calm down. When they have cooled off, they can leave their corners.

2. **Deep breathing** to relax them (this is called **counter-conditioning** because it conditions students to respond in a way that is counter to being angry and hostile):

   a. Take slow, deep breaths while you count to ten and then back to one again.

   b. Tense all your muscles and breathe in. Keep your muscles tense and hold your breath for five seconds. Then slowly exhale and relax your muscles for five seconds. Repeat this process several times.

c. When you become skilled in breathing deep and relaxing your muscles, imagine your anger leaking out of toes as you relax. Let your anger and tension drain away through your feet. Then walk away from it.

3. **Exhausting physical activities** such as walking around, pushups, or hitting a punching bag to give them the opportunity to get rid of their anger.

4. **Conflict forms** for each participant to complete.

Cooling off deescalates and postpones a conflict; it does not resolve it. Sometimes after two students have cooled off they want to skip the whole thing. If no hard feelings remain, let them do so. Most of the time, however, cooling off the disputants is a preliminary step to mediating the conflict.

Conflict Forms

The process of mediation is often helped if students reflect on the conflict, define it, and think of alternative ways of resolving the conflict before the mediation process begins. One procedure for doing so is the conflict form. **First**, the mediator gives each student involved a conflict form to fill out. If a student cannot read or write well, a partner to help fill out the conflict form is provided. **Second**, when each student finishes the form, the mediator reads over the answers with the student and helps the student with any answers he or she is unsure of. **Third**, the mediator (a) begins mediation, using the conflict form to help students communicate their views of the conflict to each other (this may be done orally or the students can exchange conflict forms and write their reactions to each other's accounts) or (b) discusses what the students will do in a situation similar to the conflict situation in the future (for each alternative suggested, ask, "Will this action solve the problem better than open hostilities such as fighting?").

The conflict forms will give the mediator a clear idea of how to proceed in helping resolve the conflict. The conflict form should highlight the cooperation and negotiation procedures and skills the students need to learn to get along better with classmates, such as:

1. Who was your conflict with?

2. What did you want? How did the other's actions stop you from getting what you want? How did you feel?

3. What did the other person want? How did your actions stop him or her from getting what he or she wanted? How did the other person feel?

4. What are three potential agreements that might resolve the conflict and reestablish a good relationship between the two of you?

5. What are three things you might try if this happens again?

7. Is there anything you would like to say to the person you fought with?

Step 2: Ensure Commitment To Mediation

Once the hostilities are stopped and the students have cooled down emotionally, the mediation session can begin. Having their conflict mediated is the students' choice. If students decide to accept help from the mediator, they must agree to work hard to solve the problem.

Arranging The Mediation Area

Sometimes there is a special area or office for mediation to occur. How the area is arranged gives a message as to whether or not the mediation will be fair. Before mediation begins the mediator has to arrange the area. The mediator makes sure the area is neat and clean. The mediator arranges the chairs around a table so that he or she sits at the end of the table. The disputants should sit at the table across from one another and close to the mediator. The mediator places a pad of paper and a pencil on the table for each disputant and for him or herself. When the mediator is ready, he or she brings the disputants into the area or room.

One disputant says that she will participate in mediation only if the mediator sits next to her and lets her speak first. The mediator refuses. Do you know why?

Introducing Yourself And Mediation

1. Introduce yourself if the disputants do not know you and confirm the names of the disputants,

making sure you know how to spell their names correctly.

2. Ask both students if they wish to solve their problem with the help of a mediator. Do not proceed until both students say "yes." To say "yes" students have to acknowledge publicly there is a conflict and they will participate in mediation.

3. State that mediation is voluntary and your role is to help them find a solution to their conflict that is acceptable to both of them. The solution must meet the needs of both parties. Your role is to hear both sides of the dispute, facilitate negotiation, encourage communication, help them see each other's viewpoint, and help them to overcome emotions that block settlement. Mediation is necessary because the students were not able to negotiate a constructive resolution of their conflict. Your overall role as a mediator is to help the students negotiate more effectively with each other.

4. State that each person will have an opportunity to state his or her views of the conflict without interruption. While one student is talking, the other disputant cannot interrupt or comment.

5. State that you, the mediator, will not take sides or attempt to decide who is right or wrong. You will be neutral. You will be unbiased and fair. You will help them decide how to resolve the conflict. You will help them work towards a solution that they both like. You are an objective person who has no biases regarding the dispute.

6. Establish the **ground rules** for the session:

   a. Agree to solve the problem.

   b. No name-calling.

   c. No interrupting.

   d. Be as honest as you can.

   Ask each disputant if they agree to the rules. Ask if they have any questions about mediation.

7. State that the disputants themselves must come up with a variety of options and decide on the solutions. You will not tell them what to do.

8. State that when the two reach an agreement, they must try to abide by the agreement. They must do what they have agreed to do. Make it clear that they will have to be flexible, will have to think creatively of options that meet both person's needs and goals, and may even have to be willing to compromise. A mediation session is considered successful when both students sign an agreement containing the elements of their settlement.

9. Explain that everything said during mediation sessions is **confidential** except for information on drugs, weapons, or alcohol on school property or at school events.

You then take the disputants through the steps of negotiation. When an agreement is reached, you complete a **Mediation Report Form** and the students sign it. This formalizes their agreement.

The above points must be covered, but different mediators may use different phrases and words to do so. The basic procedures and rules for mediation sessions have to be formulated so that students can understand and accept them. Younger students need a simpler explanation of the procedures and rules than do older students. Mediators will need to develop their personal version of the opening statement, so that they are comfortable and confident in saying it. They must then practice their opening statement **before** each session so that they can give it naturally without making any mistakes.

Step 3: Facilitate Negotiations

Define The Conflict

After the hostilities have been cooled and the students have committed themselves to the mediation process, negotiations begin with the mediator's help. The first step of negotiating is defining the conflict. The mediator helps both disputants define the conflict and communicate their goals and needs (that is, interests) in ways that do not escalate the conflict. In order to determine the facts and events that created the conflict and kept it going, the mediator decides who will talk first and then does the following:

1. Asks Student A what happened, what he or she wants, and how he or she feels.

2. Paraphrases what Student A said.

3. Asks Student B what happened and how he or she feels.

4. Paraphrases what Student B said.

5. Helps the disputants separate their interests from their positions.

6. Helps the disputants see their common interests and the need to maintain a constructive long-term relationship with each other.

In other words, **four of the more important skills for mediators are helping students give a factual and calm account of the conflict, paraphrasing or reflective listening, helping students separate each interests from positions, and highlighting the common interest in maintaining a constructive long-term relationship.** In addition, all of the guidelines for defining negotiating positions discussed in Chapter 3 need to be applied, such as defining the conflict in the smallest and most precise way possible.

Asking Students What Happened, What They Want, And How They Feel

In order for students to talk with each other about their conflict a set of **pre-stages** may need to be gone through. **First**, students may refuse to talk calmly to each other. They may yell or accuse instead. **Second**, students may demand that the mediator agrees that they are right and the other person is wrong. There often is pressure to take sides. **Third**, students may ask the mediator to understand them. **Fourth**, once the mediator understands, students often ask how come the other student cannot understand. At that point the students are able to talk and listen to each other. The mediator's role at this point is to ask each disputant to describe:

1. **What happened.** Each student is to state the facts as calmly as possible and to refer primarily to the present, not the past or future.

2. **What he or she wants.** This defines their interests. A joint definition of the conflict is then possible. It is not enough, however, for a student to understand what he or she wants. It must be communicated and explained to the opponent. The mediator helps disputants describe what they want without making the other person mad or upset. They need to describe what they want without building hills in front of them, sabotaging their chances for agreement by alienating others, or guaranteeing closed-minded rejection.

3. **How he or she feels.** Each student describes how he or she feels without making negative remarks about the other.

Students should be allowed to state their views and feelings without being interrupted. Mediators enforce the no interruptions rule. The mediator's body language should show that he or she is interested in what each student is saying. Mediators make eye contact and sit attentively. They say, "Tell me what happened." They never say, "Tell me your side of the story." Do you know why?

Many times students will not fully understand what the issue or the problem is. Having them fill out the conflict form before mediation begins will help, but further clarification may be necessary after mediation has begun. Even more frequent is not knowing how they feel. Students often feel and say "I don't know how I feel and I don't know what I want." Usually, the students are angry at each other and frustrated because negotiating has already failed. This means that in their description of the conflict a number of angry statements may be included. They may have to be reminded that no name calling is allowed. Having both persons explain how the conflict makes them feel increases their willingness to solve the problem.

If it is not clear yet, mediators help each student figure out what he or she wants by asking questions about anything they do not understand:

1. "Tell me more about..."

2. "How long has this been going on?"

3. "When did this happen?"

4. "What would you like to see happen now?"

Mediators listen very carefully to students' answers to gain an understanding of what issues have to be resolved in order for an agreement to be reached. Often it is helpful to determine what each person wants to keep the other from getting as well as what each one wants.

As mediators clarify, they need to help disputants be realistic about possible solutions. For example, Davy and Terry got into a fight over which group would use the basketball court on the playground. Terry states, "The only sure way to avoid future fights is for Davy to transfer to another school." How should you respond?

Sometimes, it helps students give a factual and calm account of the conflict if they are asked to describe it as a neutral, third-party observer. This may provide just enough distance for the students to analyze the situation and their behavior without feeling threatened.

Finally, mediators make sure the conflict is defined as a small and specific mutual problem that can be solved.

Paraphrasing What Each Student Says

Mediators must help students clarify their views of the problem and their feelings about it. An essential skill for such clarification is paraphrasing. Mediators need to be expert listeners who can listen attentively to the content and feelings of students' statements and summarize them accurately. Paraphrasing consists of:

1. **Restating the facts and summarizing the events.** Phrases that may help you paraphrase more effectively are:

   a. "Sounds like..."

   b. "In other words,..."

   c. "You're saying..."

   If these above phrases sound stilted and unnatural, do not worry. If you use them frequently while mediating, you will soon adapt them to your natural speech patterns.

2. **Reflecting feelings.** Pay attention to the emotional aspects of each person's position. A phrase that will help you do so is, "You feel...because...." When you paraphrase, try to reflect the emotional as well as the cognitive content.

3. **Remaining neutral.** Do not take sides. Use words and phrases that are impartial and non-judgmental. Identify and refer to all of the issues in a neutral way. Do not say, "She is angry because you stole her purse." Do say, "She is angry because you had her purse." Do not say,

"The two of you were yelling at each other about the $32." Do say, "You talk to each other in unhelpful ways when the topic of the money comes up."

Jose claims that Bobby stole his lunch tickets. Bobby denies it. The mediator asks Jose if he knows anything about "the missing lunch tickets," but would never ask him about "the stolen lunch tickets." Do you know why?

Roger claims that Terry stole his social studies report. Terry says he didn't. The mediator asks Roger to describe in more detail why he believes that Terry stole his report, but Roger states, "You are not a judge and this is not a courtroom. I don't have to prove anything. I said he took it and that's that. Your job is to make him confess." What should you say?

4. **Refusing to give advice or suggestions.**

5. **Avoiding bringing up similar feelings and problems from your own experience.**

There are a number of reasons why paraphrasing is one of the most essential skills for a mediator:

1. **Through paraphrasing the mediator helps make each disputant feel understood and supported.** As the disputant feels understood and accepted, his or her defensiveness will be decreased, allowing the student to think of new ways to resolve the conflict. Or it may simply help the student state the problem and his or her position more clearly.

2. **Through paraphrasing the mediator helps students clarify their goals and needs and their feelings about the conflict.** By reflecting back what the disputant has said, the mediator provides the disputant with the opportunity to reconsider and either affirm or correct the mediator's understanding of the disputant's interests and feelings. Doing so clarifies the disputant's goals, needs, and feelings not only for the mediator, but also for the disputant him- or herself.

3. **Through paraphrasing the mediator helps disputants listen to each other in a more neutral and objective way.**

4. **Paraphrasing each disputant's position helps the mediator organize the issues so that he or she knows in what order they should be discussed.** Usually the mediator will wish to focus attention first on the issues seemingly easiest for the disputants to

resolve. If they agree on some things quickly, they will develop a **momentum** for resolving all their issues. In addition, it will provide an opportunity to separate the person from the problem. This may help the other disputant to think more rationally about the conflict.

5. **Through paraphrasing the mediator slows down the interaction between the disputants and, therefore, allows a continual cooling off process.**

In the following example a mediator, Ree Flect, is helping two students, Jeremy and Mark, resolve a conflict about working jointly on a report.

Jeremy: *I went to the library to get a book I need to do the assignment. Mark jumped in front of me and grabbed the book just as I was about to take it off the shelf! It really makes me mad!*

Ree Flect: *You are angry and frustrated because Mark took the book you needed just as you were reaching for it.*

Jeremy: *Right. The only reason he knew about the book was because I told him about it.*

Ree Flect: *You want Mark to give you the book.*

Jeremy: *Yeah.*

Mark: *I knew about the book long before Jeremy found out about it. I've used it before; that's how I knew where it was. I knew that once Jeremy got it, he would never share, so I had to get it first. He can use it after I'm done.*

Ree Flect: *You are feeling hurt. You believe you knew about the book first. You are afraid that if Jeremy checked the book out, you would never get to use it.*

Mark: *Yeah. Jeremy keeps things at home and does not share them.*

Ree Flect: *I'm beginning to understand. Both of you need to use the book. Mark wants to use the book right now. Jeremy wants to take the book home and use it over the weekend. Jeremy is frustrated and angry. Mark, you are hurt and anxious. Right now you are trying to use the book in ways that keeps the other person from using it.*

So far, you have not discussed how to use the book together or share it. Does that sound right?

Jeremy & Mark: *Yes.*

Ree Flect: *We can start thinking of optional solutions now.*

In the above example each student stated his view of the conflict and the paraphrasing of the mediator (Ree Flect) helped Jeremy and Mark accurately identify each other's position.

Separating Interests From Positions

As a mediator you need to be skilled in **separating each student's interests from his or her position**. To do so you have to define each person's position and each person's interests and not confuse the two. One example is that of Meg and Jim who both wanted the baseball. Meg wanted the ball to practice catching. Jim wanted the ball to practice throwing. Their positions ("I want the baseball") were opposed, but their interests were not. Often when conflicting students reveal their underlying interests, it is possible to find a solution that suits them both.

Highlighting Cooperative Context (Enlarging Shadow Of The Future)

The mediator reminds disputants that in the long run, they are going to sink or swim together. When what one person wants conflicts with what another person wants, both cooperative and competitive interests are present. The **cooperative interests** are:

1. **We need each other to reach an agreement.** If we do not cooperate and solve this problem, neither one of us will get what we want.

2. **We will work together in the future.** If our relationship is damaged we will have future difficulties that will be far more damaging than not getting what we want today. In the long run, we will benefit far more from continually maximizing joint gains rather than trying to gain at the other's expense on this one issue.

The **competitive interests** are getting what we want and need right now. In a conflict people can think cooperatively and work to maximize joint gain or think competitively and work to maximize own gain at the expense of the other person.

An essential aspect of mediating is to highlight the cooperative interests among the disputants by:

1. Highlighting any common and compatible interests shared by the disputants and describing any opposing interests as a mutual problem to be solved rather than a "win-lose" situation.

2. Pointing out the ways in which disputants:

    a. Share a mutual fate.

    b. Depend on each other for resources and assistance.

    c. Need to value the long-term relationship over short-term gain.

    d. Will lose if you become enemies.

3. Pointing out that one of the potential costs of not resolving the conflict is teacher arbitration. This is known as "outside enemy interdependence." If students do not resolve the conflict, then the teacher or the principal will decide in a "winner take all" fashion. Since mediation is aimed at helping others negotiate constructive resolutions of conflict, there is a greatly likelihood of having an outcome favorable to oneself through mediation than through arbitration.

Exchange Proposals And Give Reasons

If after defining the conflict the dispute still exists, the mediator helps the disputants exchange reasons. This is done by:

1. **Helping disputants present their reasons and the rationale for their positions.** It is important to assess how important the interests of each disputant are. And it is important to provide disputants with the support they need to take risks in disclosing their reasons and search for common ground. To engage in spirited negotiation students have to feel supported. A critical role of the me-

diator is to provide support to both students. Negotiating and trying to resolve a conflict is risky and feelings can be hurt easily. When the mediator clearly affirms the competence of both students and provides support, the students feel less vulnerable and are more willing to take risks.

Students must explain their reasons without sabotaging the chances to reach an agreement later. They must describe the other person's actions, not accuse or label. Presenting reasons in a way that promotes open-minded consideration rather than closed-minded defensiveness is a skill that often requires the help of a mediator.

2. **Helping disputants understand the differences between their position and interests.** In order to think of good alternative agreements, disputants must understand the differences in what they want (position) and why they want it (interests).

3. **Avoiding tangents by keeping disputants focused on the issue, not on their anger toward each other.** A common occurrence within conflicts is that one person will make an angry remark, the other person will object, and soon the two are fighting over each other's insults rather than over the issue that began the conflict in the first place. "Did you hear what he said? He always tries to hurt me!" is a statement by one student that can change the topic of conversation to the tangent of whether the remark was really meant to hurt or not. A key mediation skill is keeping students focused on the issue to be resolved, not on emotional hurt, rejection, and anger. Mediators redirect the conflict back to the issue rather than on emotional tangents.

4. **Equalizing power.** It is hard for a low power person to negotiate with a high power person and vice versa.

5. **Recognizing constructive behaviors during negotiations.** Compliment what the students are behaving skillfully and shape their behavior by reinforcing "successive approximations" of skillful negotiating.

6. **Reframing the issue by helping disputants change perspectives.** This is discussed below.

Mediator's Role In Reframing Students' Definitions Of The Conflict

An example of reframing may be found in the book, **The Adventures Of Tom Sawyer**. Tom was ordered by his aunt to white wash their fence. Tom began to think of all the fun he had planned for this day, of how everyone else would have a great time while he was stuck white washing the fence, and of how they would tease him about it. Tom went tranquilly to work and soon one of his friends, Ben Rogers, came along. Ben began to tease Tom about getting stuck white washing the fence and Tom said nothing while critically surveying his work. Ben finally got Tom's attention and said, "Say--I'm going in a-swimming, I am. Don't you wish you could" But of course you'd druther work, wouldn't you? Course you would!" Tom contemplated Ben a little, and said, "What do you call work?" "Why, ain't that work?" "Well maybe it is and maybe it ain't. All I know is, it suits Tom Sawyer." "Oh, come now, you don't mean to let on that you like it?" "Like it? Well I don't see why I oughtn't to like it. Does a boy get a chance to whitewash a fence every day?" That put things in a new light. Tom went on working but soon Ben interrupted and said, "Say, Tom, let me whitewash a little." "No-no-I reckon it wouldn't hardly do, Ben. You see, Aunt Polly's awful particular about this fence right here on the street, you know-but if it was a back fence I wouldn't mind and she wouldn't. Yes, she's awful particular about this fence; it's got to be done very carefully; I reckon there ain't one boy in a thousand, that can do it the way it's got to be done." Ben said, "No-is that so? Oh, come, now-lemme just try. Only just a little-I'd let you, if you was me, Tom." By the time he was finished Tom Sawyer had done no more white washing and had sold the opportunity to his friends for an apple, a kite, a dead rat on a string to swing it with, twelve marbles, a piece of blue bottle-glass to look through, a spool cannon, a fragment of chalk, a glass stopper, a tin soldier, two tadpoles, six firecrackers, a kitten with one eye, a brass doorknob, a dog collar, the handle of a knife, four pieces of orange peel, and a dilapidated old window sash. The fence had three coats of white wash on it and if he hadn't run out of white wash, he would have bankrupted every boy in town. **The moral of this story is that the resolution of any conflict is possible if you can get the participants to look at it from the proper perspective.**

One of the major tasks of a mediator is to get the two persons to "reframe" their perception of the conflict. Ways to help disputants reframe their perception of the conflict and the other person's actions are:

1. **Framing as a mutual problem to be jointly solved.** The first reframing the mediator works towards is for students to view the conflict as a mutual problem to be solved rather than as a "win-lose" situation.

2. **Changing perspectives.**

3. **Distinguishing between intention and behavior.** Students need to distinguish between what was intended and the actual result of a person's actions.

4. **Continuing to differentiate the interests and reasoning of the disputants until a new frame is achieved.** If additional information about the other person's reasoning is sought, sooner or later a new "frame" will emerge. Differentiating goals and needs as well as reasoning leads to the reframing necessary for integration and synthesis.

5. **Exploring the multiple meanings of any one behavior.** When students seem stuck ask, "What else might that behavior mean?" The more different answers a student can think of to that question the more likely the student is to perceive a way to resolve the conflict. When students are complaining about each other's behavior, "He's too mean," "She's too picky," it helps to ask, "Think of situations in which the other's behavior would be positive." Once a positive context is thought of, the meaning of the behavior changes.

Another example of reframing is from the tale of Brer Rabbit. Brer Rabbit had got himself caught by Brer Fox and was well on his way to becoming evening dinner. Brer Rabbit was in a great deal of deep trouble. And all because he tried to win a fight with a tar baby. There did not seem much he could do about the situation but he did not seem concerned at all at being Brer Fox's dinner. He just said, "Brer Fox, I don't mind if you eat me. But oh, whatever you do, don't throw me in that briar patch." Now Brer Fox was surely looking forward to eating his old enemy but he was curiouser and curiouser about Brer Rabbit's sweating and crying about being thrown into the briar patch. And the more he questioned Brer Rabbit the more Brer Rabbit wailed about how much he feared that briar patch. Pretty soon Brer Fox became convinced that Brer Rabbit would rather be eaten than be set among those briars. So Brer Fox threw Brer Rabbit right into the briar patch. You know the rest.

Reverse Perspectives

There are many times when mediators will need to insist that the disputants understand each other's perspective. Reaching an agreement that is fair to both sides requires that they do so. There are also times when one person may not understand why another person is upset. They may say that an issue that the other cares about is "no big deal." Joan claims that Ron "bugs her" by calling her on the phone all the time. Joan and Ron have dated a few times and Ron wants to "go steady." Joan wants to date other boys. She is very angry that Ron keeps calling her every night. Ron says, "What's the big deal. So I call her. That's no crime. She's just looking for a fight." Ron needs to put himself in Joan's shoes and see the conflict from her perspective and understand why she believes the problem is important.

Perspective taking has been thoroughly discussed in previous chapters, so little will be said about it here. The mediator's role includes helping students take each other's perspectives accurately and fully by asking:

1. Student A to present Student B's wants, feelings, and reasoning.

2. Student B whether Student A was accurate.

3. Student B to present Student A's wants, feelings, and reasoning.

4. Student A whether Student B was accurate.

Disputants must be able to present and summarize each other's wants, feelings, and reasoning accurately. It is by seeing a situation from a variety of points of view that individuals demonstrate maturity and membership in the broader moral community. By seeing the situation from the opponent's perspective students (a) remain moral persons who are caring and just and (b) realize that the other person is someone who is entitled to caring and justice.

Invent Options For Mutual Benefit

The mediator's job is **not** to solve problems for other students. It is to help other students think of ways to solve problems for themselves. As student mediators have said, "The only right solution is **their** solution. We're not there to suggest **the** answer. We're there to listen." "Check your ego at the door. You're in it for two people. You have to put your own feelings aside."

The mediator's role at this point is to (see Chapter 3):

1. Help disputants avoid the obstacles to creative problem solving.

2. Invent creative options that are in everyone's best interests.

3. Realistically assess the advantages and disadvantages of each optional agreement. This usually involves using the balance sheet.

Sometimes agreements are not possible unless one student agrees to repair the damage caused by his or her actions. **Restitution** is the making amends for injury, mistreatment, or insult. If a student breaks a window, restitution is made by paying for the cost of installing a new window. If a student borrows a classmate's book and loses it, restitution is made by replacing the book. Many times disputes will revolve around damages that require some restitution by one of the students.

The mediator's job is to help students develop solutions to their conflict they can accept. Mediators never tell students that they are being unreasonable or silly. Mediators never tell students what the agreement should be. Instead, mediators:

1. **Ask Student A and then Student B what they can do here and now to resolve the conflict.** "We've talked about what's already happened. Where do we go from here?" Sometimes students become **fixated** on one possible agreement and are unable to think of alternatives. Such fixation is one of the enemies of effective negotiating. Generating a series of options requires divergent thinking and creative problem solving. **Divergent thinking** is generating a variety of ideas about how to solve a problem. Mediators have disputants think divergently before they converge on an agreement. In generating options, the disputants tell what they can do to resolve the conflict. At least three options are generated. The options should represent the ideal outcome of the conflict that they both can accept because it meets both their needs. Mediators sometimes suggest possible alternative agreements students overlooked. One of the most helpful procedures for encouraging students to think of options is role playing.

2. **Ask Student A and then Student B what they could do differently in the future if the same problem arises.**

3. **Point out any common ground.** "I hear you both agreeing that..."

4. **Help students focus on the future, not on the past.** Jose claims that Bobby stole his lunch tickets. Bobbie denies it. There are no witnesses. So who do you believe? Often, you will never know what "really" happened in the past. No one will ever know. So what can students do? How will Jose and Bobbie resolve their conflict if they disagree about what happened in the past? The answer is: Focus on the future. Jose and Bobbie may never be able to agree on what happened to the lunch tickets but they can agree that they

are in crisis now and they can develop an agreement that will specify how they will relate in the future. A future-oriented agreement will not force any one to admit he or she was wrong. It will only specify what they are to do now.

5. **Help students find a number of solutions they both think are good.** Each alternative should be evaluated against the following criteria:

   a. Is it specific? Does it tell when, where, who, and how?

   b. Is it realistic? Can each person do what they say they will?

   c. Are responsibilities shared? Are both students agreeing to do something? Say, "Is this solution acceptable to you?" You would never say, "That's a fair solution, isn't it?" Do you know why?

6. **Help disputants complete a balance sheet on each alternative.**

7. **If necessary, increase disputants motivation to resolve the conflict by highlighting gains and losses for doing so:**

   a. Analyze carefully what each student has to gain by reaching an agreement. Remind them of the benefits of resolving their conflict. For example, "Ron, you may not want to apologize to Joan, but you do want to date her. If she is angry at you, she won't date you. Her friends won't invite you to their parties, which means that you won't see her very often. What would you be willing to do to have Joan and her friends happy with you?"

   b. Analyze carefully what each student has to lose by not reaching an agreement. Sometimes students get so angry that they refuse to agree to anything . Part of your job, as a mediator, is to highlight the costs of refusing to agree. The price of not agreeing may be to have the teacher arbitrate the conflict or, in some cases, to be suspended from school. Another cost is having the strain of dealing with an enemy at school.

8. **Help disputants develop trade-offs.** A **trade-off** is the exchange of two different things of comparable value. If Ron proposes a trade-off where he will not call Joan every night if she will date no one but him, would this be acceptable? The answer is no. Not dating anyone but Ron is "worth" much more than limiting the number of phone calls. Be certain that the proposed items to be traded are of comparable value.

9. **If an agreement is not reached right away, the mediator returns to students' feelings and definitions of the conflict.** "What did you do that made A so upset with you?" Why are you upset at A?"

10. **If time runs out, the mediator may wish to help disputants develop a compromise that both can live with.**

Sometimes if students will not agree to resolve an issue, the mediator can get them to agree to a principle. While two students may not agree on whether one should replace a lost book, they may be willing to agree to the principle that it is wrong to solve problems by fighting. Once they agree on a principle, then perhaps they can agree not to fight each other in the future when they have a conflict.

Reach An Agreement

The goal of mediation is to arrive at an agreement that is written down and signed by everyone involved. When mediation has been successful, the conflict will be resolved, the relationship between the students will be as good as or even better than ever, and students' negotiating skills and self-confidence in using them will be increased. The mediator:

1. **Makes sure that both students agree.** The mediator fills out the Mediation Report Form and has students sign it. This involves writing out the agreement clearly and concisely, noting what disputants have agreed to do, making sure disputants' names are spelled correctly, and all dates are written out completely. A separate paragraph should be used for each issue. The agreement should include only the promises and commitments each person has made to the other. Each paragraph should begin, "Joan Johnson agrees to..." Only the present tense is used. The agreement should be as specific as possible. It should not include phrases that contain an implication of wrongdoing, such as "Ron agrees never to harass Sally again." If only part of the issues are resolved, the mediator may wish to list the issues that still need resolution. Finally, each student signs the agreement and then the mediator signs as a witness. Each student receives a copy of the agreement. The mediator keeps a copy. After the agreement is signed the mediator congratulates them both.

2. **Helps determine restitution if one side has been injured.** If a shirt has been ruined, restitution consists of paying for the cost of replacing it. When a person has been insulted, restitution may be made through an apology. Getting two people to agree on how restitution may be made is an important aspect of mediation.

3. **Rips up any notes he or she has made in front of students.**

4. **To prevent rumors, asks students to tell their friends that the conflict is ended.**

5. **Congratulates him- or herself after the disputants leave.** Mediators should take satisfaction from helping others. "We're all like hidden gold mines."

6. **Ends the discussion if the students fail to reach an agreement.** It is important to end on a positive note. Mediators tell disputants they (a) appreciate that the disputants tried to reach an agreement, (b) are sorry disputants did not resolve the conflict, and (c) are hopeful that disputants will be able to resolve the conflict constructively in the future.

7. **Uses humor.** Laughter is the best cure for conflict.

Step 4: Formalize The Agreement

When an agreement is reached, the mediator completes a **Mediation Report Form** and has both students sign it. This formalizes their agreement. Students must agree to abide by their final decision. Mediation is successful when disputants sign an agreement telling what each will do to resolve the conflict. The mediator becomes the keeper of the contract who verifies that students are doing what they have agreed to do. If the agreement breaks down, the mediator reconvenes the mediation session and helps the disputants negotiate again.

Being A Mediator

A good mediator is impartial, neutral, nonjudgmental, patient, understanding, imaginative, knowledgeable, analytical, respectful, and trustworthy. As a mediator you act and talk in ways that show you have these qualities. Some guidelines for doing so are as follows:

1. **Listen, don't talk.** You can't listen and talk at the same time. When you do talk, use words and phrases that are impartial and non-judgmental.

2. **Find out the facts.** Find out what happened and what must be done to resolve the conflict. Ask each student, "What has to happen in order for this conflict to be resolved to your satisfaction?"

3. **Analyze what you hear to see if agreement is possible.** You must do more than listen. You must think about what is being said so that you can help students separate their interests from their positions and think of creative solutions to their problem.

4. **Be firm in enforcing the rules.** You will not help anyone if you permit students to interrupt, insult, or shout at each other. The rules ensure that the procedures are fair.

5. **Be patient.** Some things take time resolve.

6. **Respect each disputant.** They will not participate effectively unless they believe that you respect them.

Teacher Implementation Of Peer Mediation Program

Each day the teacher selects two class members to serve as official mediators. Any conflicts students can not resolve themselves will be referred to the class mediators. The mediators wear mediator t-shirts, patrol the playground and lunchroom, and are available to mediate conflicts that occur in the classroom or school. The role of class mediator is rotated throughout the class so that each student serves as class mediator an equal amount of time. Refresher lessons are periodically taught to refine students' negotiation and mediation skills.

Teacher As Mediator

When a student mediator is not successful in helping the disputants resolve the conflict, then the conflict is referred to the teacher. The teacher then mediates the conflict. If that fails, the teacher arbitrates. How successful mediation is, both peer and teacher mediation, depends on how well the teacher has trained students to negotiate and mediate. For younger students the teacher may use the story-telling procedure. For older students role playing may be used.

Story-Telling Procedure

For **younger students** the storytelling procedure is especially good for teachers students how to resolve conflicts and for whole-class mediation. The procedure is:

1. Tell the story of the conflict situation using a "once upon a time" format.

2. When the story reaches the point of conflict, stop and ask the class for suggestions on how to resolve it. Make sure students give specific (rather than general) suggestions. Requiring specificity helps prevent the "give-the-teacher-what- she-wants-to-hear" response.

3. Incorporate one of the suggestions into the story, and then bring it to a conclusion.

4. Ask the participants if this would in fact meet their needs and if it is something they might try the next time they have a problem.

An example is the following kindergarten class.

T: *Once upon a time, Jack and Jill were playing with the toy train. Jill was playing with the engine and Jack decided he wanted the engine. Jill refused to give it to him, so Jack yelled at her and gave her a push. She pushed him back. What could they do?*

1: *Say they were sorry?*

T: *That does not solve the problem with the engine. They both want to play with the engine.*

2: *You could take the engine away from both of them.*

T: *The teacher is too busy. They have to solve this by themselves.*

3: *They each could try to grab the train cars.*

T: *They tried that. It didn't work.*

4: *Why don't they share and play with the engine together?*

T: *Actually, that is just what they did. Jill asked Jack if they could play with the engine together. Jack said yes, and then they both pushed the engine together. Do you think that would work with the real Jack and Jill?*

1, 2, 3, 4: *Yes.*

T: *Well, from that day on they played happily ever after.*

Problem Puppets

Margaret and Sarah were arguing over a set of blocks. Each believed that it was their turn to get the blocks. The teacher intervened, called the class together, and showed students two puppets. "These are the problem puppets, and they will help us solve the problem Margaret and Sarah are having," the teacher says. With younger students negotiation and mediation procedures may be taught with problem puppets. Puppets can provide young children enough distance from a conflict to discuss their behavior without feeling threatened.

1. Use the puppets to reenact the conflict.

2. Freeze the puppet role play at a critical point in the conflict. Ask the class for suggestions on ways to resolve the conflict. Incorporate one of these suggestions, and finish the puppet play.

3. Repeat the puppet play until several different suggestions for solving the conflict have been suggested. Discuss whether or not each one will work. This helps children learn to think through the consequences of their suggestions.

4. Ask the children to pick the suggestion they think will work best. The problem puppets can then be retired.

Role Playing To Master Negotiation And Mediation

Role playing is a tool for bringing conflict skills and their consequences into focus by:

1. Allowing students to experience concretely the conflict situation.

2. Identifying effective and ineffective behavior.

3. Gaining insight into their behavior in conflict situations.

4. Practicing the skills required to manage the conflict constructively.

Role playing is a helpful tool for teaching students conflict skills. Role playing can simulate real-life situations, making it possible for students to try new ways of managing conflicts without suffering any serious consequences if the methods fail.

Within role playing an imaginary situation is set up so students act and react in terms of the assumptions they are asked to adopt, the beliefs they are asked to hold, and the characters they are asked to play. The outcome of a role-playing situation is not determined in advance, and the situation is not rehearsed. Initial instructions are given and the actors determine what happens.

Role playing is especially useful in teaching students to generate a number of optional agreements. Sometimes students in a conflict cannot "unlock" from their perspective sufficiently to generate a number of possible solutions that will be acceptable to both parties. A class role play often will help. Before using the procedure with a real conflict, have your students practice it with hypothetical situations. Be sensitive to the fact that not all students like to participate in role plays.

1. Describe the conflict situation, giving time, place, and background and any other information that will help the students "get in role." Define the roles to be played. Ask the students who are involved in the conflict to play the roles, or use volunteers. Help the students get into the situation and their roles by introducing it in such a way that the players are emotionally involved.

2. Have the players act out the conflict. If they do not know what to say or do, asking them some leading questions may help them get unstuck. Keep the role play short.

3. Freeze the role play at critical points in the conflict. Ask the class for suggestions as to what could be done next. The players then incorporate one of the suggestions into the role play and finish it.

4. Always discuss the role play when it is finished:

   a. How could the conflict have been prevented?

   b. How did the characters feel in the situation?

   c. Was it a satisfactory solution?

   d. What other solutions might have worked?

5. Be sure to "de-role" after the role playing has ended. Some students may have trouble "getting into the role" and other students may have trouble "getting out of their role."

Announce clearly that the role play is over and students should reflect on and analyze the role play, not continue it.

Role Reversal

A more sophisticated and powerful procedure is the addition of role reversal to the role play. **Role reversal** is having two participants in the conflict reverse roles and play each other during the role play. It can be a dramatic way to help solve stubborn conflicts.

1. Establish the role play as above. Try to use the participants in the original conflict as players.

2. Freeze the role play at the point after which the conflict has begun.

3. Have the participants switch roles and replay it, so that they are taking the role of their opponent and, in effect, arguing against themselves.

4. Stop the role play after the players have gotten the feel of their opponent's point of view. Discuss the role play and see if any new alternative solutions have occurred to the students engaged in the conflict.

Instructions To Students

When participating in a role playing exercise, remain yourself and act as you would in the situation described. You do not have to be a good actor to play a role. You only need to accept the initial assumptions, beliefs, background, or assigned behaviors and then let your feelings, attitudes, and behavior change as circumstances seem to require. The role play instructions describe the point of departure and the beginning frame of reference. You and the situation then take over.

Your experiences in participating in the role play may lead you to change your attitudes and future behavior. You may have emotional experiences that were not expected when the role playing began. The more real the role playing and the more effective the exercise, the more emotional involvement you will feel and the more you will learn.

In role playing, questions may be raised that are not answered in your briefing sheet. When this happens, you are free to make up facts or experiences that accord with the circumstances. Do not make up experiences or facts that do not fit the role.

In participating in role playing, you should not consult or look at your role instructions. Once they are used to start the action, you should be yourself. A role player should not act the way she feels a person described in the instructions should behave. The role player should act as naturally as possible, given the initial instructions of the role.

Arbitration

Aesop tells of the bees, the wasps, and the hornet. A store of honey was found in a hollow tree, and the wasps declared positively that it belonged to them. The bees were just as sure that the treasure was theirs. The argument grew very heated, and it looked as if the conflict could not be settled without a battle, when at last, with much good sense, they agreed to let an arbitrator decide the matter. So they brought the conflict before the hornet, who was a judge in that part of the woods. Witnesses were called, who testified that striped, yellow and black winged creatures (like bees) had been seen near the tree. The wasps declared that the description fitted them exactly. With some thought the hornet stated that if a decision was not made soon, the honey would not be fit for anything. He, therefore, instructed the bees and the wasps both to build a honey comb. "Whoever makes the best honey comb obviously is the owner of the honey," the hornet declared. The wasps protested loudly. The hornet quickly understood why they did so--they could not build a honey comb and fill it with honey. "It is clear," said the hornet, "who can make the comb and who can not. The honey belongs to the bees."

When all else fails, the teacher must arbitrate. **Arbitration** is asking a disinterested person, an arbitrator, to make a final judgment as to how a conflict should be resolved. Technically, arbitration may be voluntary, when it is requested by the persons in conflict, or compulsory, as in the case where a judge may order arbitration. Within the classroom arbitration will be voluntary when two students ask the teacher to decide how a conflict should be resolved and all other methods of conflict resolution have been tried and have

failed. Or arbitration may be compulsory when a conflict between two students (or groups of students) becomes so severe that the teacher has to step in and arbitrate it. While mediation is an extension of negotiating, and the mediator assists the two persons in negotiating a constructive resolution to their conflict, arbitration is a judgment made by an outside person and, therefore, does not assist the persons in conflict in improving their conflict skills. In arbitration the students leave the decision to the arbitrator, who hears both sides and then makes a judgment.

The process of arbitration consists of:

1. Both people agree to abide by the arbitrator's decision. Most people agree to abide by the arbitrator's decision on the assumption that after they have had their chance to present fully their side of the conflict, the arbitrator will be able to make a fair decision.

2. Each person submits his or her desired goal to the arbitrator. At the beginning, each side has to define what he or she wants and tell the arbitrator what he or she would like to see happen. The arbitrator then starts out with an understanding of what the focus of the decision has to be.

3. Each person defines the problem as he or she sees it. Both persons get the opportunity to tell their side of the story.

4. Each person presents his or her case with documented evidence to support it. One person may not interrupt the other and both people are given an equal opportunity to present his or her views.

5. Each person may attempt to refute the other's contentions. After each person has made a presentation of his or her case, the other person is given an opportunity to refute the person's contentions. Both people have the opportunity to give the arbitrator a different perspective on the issues.

6. The arbitrator makes a decision. Each person makes a closing statement. When both people have nothing more to add to the presentation of their case and the refutation of the other's case, the arbitrator has to decide. The decision most often is one wherein one person wins and the other person loses. Whether a person wins or loses is assumed to be secondary to having had a fair opportunity to be heard. In essence, they have had their day in court.

Arbitrators should have certain qualities. They should be disinterested parties, who are extremely familiar with the particular subject matter of the case, and who are allowed to examine all the available documents and evidence.

A teacher or administrator will want to be as objective and fair an arbitrator as possible. They will also want to leave arbitration as the conflict resolution method of last resort. Make sure that students have tried to negotiate a resolution to their conflict and have gone to mediation before you think about arbitrating.

Summary

A **mediator** is a neutral person who helps two or more people (called disputants) resolve their conflict. There is considerable value in having students serve as peer mediators. Conflicts become resolved, discipline problems decrease, school climate improves, and conflict resolution skills are transferred to a number of nonschool settings. Mediating teaches students both interpersonal and academic skills, improves cooperative work, increases students' commitment to education, and prepares students to be citizens in a complex and conflict-filled world.

To establish a peer mediation program, teachers (a) build a cooperative classroom context by using cooperative learning the majority of the time, (b) frequently use structured academic controversies, (c) instruct students in how to negotiate, (d) teach all students mediation procedures and skills, and (e) implement the peer mediation process within the classroom and school.

To implement a peer mediation process the teacher selects each day two students to be the class mediators. Any conflicts that students can not negotiate resolutions to are referred to class mediators. The role of class mediator is rotated throughout the class so that each student serves as class mediator an equal amount of time. Students need to know how to arrange for a mediator when they need one.

The **procedure for mediation** consists of a series of steps. First, you **end hostilities**. Break up fights and cool down students. Second, you **ensure both people are committed to the mediation process**. To ensure that both persons are committed to the mediation process and are ready to negotiate in good faith, the mediator introduces the process of mediation, sets the ground rules, and introduces him- or herself. Third, you **help the two people negotiate with each other successfully**. This includes taking the two persons through the negotiation sequence of (a) jointly defining the conflict by both persons stating what they want and how they feel, (b) exchanging reasons, (c) reversing perspectives so that each person is able to present the other's position and feelings to the other's satisfaction, (d) inventing at least three options for mutual benefit, and (e) reaching a wise agreement and shaking hands. Fourth, you **formalize the agreement**. The agreement is solidified into a contract. Disputants must agree to abide by their final decision and in many ways the mediator becomes "the keeper of the contract."

Peer mediation gives students an opportunity to resolve their dispute themselves, in mutually satisfactory ways, without having to engage the attention of a teacher. This empowers the students and reduces the demands on the teacher. The teacher can then devote less time to arbitration and discipline in general, and more time to teaching.

One of the major sources of conflicts of interests is the demands that physical, social, and cognitive development make on children and adolescents. As you get older, you get taller, stronger, smarter, more skilled in relating to others, more able to see issues from a variety of perspectives, and more able to be an equal in relationships with a wide variety of people of many different ages. The maturation and development process requires that relationships change with adults as well as with peers. Conflict results. Such developmental conflicts are discussed in the next chapter.

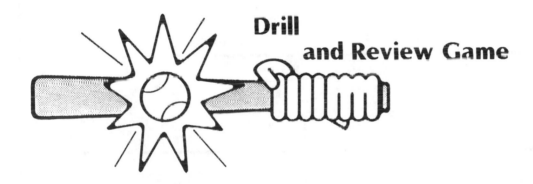

Drill and Review Game

Mediation Baseball: Form teams of four members. Divide each group into two pairs (Pair A and Pair B). They will be competing against each other. Write out a deck of cards listing the four steps of mediation (ending hostilities, ensuring commitment to mediation, facilitating negotiations, formalizing the agreement). Make at least four copies of each step. Shuffle the cards and place them in the center of the group. A member of Pair A draws a card and gives a mediator statement from the step on the card. If he or she makes a correct statement, he or she advances to first base. Then a member of Pair B draws a card. On the second round a member advances to second base. At the end of ten or fifteen minutes the game is stopped. The pair with the most "runs" wins.

Creative Conflict Contract

Major Learnings	Implementation Plans

Date _____ Date of Progress Report Meeting _____

Participant's Signature _____

Signatures of Other Group Members _____ _____

_____ _____ _____

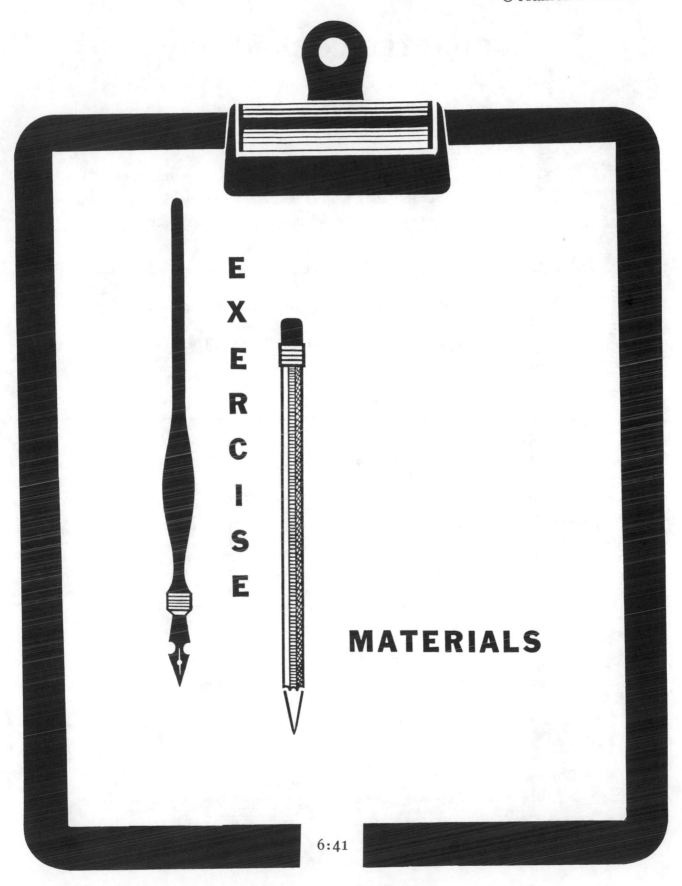

CHAPTER VOCABULARY

Working with a partner, learn the definitions of the following words.

1. Define each word in two ways.

    First, write down what you think the word means.

    Second, look it up in the book and write down its definition.
    Note the page on which the definition appears.

2. For each word write a sentence in which the word is used.

3. Make up a story in which all of the words are used.

4. Learn how to spell each word. They will be on your spelling test.

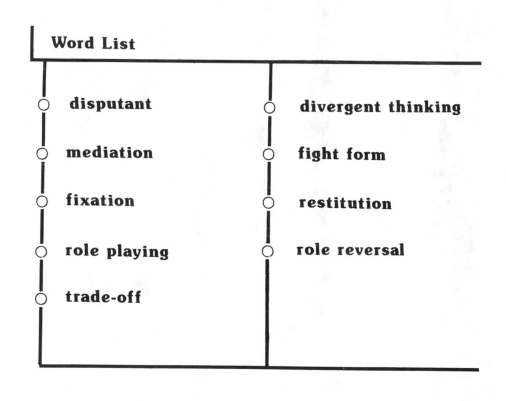

Word List

○ **disputant**	○ **divergent thinking**
○ **mediation**	○ **fight form**
○ **fixation**	○ **restitution**
○ **role playing**	○ **role reversal**
○ **trade-off**	

Name_____   Date_____

Crack the Conflict Code!

Using the key at the bottom of the page, see if you and your partner can solve the puzzle to define one of your conflict terms. Above each of the numbers, place the letter which it represents and your work will be done for you.

—	— — —	— — — — — —	— —	—
6	15 20 8	11 6 17 19 1	11 13	6

— — — — — — —	— — —	— — — — —
13 17 12 8 20 7 17	3 16 19	16 20 10 9 13

— — —	— — — — — — — — — —
17 3 19	2 10 6 13 13 15 6 17 20 13

— — — — — — —	— — — — —
1 20 13 19 10 24 20	17 16 20 11 1

— — — — — — — —	— — — —	— — —
2 19 7 26 10 11 2 17	3 16 20 7	22 19 12

— — —	— — — — — — — — —	— — —
6 1 20	6 15 20 8 11 6 17 19 1 '	22 19 12

— — —	— — — — — — —	— — —
6 1 20	7 20 12 17 1 6 10	6 7 8

— — —	— — — —	— — — — — — — — — —
22 19 12	25 20 20 9	20 24 20 1 22 17 16 11 7 5

— — — — .
26 6 11 1

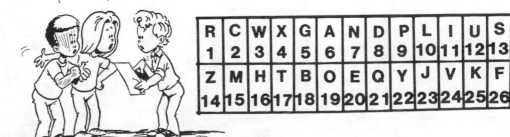

R	C	W	X	G	A	N	D	P	L	I	U	S
1	2	3	4	5	6	7	8	9	10	11	12	13
Z	M	H	T	B	O	E	Q	Y	J	V	K	F
14	15	16	17	18	19	20	21	22	23	24	25	26

Warm Up:

A Difficult Situation

Form triads. Read the following case study. Assume that you are Ms. or Mr. Fair. Make a plan for mediating the conflict between Brightness and Foggy. This is a cooperative task, everyone in the group should agree on the plan and be able to describe and explain it to the class as a whole.

Brightness was always an A student. She seemed to be able to remember and understand new things very easily and, therefore, never had to study very hard. Her best friend, Foggy, was not as smart and found school work difficult. They were both in the Ms. Fair's English class. Ms. Fair announced that there was a very important test coming up and, to reward the best students, anyone who got over 90 percent correct on the test would be given a part in a short play to be presented to the entire school. Everyone in the class seemed to want to be in the play and, therefore, there was considerable discussion as to who would score 90 percent or better on the test.

Foggy asked Brightness to help her study. Since Brightness never put much effort into preparing for a test, she was not very helpful. Foggy went to another friend, Bugoff. Bugoff told her to get lost because he was too busy. Foggy was close to tears. Brightness offered to try to give more help, but Foggy told her to bug off. Brightness felt terrible.

During the test Innocence passed a note from Foggy to Brightness. In the note Foggy asked Brightness for several answers. Brightness debated whether or not to respond, but finally decided she had to or risk losing Foggy as her best friend. She wrote the answers on the note. Ms. Fair caught her, and tore up her test and declared her ineligible for the play. Foggy said nothing.

Much to everyone's amazement, Foggy scored 91 percent on the test. She accepted a major role in the play. Brightness decides she is never going to speak to Foggy again.

6:44

CONFLICT FORM

Who was your conflict with?

What did you want?

How did the other's actions stop you from getting what you want?

How did you feel?

What did the other person want?

How did your actions stop him or her from getting what he or she wanted?

How did the other person feel?

What are three potential agreements that might resolve the conflict and reestablish a good relationship between the two of you?

a.

b.

c.

What are three things you might try if this happens again?

a.

b.

c.

Is there anything you would like to say to the person you had the conflict with?

Referral to Mediation

Your Name: _____ Date: _____

Your Relation To People Involved: _____

People Involved In Conflict: Agreed To Mediation :
                                                                   Yes   No   Unknown

_____   __   __   __

_____   __   __   __

_____   __   __   __

_____   __   __   __

What Is The Conflict About? _____

_____

Mediation Reminder / Pass

This is to remind you that mediation between you and

_____ has been scheduled for

_____ (time) on _____ date)

at _____ (place).

MEDIATION RECORD

Name _____ Date _____

School _____ Grade Level _____

NATURE OF CONFLICT	WITH WHOM		TIME SPENT	AGREEMENT REACHED		COMMENTS
	Person I	Person II		Yes	No	

MEDIATION SUMMARY

Mediator(s): _____

Date, Time, Place of Mediation: _____
_____

People Involved in Conflict:

Name	Grade
_____	_____
_____	_____
_____	_____
_____	_____

What Is the Conflict? _____
_____
_____

Was an Agreement Reached?   _____ Yes   _____ No

Person I Agrees to: *Person II Agrees to:*

_____   _____
_____   _____
_____   _____
_____   _____
_____   _____
_____   _____
_____   _____

Signature: _____   Signature: _____

Follow-Up: _____
_____
_____
_____
_____
_____

Name _____ Date _____

MEDIATION MENU

As a **mediator** you help two classmates resolve their conflict. You are neutral. You keep everything fair. You stand in the middle and help them go through each step of negotiating.

You Say: ─────────────────────────────

My name is _____. I am a mediator. Would you like help in solving your problem (make sure both answer "yes")? Mediation is voluntary. I cannot make you do anything. I will not take sides or attempt to decide who is right or wrong. You will have to decide for yourselves how best to resolve your conflict. Our goal is to reach an agreement that is acceptable to each of you. I will not take sides.

Each of you will have a chance to state your view of the conflict. In order for us to resolve your conflict we must agree on a set of **rules** are:

1. You must agree to solve the problem.

2. No name calling.

3. Do not interrupt.

4. Be as honest as you can.

If we are successful, we will reach an agreement.
You must live up to your side of the
agreement. You must do what you have agreed to do.

Anything you say in mediation is confidential.
I will not tell anyone.

We will now proceed across the bridge:

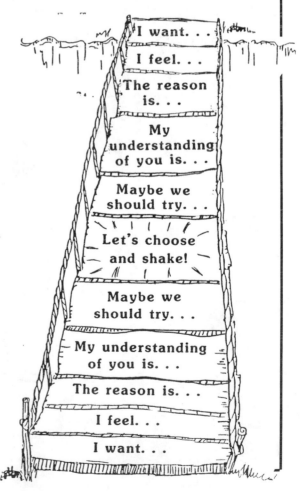

The agreement is good if:

1. It tells when, where, who, and how.

2. Each student can do what he or she has agreed to.

3. Both students agree to do something.

Fill out the **Mediator Report Form** and have both students sign it.

You Say:

"We now have a signed agreement. Shake!"

"I am the keeper of the contract."
"I will check back with you tomorrow to see if the agreement is working."

Ending Hostilities

Mediation begins with the ending of hostilities among students and cooling students down enough so that constructive negotiations may take place. There are no magic formula's for breaking up hostilities, but a few suggestions are given below.

Working with your partner, rank order the suggestions given below from the one you think will work best (1), second best (2)...to the one you think will be least effective in ending hostilities (6). Both of you must be prepared to tell the class **why** you ranked each suggestion the way you did.

_____ Get a teacher to tell the hostile students to stop.

_____ Get several students to help you separate and restrain the hostile students.

_____ Distract their attention.

_____ Take away the audience (all students leave).

_____ Get several students to chant, "Stop fighting, stop fighting."

_____ Get several students to sing a happy song such as "Ring Around The Rosy"

As a pair, lead the class in a practice role play of implementing your choice for the most effective strategy. Your purpose is to train classmates to break up hostilities on the playground and in the lunchroom.

COOLING DOWN

Before you can successfully negotiate with another person you must first cool down. Anger usually interferes with problem solving. Sometimes you must wait until you are not so angry so that you can think clearly and talk calmly.

Your **task** is to read the following story and to answer the questions. Work **cooperatively** with a partner in doing so. One of you is to read the story and the other listen carefully and then summarize it in your own words. Flip a coin to choose who is the reader. Once the story is finished, answer the questions--one set of answers for the two of you, both of you have to agree, and both of you have to be able to explain.

Story

Keith asked Dale to loan him his new sport coat for a big date. Dale said "no," but Keith was so persistent that finally Dale agreed that Keith could wear the coat if he took absolutely great care of it. The next day Dale found his coat. It had mud all over it and one of the sleeves was ripped. He was furious. He wanted to find Keith and physically demolish him. He looked at the clock, however, and noted it was time for track practice. He went to track practice and ran for an hour. Later, physically exhausted, he found Keith. "What happened to my coat?" he calmly asked.

1. How did Dale feel when he found Keith? Why?

2. What happened to Dale's feelings while he was running?

3. What do you think would have happened if Dale had tried to solve the problem before he cooled off?

4. Why is cooling off important before you start negotiating? Give three reasons.

5. What are five ways to cool down before you start negotiating?

Introducing Yourself
and
Mediation

Form a cooperative group of four. Number off from 1 to 4. Form two pairs (1 and 2, 3 and 4). One person becomes the presenter, the other person becomes the accuracy checker.

1. First one person gives the introduction while the other listens, checks for accuracy, and gives feedback.

2. The two reverse roles.

3. Discuss how the introduction to mediation could be improved.

4. Combine into new pairs (1 and 3, 2 and 4). Repeat Steps 1, 2, and 3.

5. Combine into new pairs (1 and 4, 2 and 3). Repeat Steps 1, 2, and 3.

6. In the group of four, list the three most important pieces of advice for introducing mediation.

Planning Your Opening Statement

1. Divide into pairs. Your **task** is to write out your opening statement in mediating a conflict among classmates. Work **cooperatively** to produce one statement from the two of you that each of you can give. Both of you need a written copy of the opening statement. Include:

   a. An introduction of yourself.

   b. A description of the process of mediation.

   c. A description of the role of the mediator.

   d. Asking both students if they wish to solve their problem and will abide by the mediation rules.

   e. A statement of the confidentiality inherent in mediations.

   f. A statement of the goal of finding an agreement that meets both persons' needs.

2. Divide into new pairs. Give your opening statement to the other. Listen to his or her opening statement. Discuss how the statement can be given better next time.

3. Find a new partner. Give your opening statement. Listen to his or her's. Discuss how the statements could be given better next time.

4. Form groups of four. Write out at least four pieces of advice on how to make an effective opening mediation statement.

5. Participate in a whole class discussion on how to make an effective opening mediation statement.

Remaining Neutral,
Not Taking Sides

An important skill for a mediator is to remain neutral and not take sides. You do so by using words and phrases that are impartial and nonjudgmental. You have to identify and refer to all of the issues in a neutral way.

Do not say, "She is angry because you stole her purse." Do say, "She is angry because you had her purse." Do not say, "The two of you were yelling at each other about the $15." Do say, "You talk to each other in unhelpful ways when the topic of the money comes up."

Jose claims that Bobby stole his lunch tickets. Bobby denies it. The mediator asks Jose if he knows anything about "the missing lunch tickets," but would never ask him about "the stolen lunch tickets." Do you know why?

Roger claims that Terry stole his social studies report. Terry says he didn't. The mediator asks Roger to describe in more detail why he believes that Terry stole his report, but Roger states, "You are not a judge and this is not a courtroom. I don't have to prove anything. I said he took it and that's that. Your job is to make him confess." What should you say?

When paraphrasing or reflective listening is used, it is important that the mediator does not impose his or her own opinion or bias on what the students say. The mediator must be able to state each student's position and feelings to that student's satisfaction.

Being An Umpire: Calling Fouls

While disputants may wish to fight fair, when they are frustrated and angry, they may try to "foul" each other. A mediator's responsibilities include being an umpire. An **umpire** makes sure that disputants' statements and actions are in the "fair" zone. Mediators must recognize and call fouls.

Task 1: With a partner, make a list of what is **fair** and what is **foul** in a conflict. An example of a list is given below. Share your list with the entire class. When other pairs are giving their lists, write down any good ideas that you did not already have on your list. When you finalize your list, use it to make a table similar to the one below.

Task 2: With your partner, for each foul on your list write out:
1. How a person would feel if they were fouled in this way?
2. How you recognize when the foul is occurring, that is, what a person says or does to foul someone in that way.

Foul	Feelings	Actions
Name Calling		
Blaming		
Put-Downs		
Making Excuses For Own Actions		
Bringing Up The Past		
Threats		
Pushing, Hitting, Shoving		
Bringing Others Into The Conflict		

Task 3: Pick a conflict you have recently seen between two class members. Plan a role play of the conflict that **first** includes several fouls and **second** shows how to resolve the conflict fairly.

Practicing Mediation

1. Divide into triads. These are called **role-playing triads**. Assign the roles of "the Giant," "Jack," and "mediator."

2. Combine with another triad. Then form pairs. These pairs are known as **preparation pairs**. The two Jacks get together, the two Giants get together, and the two mediators get together. They are to prepare each other to play their role. They read their instructions carefully, and plan how to present their wants, feelings, and reasons. They should make a visual to help them present their best case.

2. Return to your role-playing triad. The mediator gives the opening statement to ensure commitment to the mediation process. Both Jack and the Giant state what they want and how they feel. Each position is defined using the rules listed in Chapter 3.

3. Both Jack and the Giant present the reasons why they want and feel as they do. The mediator helps them separate their interests from their positions.

4. The Giant and Jack reverse perspectives and present each other's wants, feelings, and supporting facts and experiences. The mediator helps them reframe their views of the conflict.

5. Jack and the Giant invent at least five optional agreements that would give both what they want and build a better relationship between them. They star the three they like the best.

6. Jack and the Giant reach an agreement. The mediator gives the closing statement. The triad writes an ending to the story.

7. As a triad, write out at least three advice statements for peer mediators based on what you have learned about mediation from the role play.

8. Meet in your preparation pair. **Share** your list of advice. **Listen** carefully to your partner's advice. **Create** a new list that integrates the best ideas from both of you.

9. Return to your role-playing triad. Share your new list.

   Tell each member one thing
   you enjoyed about working with them.

Jack's Position:
I'M A HERO!

My name is Jack. I lived with my mother on the edge of town. My father is dead and my mother and I were very poor. All we had was our cow Bertha. Finally, in order to eat, we had to sell Bertha. I felt so proud that my mother would trust me with such a responsibility. I lead Bertha to the market where I met an old man who convinced me to sell him Bertha for five magic bean seeds that would grow so tall that we would have enough beans to last us forever. I was so excited. Lots and lots of food forever! We would never be hungry again! But when I took the seeds home my mother told me I had been cheated and now we would starve. She threw the beans out the window and sent me to bed. I felt so bad. Somehow I had to find the money to support my mother. I cried myself to sleep. The next morning, when I woke up, I saw the beanstalk growing up into the clouds. I started climbing to find beanpods. But what I found instead was a magical land where there was a huge giant. Giants are evil, rotten creatures who like to eat boys like me, so I hid until he was asleep. Then I took his hen and ran to the beanstalk and came home. It turned out so wonderful. The hen lays golden eggs and my mother and I now have lots of food and clothes. My mother is so proud of me and so happy! She thinks I'm a hero. Several of my friends, however, think it was just luck. I keep thinking about the giant's golden harp. I would really be a hero if I could get that harp! And if I could kill the giant in the process, I might even marry a princess!

Giant's Position:
I WAS ROBBED!

My name is Ralph. I've always tried to be friendly and helpful to everyone, but no one likes me. They think I'm a freak and make fun of me because I'm so big. My eyesight is poor, but I have a good sense of smell. When I smell something, I often say, "Fe, Fi, Fo, Fum." One of my problems is that I suffer from insomnia. I love music. It's my only source of happiness. The only way I can get to sleep is to listen to my golden harp play its music. It's an old family treasure. The only thing my father left me. I have no human friends. Whenever I try to make friends people are either frightened of my size or make fun of me. Because my feelings are so easily hurt I tried to avoid people. I live in a magical land in the clouds that humans can not reach and, thanks to my hen and my harp I am fairly happy. My hen lays golden eggs and my golden harp plays the most beautiful music. Without my hen and harp I would have nothing.

Recently a boy named Jack found a way into my magical land. He hid in my house and stole my hen. I'm devastated. How could he be so cruel and dishonest! I never did anything to him! I've never taken anything from him. He seems to think that because I'm big, clumsy, and ugly he can do anything he wants to me and my things. That is not right. All I have left is my golden harp and I'm afraid Jack means to come back and steal it too. What am I to do? I hate violence but I have to defend my possessions and I have to stick up for my rights.

Mediation Training Role-Play Round Robin

1. Divide into new role-playing triads. Decide who is Person A, B, or C. Person C becomes the mediator. There are six role plays. For each role play, the roles within the group will rotate so that each student will get a chance to practice mediation.

2. Combine with another triad. Then form pairs ("A's," "B's." and "C's). These pairs are known as **preparation pairs**. Pair members work together to prepare each other to play their role. They read their instructions carefully, and plan how to present their wants, feelings, and reasons. They should make a visual to help them present their best case. The mediator prepares by reviewing the steps in mediation.

3. Return to your role-playing triad. Students have 10 minutes for each role play. The intent of the role play is to provide students practice in mediating conflict. The mediator gives the opening statement to ensure commitment to the mediation process. Both A and B state what they want and how they feel. Each position is defined using the rules listed in Chapter 3 and each person gives his or her reasons. The two reverse perspectives, invent options, and reach an agreement.

4. The members of the triad rotate roles and follow the above procedure for the second role play. The same preparation pair is used every time. After the second role play has been finished, the members rotate roles once more and engage in the third role play. The rotation continues until all six role plays have been conducted. Each member will now have experienced being a mediator twice.

5. After the role plays are completed, the triad, working cooperatively:

   a. Discusses the issues that arose in practicing the mediation procedure.

   b. Discusses the way in which each mediator managed the resolution of the conflict.

   c. Writes out three conclusions about how mediation needs to be managed.

6. Meet in your preparation pair. **Share** you list of advice. **Listen** carefully to your partner's advice. **Create** a new list that integrates the best ideas from both of you.

7. Return to your role-playing triad. Share your new list. Tell each member one thing you enjoyed about working with them.

Role Play 1

WHY DIDN'T YOU KEEP YOUR HANDS OFF?

Megan and Penny are in the same class. Megan worked hard on a tooth-pick sculpture. Penny, without asking, picked it up to look at it, dropped it, and it broke. Ask Megan to speak first.

Megan Says: "I'm so mad! I'm going to find something Penny made and smash it. She broke my sculpture. I **told** everyone not to touch it! I hate it when other people 'trash' my things!"

Penny Says: "It was an accident. I didn't mean to break it. I liked it and wanted to see how she did it. And now she's mad! It was just a bunch of toothpicks. She can put it back together. But if she thinks she's going to break something of mine she is mistaken. I'm mad at her just thinking about what she might try to do!"

Role Play 2

CAN'T YOU STAY ON TOPIC?

Dan and Sam are working on a report together. Ask Dan to speak first.

Dan Says: "Sam's always interrupting and trying to change the subject so we can never get anything done! It's so frustrating! Whenever we're discussing how to organize the report he starts talking about completely unrelated things! I can't get him to pay attention and think about the report!"

Sam Says: "I try to think creatively. I get new ideas about the report by trying to make new associations. I want to use my fantasy and spontaneous ideas to make our report different from those the rest of the class are doing. But I never get a chance to explain what I'm doing. Dan is so power hungry!"

Role Play 3

WHERE'S THE BOOK?

Fred and Ralph: Although the two are friends, they got into a fight about lost library books. Ask Fred to speak first.

Fred Says: "Ralph and I were doing reports on the same topic. He wanted to borrow a book from me that I took out of the library. He promised to return it, so I loaned it to him. Then I got a notice that the book is overdue and I'm being fined. If the book isn't returned, I will have to pay for it. He didn't even tell me that he lost the book!"

Ralph Says: "I meant to return the stupid book. I always do what I say. Someone broke into my locker last week and took a bunch of my things. The book must have been one of them. I forgot all about it. Now he's calling me a liar. Some friend. He didn't ask for an explanation."

Role Play 4

YOU SHOULDN'T HAVE SAID THAT!

Todd and Tim: The two are classmates who have been friendly but don't spend much time together. They were caught fighting in the hall. Ask Todd to speak first.

Todd Says: "I was just standing around in the hall talking to Chris when Tim came up and pushed me and starting yelling about how he's not on drugs. He was yelling that he's going to kill me for telling people he's doing drugs. I thought he was! I heard someone say he saw Tim doing drugs. I though we should figure out a way to help him!"

Tim Says: "I have never taken drugs. I hate people who do drugs! I have an ear infection, have been dizzy and nauseous much of the time, and have been taking medicine. Suddenly people started spreading rumors I was on drugs. Todd is supposed to be my friend but he just went along with everyone else. So I punched him out."

Role Play 5 ———————————————

DON'T HURT THAT DOG! ———

Meggy and Ensley: Meggy was walking home from school. She saw Ensley and one of her friends throwing rocks at a puppy that was tied up in a yard. Meggy wanted to help the puppy. She told Ensley to stop and Ensley began to call her names and chased her home.

Meggy Says: "That poor little puppy was all tied up and couldn't run and hide. Ensley was trying to hurt it! It was so sad. It makes me mad every time I think of it. Ensley should have tried to pet the puppy and make friends with it, not try to hurt it."

Ensley Says: "I don't like dogs. I'm scared of them. That puppy was barking at me. If it wasn't tied up, who knows what it might have done to me. I was trying to teach it not to bark or try to bite me. Meggy had no right to tell me to stop. She acted like I was a nasty person for trying to defend myself. I'm really mad at Meggy and I'm going to make her sorry she stuck her nose in my business."

Role Play 6 ———————————————

WATCH OUT FOR MY CHAIR! ———

Joan and Jane: Jane is confined to a motorized wheelchair. She is being mainstreamed into a regular fourth-grade class. She often bumps other students with her chair and frequently runs over their feet and then laughs. Today she ran over Joan's foot. Joan got angry and kicked Jane's chair several times.

Joan Says: "Jane is always running over someone's foot and laughing about it. It's not funny for the person whose foot just got crushed. She always wants us to move rather than going around. I know we're all supposed to like Joan, but I don't. She seems mean to me. If she thinks she can run over my foot and get away with it, she has another think coming!"

Jane Says: "It's hard to steer my chair. The classroom is crowded with desks and chairs, and all the students sit around on the floor and in the aisles. No one moves when I have to get by. I could complain, but I don't want to seem like a nag. So I try to make a game of it, and occasionally run over someone's foot to give them the message to move out of the way when I have to get by. My chair isn't heavy. It doesn't hurt them. I'm really mad at Joan for being so inconsiderate and using my running over her foot as an excuse to get everyone to not like me."

Role Play 7
∾ RETURN MY THINGS! ∾

Jill and Jack: Jill and Jack are seniors in high school. For the past two years they went steady with each other. Jill broke up with Jack two months ago but wanted to remain friends. For several weeks Jack followed Jill around asking her to go out with him again. She refused. One day she lost her temper and told him to "get out of her life."

Jill Says: Jack calls me at home all the time insisting that I return some of "his" things. He gave me a gold necklace and four rock albums. He loaned me two other rock albums. I will gladly return the albums he loaned me. I am not, however, going to return the things he gave me. They were presents. While we were dating I gave him two sweaters and three books. I am not asking him to return those to me. He should stop hounding me.

Jack Says: After Jill told me to get out of her life I have stayed away from her. I did phone her a few times so I can get some albums and a gold necklace back from her. I have a new girlfriend now (although Jill does not know it) and I would like to give the necklace to her. In addition, I worked hard to get the money to buy those albums and it is not fair that Jill keeps them. It is true that Jill gave me two sweaters and three books, but that is different because she has no use for them and, therefore, does not want them back. Furthermore, I need them. She should give me my things.

Role Play 8
∾ I'LL GET YOU! ∾

Tyler and Chris: This morning Chris walked into first hour class, slammed the door, then slammed his book down on his desk. The science teacher told him to sit down and be quiet. Chris loudly stated that he was quiet. Tyler, who sits next to Chris, said, "Hey, stupid. Shut up so the rest of us can learn something and pass this course." Chris called Tyler a nerd and said, "I'll get you after school." During the class Chris poked Tyler with his pencil and kicked his chair several times. Tyler ignored it. During lunch Chris started pushing and shoving Tyler.

Tyler: I do not want to be around a jerk like Chris. He takes his problems out on everyone around him. I should not have to put up with his harassment and threats. He's much bigger than I am. I'm not going to fight him. But I'm not going to let him push me around either. I have to get an "A" in science if I'm going to get a scholarship for college. Chris keeps causing me trouble in class. That's not right.

Chris: Two weeks ago the science teacher accused me of cheating on a test. He said I was copying from Tyler. The teacher asked Tyler about it and Tyler said he thought I was looking at his paper. The teacher gave me an "F." I may now get a "D" in science. If I do, I'll be kicked off the basketball team. And it's all Tyler's fault. He should have kept his mouth shut.

Practicing Mediation Through Role Playing

The purpose of the role playing is to give each participant practice in mediating a conflict. Within each situation participants should authentically portray the conflict and use all the steps of mediation to resolve it.

1. Divide into triads.

2. Working cooperatively, brainstorm a list of conflicts that occur among the students in your school:

   a. Think of seven to ten conflicts that commonly occur among students. Include actual conflicts you have seen in your classroom and school.

   b. Take three that seem either the most common or the most troublesome for you as a teacher. Script each of the three by:

      1. Writing a three to four sentence description of the situation. Include the time, place, and background needed to understand the conflict and the students' positions.

      2. Writing a three to four sentence description of each student's position, feelings, and needs. The descriptions will orient the persons' role playing each student. Designate which student should be asked to speak first.

3. Within your triad decide who is Participant A, B, or C. Participant A and B become students while participant C becomes the mediator. The roles within the group rotate, so that in Role Play 2, participants B and C become the students and participant A becomes the mediator, and in Role Play 3, participants C and A become the students and participant B becomes the mediator.

4. Participants prepare for the role play by reviewing the position and feelings of the student they are to represent. The mediator prepares by reviewing the steps in mediation and planning how to manage each stage.

5. Participants have 15 minutes for each role play. The intent of the role plays is to provide each participant with the opportunity to practice the entire mediation procedure.

6. After the three role plays have been completed, working cooperatively, the triad:

   a. Discusses the issues that arose in practicing the mediation procedure.

   b. Discusses the way in which each mediator managed the resolution of the conflict.

   c. Writes out three conclusions about how mediation needs to be managed.

One-Text Procedure

The **one-text procedure** is conducted in the following way (Fisher & Ury, 1981).

1. Listen to each student's views and ask:

   a. What does the student want?

   b. How does the student feel?

   c. What are the student's reasons?

2. Develop a rough draft of an agreement that achieves the goals of each person.

3. Ask each student to review the draft agreement. Incorporate their corrections until you believe that the proposed agreement cannot be improved further.

4. Formally present the final draft as the agreement and recommend that they accept it.

The Problem-Solving Rug

When students cannot agree, the teacher (or administrator) can send them to the problem solving rug to keep negotiating until they reach agreement. The rules for the rug are:

1. Both students must sit on the rug until the conflict is resolved.

2. No touching. Verbal exchanges only.

3. Be patient. It may take them a long time.

4. When they resolve the conflict, praise them and ask what the resolution is.

7 Managing Developmental Conflicts

What Are Developmental Conflicts?

In a second-grade classroom students are crowding around the teacher, wanting to sit on her lap, be helped by her, given a compliment by her, and generally seeking her attention. "I've had it with second grade," the teacher complains. "Every time I try to take a step there are three kids hanging onto my leg." In a eighth-grade science class, a teacher asks several students to quiet down and get to work. "We are working!" they reply. "I've had it with eighth-graders," the teacher complains. "Every time I tell them to do something all I get is grief and smart-aleck remarks."

Both teachers are involved in the same developmental conflict. In the second grade, students are struggling with their dependence on the teacher; in the eighth grade, students are wrestling with establishing their independence from adult authorities such as teachers. The conflicts children and adolescents initiate in their attempts to resolve issues of dependence and independence from adults and peers are just one of the developmental conflicts students face every day of the year. Such conflicts are an essential aspect of human development, and their constructive resolution is essential for psychological health and social maturity. Yet many educators believe that if the teacher is competent, conflicts won't occur in the classroom. Nothing could be farther from the truth. Developmental conflicts, as well as other types of conflicts, are absolutely essential for effective socialization and for gaining maturity. For the sake of their students, teachers need to promote such conflicts and help in their constructive resolution, not avoid them.

As individuals develop from infancy to adulthood, there are a number of developmental conflicts that must be repeatedly faced and resolved (Berger, 1974; Erickson, 1950, 1968; Freud, 1930; Johnson, 1975). A **developmental conflict** is a recurrent conflict that cycles in and out of peak intensity as the person develops socially, physically, and cogntively. There are a number of overlapping developmental conflicts. Each comes to the fore at a particular time, reaches a peak intensity, is worked through or put aside as another developmental conflict builds up, and reappears in a new form later on. Each is a continuum. Conflicts appear at either end. These overlapping conflicts are:

1. Dependence - independence.

2. Security in the status quo - demand for growth and change.

3. Impulsive satisfaction of needs - delay of gratification.

Each time a developmental conflict arises, there are a series of steps it progresses through. Taking the independence of two year olds as an example, the child declares its independence by saying, "no" and "I want to do it myself." The child pushes his or her new spirit of independence to extremes, creating conflicts with parents that leave them no alternative but to place limits and constraints on the child's independence. After repeated conflicts over such issues as whether the child will or will not go to bed, the child realizes that the parents are in fact bigger and stronger, and that he or she has to do what they say. The child accommodates the constraints the parents place on his or her independence by behaving appropriately, that is, by going to bed when he or she is told. The child then either identifies with the parents and integrates the constraints into his or her internal value system, or does not identify with the parents and dissociates the constraints from his or her internal value system. The issue of independence then fades into the back group as the child moves toward a new dependence, and another developmental conflict, such as anxiety about growth and change, may take arise.

Developmental conflicts occur and are resolved through the following process. **First, the child overassimilates new skills, competencies, and opportunities**. Developmental conflicts arise when the child pushes new skills and opportunities to their limits, that is, **overassimilates**. The child of two, for example, pushes his or her new skills, competencies, opportunities, and spirit of independence to the limits by demanding independence in everything. At the onset of a new stage of development there is a tendency to overdo things, for the child to see his or her skills as so powerful and his or her needs as so important that other people's actions will be determined and controlled by what he or she does and demands. The child makes the egocentric assumption that he or she is the center of the family, around whose wishes and actions parents, siblings, and others resolve. This overassimilation of one's competencies, power, and needs leads to conflicts with others such as parents, peers, older siblings and children, and teachers, and is countered by social constraints being imposed on the child.

Second, the adult (or older children) place social constraints on the child. In response to the child or adolescent's pushing new skills and opportunities to their limits, adults and older children place social constraints on the student by enforcing classroom rules and general standards of conduct. **Social constraints** define what is realistic and unrealistic behavior within the relationship and setting. It is important that the social constraints are placed on the child in a caring and consistent way, rather than in a hostile and inconsistent way. Despite saying "no" and "I want to do it myself," for example, the child finds that parents are more powerful and that the child has to behave according to their expectations and standards.

Third, the child accommodates the social constraints by modifying his or her behavior. The child then tests the limits over and over again until he or she becomes convinced that the older person is more powerful and cannot be controlled or ignored, and that the social constraints cannot be overcome or avoided. In other words, the child is forced to **accommodate** to the social constraints by adjusting his or her's behavior to conform to them.

Fourth, the child either identifies with the more powerful person and internalizing the social constraints as his or her own guidelines or does not identifies with the more powerful person and dissociating the social constraints as alien to him- or herself. Once the child is convinced that he or she must accommodate the social constraints, one of two things can happen. The child either identifies with the older person and internalizes the social constraints or does not identify with the older person and dissociates the social constraints. **Identification** occurs when a person tries to be like someone else, usually someone he or she loves or admires, and sometimes someone he or she fears. Through identifying with other people, a person incorporates their qualities and attributes. A student can admire a teacher's scholarship and strive to become a scholar himself. A student can like a teacher and imitate that teacher's friendliness and warmth. By actively selecting people to identify with, a person constructs his or her own personality and transforms him- or herself into the kind of person he or she wants to be. By identifying with the "stronger" and "more powerful" adult, the student internalizes the social constraints and integrates them into his or her expanding sense of self by accepting the social constraints as a good idea that originates within one's own value system rather than from without. **Integration** is the internalization of social constraints and adult values and accepting them into

one's own value structure. "Not playing in the street," for example, becomes one's own guideline rather than an adult- enforced rule. If, on the other hand, the child does not identify with the adult and rejects the adult's authority, the child will conform on the surface (out of fear) while rejecting the social constraints privately by dissociating them from his or her sense of self. **Dissociation** is the internalization of social constraints and adult values but rejecting them by seeing them as alien to one's own value structure. Through dissociation the social constraints are taken in and followed but are experienced as "not mine" and resented. "Not playing in the street" becomes an internal guideline that is followed out of fear while being resented and rejected.

Fifth, the child retreats towards the other end of the continuum as another developmental conflict arises. Regardless of whether social constraints are integrated or dissociated, the child then retreats toward the other end of the developmental conflict (for example, moving from independence to dependence) while another developmental conflict arises.

The first few rounds of developmental conflicts are between child and parents. As children grow older, the conflicts are expressed in relationships with other children. This is especially true during the school years. As children continue to mature and develop, the conflicts become central in relationships with adults other than parents, such as teachers. Each time the conflicts reoccur children resolve them at the level allowed by their cognitive and social development. At each age children are different in the type of experiences they can initiate, the ways they can process information about their experiences, and the amount of accumulated experience they can bring to bear to aid understanding of current experiences. A two-year old may be satisfied with "because your mother says so" while a fourteen-year-old may not, because the fourteen-year old is far more capable of initiating a discussion and an intellectual challenge to the rule than is a two-year old. The greater the physical maturity of the brain, the more complex the analysis and understanding of one's experiences. Finally, all present experience is interpreted in the light of past experience. The first time an adolescent falls in love is perceived much differently than the tenth time, because there is little previous experience to aid in the understanding of what romantic love is. During adolescence, when children are fully mature physically, the conflicts are resolved in an adult and healthy way, unless something in their development prevents them from doing so.

The three developmental conflicts discussed here are those involving dependence and independence, security and change, and impulsiveness and the delay of gratification.

Dependence-Independence

The hardest part of raising children is teaching them to ride bicycles. A father can either run beside the bicycle or stand yelling directions while the child falls. A shaky child on a bicycle for the first time needs both support and freedom. The realization that this is what the child will always need can hit hard.

Sloan Wilson, 1976

Why does a child of one say, "mommy," "mommy," "mommy" over and over again when the mother is trying to take a shower or clean the house while a child of two will say, "no" and "I want to do it myself" over and over again when parents are tying to put the child to bed or cut up its food into smaller pieces. The answer is that children behave that way because they are developmentally impelled to do so. They have no choice. They are under a developmental imperative to define the limits of their dependence and independence so that they have a clear sense of social reality and an internal set of guidelines and values to help them decide how to behave.

The first developmental conflict that has to be faced by the child and its parents revolves around the child's initial dependence on the parents and the child's increasing independence as he or she physical and social matures (Breger, 1974). There is no doubt that the child begins his or her life highly dependent. The human infant cannot survive without the provision of milk and food, protection from outside dangers and shelter from wide variations in climatic conditions. The child is completely dependent on adults for survival and for information about how to adapt to the social and physical environment. Conflicts over dependence often come to a head about the age of one. A child somewhat younger than one often wants to be held all the time. The child cries whenever he or she is by him- or herself. The child's demands to be physically held by a parent are pushed to the extreme until the parents have no choice but to establish limits that define what is realistic and unrealistic dependence. The parent establishes social constraints by communicating that at times (such as when the parent is preparing dinner or leaving for work) the child cannot be held and must be physically separate from the parents.

A year or so later, when the child is older and more confident, the situation reverses. The child cycles out of dependence into an independent stage and struggles to define himself or herself as an independent being, one who can say "no" and "I want to do it myself." Because of emerging skills and a spirit of independence, the child's demands are pushed to the limit until the parents have no choice but to constrain the child's independent action and clarify what is realistic independence and what is unrealistic independence. When the child says "no" to bedtime, runs onto the street as soon as the parent's back is turned, says "no" to cleaning up, and refuses to eat vegetables, the parent makes it clear that the child does have to go to bed, cannot play in the street, has to clean up, and must eat vegetables. These social constraints have to be enforced over and over again.

A later version of the dependence-independence conflict is encountered in adolescence and young adulthood, as childhood finally passes and the person is faced with shaping his or her own life. Adolescents enter into an intense struggle for independence, beginning the task of defining themselves as adults, independent of the family and their own childhood. It is identifications with the peer group and with symbolic figures such as comic strip heroes that finally resolve the dependence- independence conflict and lead adolescents into adulthood. Because we are always dependent on other people, however, conflicts concerning dependence and independence can arise within career and family settings even in adulthood.

The child's initial dependence upon parents results in identifying with them and incorporating aspects of their competencies and attitudes. As they become more and more confident, children begin to differentiate themselves from parents and other people they are identified with. In an exaggerated sense of their own power, they push this new separate identity and independence as far as possible. When the limits of independence are reached and they realize they are still less powerful, less able, and less competent than parents, older siblings and children, and other people in the environment, they make new identifications with these people and accept a new level of dependence on them. Conflict then subsides temporarily. Gradual recognition of the greater power of adults and older children leads to a more complex identification with significant people in which children play, fantasize, and dream themselves into more adult roles. The next appearance of this core conflict occurs when the child is around five or six and moves more clearly into the world of school and peers. The child must again give up some to the prerogatives of his or her special place in the family and become one of many children in a larger group.

When the child identifies with the parent and integrates the social constraints into his or her internal guidelines and values, the child in effect says:

1. I am independent. I demand complete independence in everything.

2. My parents constrain me and are more powerful than I.

3. I incorporate their power by internalizing their constraints.

4. It is now me who constrains myself, not them.

5. I am active in controlling my own fate.

6. I have internal guidelines and values.

7. I follow my values and feel satisfaction.

8. I retreat towards dependence.

When the child does not identify with the parent and rejects the social constraints, the child in effect says:

1. I am independent. I demand complete independence in everything.

2. My parents constrain me and are more powerful than I.

3. I pretend to accept their constraints and fantasize revenge.

4. They continue to constrain me, while I fantasize I am a superman (or woman) who gets revenge.

5. I am a passive victim. I resent the constraints.

6. I place their constraints on myself, but I have no values or internal guidelines.

7. I simultaneously conform to their constraints on the outside and resist them on the inside.

8. I retreat towards dependence.

Within the school years the issue of balancing dependence and independence in one's relationships with peers, older children, and adults involves the two questions of, "Do you belong?" and "Am I a separate, unique, and valued individual in my own right?" Every person needs to feel accepted and included in relationships with others who care about the person and are committed to the person's wellbeing. At the same time, every person needs to feel like a separate and unique individual who is valued in his or her own right. Balancing these two needs results only from periodically testing the limits of one's dependence on and independence from others.

Security-Anxiety

A first-grade student stands in the classroom door. She wants to enter, but she feels like drawing back and returning home. She is so proud of being older and being allowed to attend school. She is so afraid she will not be able to survive without the love and protection of her family. She wants to strike out on her own and be a student. She wants to run home and be comforted and reassured in her mother's arms. A ninth-grade student stands in the classroom door. He wants to sit down by the girl he is so attracted to, but he is afraid and feels like sitting with his friends. He has changed physically, sex is a reality he cannot ignore, and sooner or later he has to establish a friendship with a member of the opposite sex. But he is so afraid he will be rejected and ridiculed. He wants to begin a new life by initiating a friendship with that one special female. He wants to return to security of his male friendships. Both students are struggling with the same development conflict: they are caught between the security of the status quo and their desire for change (Breger, 1974).

This core developmental conflict first appears early in childhood as anxiety forms about whether or not the crucial mother-infant relationship is to be maintained. At about the age of seven to twelve months the child continually seeks the security of the mother's lap. The child will crawl away from the mother, play for a few minutes, and then come hurrying back to be reassured. At about the age of fifteen to eighteen months the child practices walking, up and down a step, and taking things out of cupboards. In this "search and destroy" stage, the child expands and perfects new skills but constant practice. Motivation to increase his or her competence is so dominant parents are forced to limit the child's activities. The child believes it is invincible and will climb out windows, take tops off jars and eat what is inside, and walk across busy streets. New competencies are pushed to their limits until adults and older children say, "no." The child then must accommodate rules regarding safety and "learn common sense." In realizing that parents and older children are more powerful than he or she is, the child either identifies with the older individuals and internalizes the limits on his or her explorations and expansion of competencies, or does not identify with others and dissociates the social constraints. The child then moves toward the other end of the continuum and at about three and one-half years wants stability and order with little change and is fearful of the unexpected.

Anxiety concerning separation from the mother and the disruption of the mother-child relationship is based on feelings of helplessness and a lack of survival. The child gains security from the mother, but development and growth force the child to move away. Anxiety is then experienced as a potential loss of the mother's love and later becomes connected to those internal impulses, wishes, and ideas that signal a potential loss of love of valued others. Thus, whenever there is a basic change in one's relationships with others or within one's self, there is anxiety concerning one's potential helplessness in the changed world.

The developmental problem for the maturing child is how to become something different and still retain the security of the past. Psychological growth and change pose a threat to identity because they demand an abandonment of past securities. They also promise a more satisfying identity and more secure relationships in the future. Change and growth are exciting, appealing, and inevitable, but they produce anxiety about losing the security of being what one now is. The forces for change and growth are the attraction of novelty, innate human curiosity, the satisfactions of competence, the need for new intellectual challenges, physiological development, and changing social demands. These forces push toward development, increasing one's competence, and understanding better oneself, one's relationships with others, and one's place in the community and society. The child is propelled into new and challenging situations in which old skills and ways of being are not necessarily effective. This, in turn, stimulates further growth and development.

The conflict between security of the status quo and growth and change will reoccur several times in childhood. As the child passes through the various stages of growth, first the need for security will dominate, then the need for growth and change. The security-seeking infant becomes the independent-minded two-year-old concerned with "doing it myself." As the child begins school and has to leave the family, conflicts concerning security and change may reoccur. Adolescence, with its great physical and intellectual changes, creates new anxiety about change. Just as infants must move beyond the security of the mother's arms, so adolescents must move beyond the security of earlier versions of themselves.

In your classroom students will intensely experience the conflict between the security of the past and the satisfactions of new growth and accomplishment. Each student may choose to deal with learning opportunities and interpersonal relationships by relying on the established modes of the past or by experimenting with new patterns of behavior and thereby change himself. The personal support and acceptance each student feels from the teacher and his peers will affect his choice of clinging to the past or risking personal change. The less support and acceptance a student feels, the more likely she is to cling inappropriately to the past.

The very process of self-development is itself a source of conflict. Past securities must be abandoned and the child must change through internalization of external constraints and expanding his or her sense of self through a developing value system and awareness of choice and control. The problem growing children face is how to become something different and still retain the security of the past. Psychological growth and development pose a threat to identity. They demand an abandonment of past securities. Change and growth, although inevitable and exciting, also produce anxiety:

1. The attraction of novelty, innate human curiosity, the pleasures of competence, the need to function all provide the motivation for change.

2. The security of the known, the tendency for self once structured to perpetuate itself, the anxiety of separation, all resist change. They are motives for the maintenance of sameness.

3. During development children are faced with a number of opportunities and must deal with them by either relying on the established modes of the past (assimilation) or by trying new ways (accommodation) and, in the process, change themselves.

4. When children need to accommodate but do not, they dissociate. When children need to accommodate and do, they integrate.

Impulsiveness Versus Delayed Gratification

A high-school student suddenly "has" to sharpen his pencil, talk to one of his friends, or shout out a greeting to someone across the room. Delaying gratification of his or her needs seems beyond all possibility. At other ages children appear almost ritualistic, having to do things the same way regardless of circumstances, and making all impulses subordinate to "the way things should be done." A young child may have a bedtime ritual of getting a drink of water, listening to a parent read three (not two or four) stories, and kissing the parent good night. An eleven year old may have to sit at the same place at the table every time, arrange his or her books in a certain order, always be next to a certain friend during math, and so forth. A third developmental conflict involves following one's impulses and learning to control impulsive behavior and to delay gratification of one's immediate needs. Although there is general indulgence of an infant's impulsive behavior, sooner of later the child must be taught to control his or her impulses and to inhibit undesirable behavior. The control of impulsive aggression, excitement seeking, sexuality, and undesirable behavior becomes a central conflict with adults and older children.

Young children tend to be centered on the present and lack the differentiated time perspective necessary for delays in gratification. Reality from their point of view consists of a string of succeeding "nows"; past and future do not exist. Aggressive impulses are usually immediately expressed, sexual impulses immediately acted upon. This focus on the present and on their own impulses and needs is replaced with the ability to take longer time perspectives, to view their needs from the perspective of others, and to ritualize their behavior in certain situations.

Learning to inhibit undesirable behavior requires that children develop some capacity to delay seeking immediate gratification and instead seek to avoid subsequent punishments or seek future rewards of greater value than the ones foregone. Without some appreciation for the long-range consequences of action, children remain victims of monetary urges to impulsive behavior. Socialization involves learning self-control of behaviors that potentially threaten the maintenance of the relationships, such as unrestrained aggression, unrestrained sexuality, cheating, deceit, and thievery. Throughout childhood and adolescence there is a continued developmental conflict between the desire to gratify one's needs and the need to delay gratification. It is parents, peers, teachers, and older friends who must again and again convince the child and adolescent to forego immediate needs in order to avoid punishments and to obtain more valuable future rewards.

The developmental conflict between impulsively seeking to satisfy needs immediately and delaying gratification is resolved as follows. The child demands immediate gratification of his or her needs. This impulsive behavior is pushed to its extreme until the parents, other adults, or older children are forced to limit it. The social constraints placed on the immediate satisfaction of the child's needs are at first resisted until the child is convinced that others are more powerful and persuasive. The child then accommodates the limits on his or her behavior by either (a) identifying with the older individuals and internalizing the constraints on immediate need gratification as part of his or her value system, or (b) not identifying with the older individuals and dissociating the requirement to delay gratification of his or her needs. Either way, the conflict subsides and the child moves toward the other end of the immediate need gratification as part of his or her value system, or by not identifying with the older individuals and dissociating the requirement to delay gratification of his or her needs. Either way, the conflict subsides and the child moves toward the other end of the continuum, which includes ritualizing situations to the extent that adults are compelled to place constraints on the child's behavior, stating that "it does not have to be done that way every time!"

Dissociation

The penalty for not identifying with the adults or older children who are placing the constraints on one's behavior is dissociation. **Dissociation** is the splitting off of conflict-producing or anxiety-arousing thoughts, impulses, or actions from one's self-conception. It is the experiencing of one's thoughts, impulses, acts, and even parts of one's body as alien. The essence of dissociation is dealing with conflicts by splitting oneself off from the conflicts because one feels unable to resolve them and then seeking a fantasy solution. Direct or "real" solutions are abandoned for fantasy, pretend, or imaginary solutions. When dissociating the person divides into:

1. **Outward compliance**: Outwardly the person pretends to cease being angry and resistant (pretends to be other than he or she really is).

2. **Inward resistance and revenge**. Inwardly the person pretends that things are other than they are. In his or her fantasy anger is expressed and demands are gratified.

An example is when a child is disciplined or threatened with a loss of love by a parent. Striking back directly does not work because the parents are larger and stronger, and because it will simply lead to more loss of love. The child gives in and accepts the parental discipline, becoming outwardly a "good child" but inwardly expresses his or her frustrated anger and wishes in fantasy. In his or her fantasy, parents are run over by cars and are vanquished by the masked marauder, the avenger of injustices to the weak. The child divides him- or herself into an outward, socially compliant good boy or girl, and an inward or fantasy self who overcomes frustrations and social constraints. The conflicts are solved in fantasy but are left unresolved (out of fear) in the real world. The destructiveness of fantasy solutions is that they are both passive and private. The child feels like a passive victim who is controlled by external, more powerful, people and forces. The person feels helpless, the victim of more powerful forces that he or she can do little to influence. The resentment and rejection of the constraints is kept hidden and, therefore, no reality testing is possible. Once a conflict goes underground (becomes dissociated from the outward self) it is no longer subject to social influence. The person cannot test his or her attempted solutions against the reality of other people. Once a dissociative direction is taken, it is likely to become fixated and maintained.

Dissociation is normal in children, as they are in fact lacking in power and influence when dealing with adults. The child is at the mercy of people whom he or she cannot control and whose actions he or she may not understand. Insofar as the child realistically cannot have or do what he or she wants at a particular age, it makes sense to settle for a fantasy or pretend gratification. Putting aside one's wishes in fantasy until such time as one is capable is the normal or adaptive thing to do in many cases. Problems arise when dissociation becomes fixed and the solutions do not get reopened when the child is older and better able to negotiate an acceptable solution. When excessive anxiety becomes connected with the original conflict, attempts to reopen the area to new, less fantasy-oriented solutions, rearouses the anxiety. The feelings of smallness and incompetence are a part of every child's life to some extent, but they will be enhanced by certain types of parental response. Being abandoned, treated with inconsistent love and abuse, and being subjected to contradictory communications all contribute to the child's sense of helplessness. Such maltreatment will result in dissociations so strong that the child becomes so anxious when the conflict reoccurs that fantasy solutions are kept without trying to establish more mature and effective resolutions. As a general rule, the greater the anxiety the more likely dissociation, and the greater the security the more likely integration. Psychological problems result.

Constructive Resolution Of Developmental Conflicts

Psychological growth results from facing developmental conflicts over and over again until they are resolved in adult and healthy ways (through identification and internalization). The perennial conflicts of human life involve growth and change, but they can also lead to psychological disturbance. People who fail to deal adequately with these conflicts are labeled "neurotic" or "psychotic." **Psychological problems develop when**:

1. No constraints are placed on the child. The child is physically or psychologically abandoned.

2. The constraints are inconsistent, illogical, arbitrary, random, or destructive, or when one is treated with inconsistent love and abuse, or when one is subjected to contradictory communications. (All of these contribute to a sense of helplessness.)

3. Children dissociate rather than identify and integrate.

Developmental conflicts are constructively resolved when children and adolescents accommodate to social reality while internalizing an independent and differentiated sense of self, the security of the relationships they are dependent on, and the necessary constraints on impulses to immediately satisfy their needs. Such integration of social constraints is commonly achieved through identification, in which the external conflicts with adults and peers are transformed into internal conflicts. An aggressive child, for example, is first constrained by parents and teachers. Through identification, he acquires self-control by internalizing the adult restraint on aggression. He begins to carry the conflict between impulses to aggress and the prohibition against these same impulses within himself. When such conflicts are internalized and made an integrated part of oneself, the conflict has been constructive. When the conflict is experienced as being an alien part of oneself, dissociated from one's psychological nature, the resolution has been destructive.

In order for teachers to help students resolve their developmental conflicts constructively, the following suggestions may be helpful.

1. **Expect repetition**. Developmental conflicts will appear and reappear throughout the person's childhood and adolescence. A teacher will be faced with these same conflicts over and over again as each student attempts to achieve a balance between dependence and independence, security in status quo and desire to grow and change, and impulsive satisfaction of needs and delay of gratification.

2. **Face the conflict**. Do not ignore or suppress it. As part of each developmental conflict a student will egocentrically test the limits of new competencies, awarenesses, opportunities, and impulses until he or she is forced again and again to take cognizance of other persons as well as him- or herself. Such continued conflict with peers and adults results in an accommodation to social reality that sets the stage for the next cycle of growth and development. A teacher cannot avoid developmental conflicts and it is destructive for the student if the conflicts are not faced and resolved constructively. Ignoring the developmental conflicts of your students will only retard their social development. Confront students directly and push towards the resolution of the conflicts.

3. **Be consistent**. Consistently place realistic constraints on students' actions and emotional expressions. While this will sharpen the conflict between you and your students, it will force them to accommodate to social reality. It is through such conflicts that students will identify with you, internalize aspects of your competence in dealing with interpersonal relationships, and move from a naively selfish and asocial infant to a social adult.

4. **Provide constructive models**. Developmental conflicts are resolved by making external relationships into internal ones via identification. Unable to defeat more competent and powerful individuals and unwilling simply to give in, the child and adolescent do the next best thing. She or he makes the other people and their competencies and power part of him- or herself.

5. **Provide support for growth and risk-taking**. Throughout a person's development a supportive network of interpersonal relationships is needed within which the developmental conflicts can be resolved in ways that promote growth and change through positive identification with the people involved. Ensuring that the classroom is a network of supportive interpersonal relationships is one of the major tasks of the teacher. Whenever possible, use cooperative goal structures as part of instruction, as this is probably the most efficient way to ensure a supportive classroom climate in which students help, encourage, care for, and accept each other (Johnson and Johnson, 1987). It is also the most effective way of creating the impression that you, the teacher, support and accept each student both personally and academically.

6. **Teach students conflict skills**. Students need to master the skills and procedures involved in resolving interpersonal conflicts constructively. It is through controversy and negotiating skills that students accommodate to the social reality that they are separate, but interdependent, individuals who have the competencies necessary for growing and changing, and who have to take other people's needs and rights into account as well as their own wishes. Learning how to negotiate skillfully with each other and with you, the teacher, is an important set of skills that will do much for ensuring that healthy resolutions of developmental conflicts will be made.

7. **Emphasize understanding the viewpoint and feelings of other people**. The ability to take the cognitive and emotional perspectives of other people is necessary to reduce the egocentrism that blocks further social and intellectual growth. When the child or adolescent overassimilates and pushes new competencies and opportunities to the limits, they partially do so out of naive egocentrism that they really are capable of complete independence or that their needs are so important that everyone will see why the needs have to satisfied right now. Viewing his or her competencies and needs from the perspectives of others helps the child

or adolescent understand the need for accommodation to and internalization of the social constraints being placed upon him or her.

8. **Do not make the impersonal personal**. By definition, all developmental conflicts are impersonal. They result from the imperatives of development, not from personal experience. If students are testing the limits of their independence by being rejecting and negative toward you, do not take it personally. Remember that if the student would act toward any teacher the way he or she is acting toward you, it is not a personal attack. It is an impersonal attack in that any adult will do to lash out at. You can save yourself countless hours of grief and anger by clearly differentiating between conflicts that are products of students trying to work through developmental conflicts, and conflicts personally directed at you as a person. You may be surprised by how few instances of the latter you will find.

Students will be working through developmental conflicts involving such things as their increasing independence from adults and peers, increasing the stability of their self-identity so that they are secure enough to change, and increasing their ability to control their impulses and delay gratification of their immediate needs. Resolving such developmental conflicts involve testing the limits of their new competencies, awarenesses, and opportunities. Thus, some aspects of perfectly normal development lead to discipline problems. The defiance and rebelliousness of junior high and high school students, for example, is both appropriate and normal. The behavior is motivated more by the natural consequences of growth and development and by a healthy inclination to defend one's integrity than by angry feelings toward the teacher and school. Not all misbehavior is abnormal. Some misbehavior is merely symptomatic of a particular developmental issue and growth period. Consider the following statement by Redl (1955):

> *We want Johnny to be respectful to his teacher but we don't want him to run after the first designing bum that offers him candy just because the man is an adult and looks like a mixture of Abe Lincoln and Santa Claus. On the contrary, we want our children to retain the capacity for intelligent rebellion--courage to stick to what they believe in even against strong-armed pressure and the fear of becoming unpopular with the mob.*

It is easy for teachers to overreact to students asserting independence from their authority or impulsively refusing to accept the validity of teachers' judgments over their own. And it is part of the **art** of teaching to balance the need to place realistic restraints on students' actions while at the same time encouraging students to develop autonomous, separate, integrated identities that contain enough self-confidence to allow further growth and development. The long run psychological health of students depends on two things: teachers being understanding people who do not overreact to the occurrence of developmental conflicts, and students learning the negotiation procedures and skills required to resolve developmental conflicts constructively.

Summary

A **developmental conflict** is a recurrent conflict that cycles in and out of peak intensity as the person develops physically, socially, and cognitively. A developmental conflict comes to the fore at a particular time, reaches a peak intensity, is worked through or put aside as another developmental conflict builds up, and reappears in a new form later on. Each is a continuum. Conflicts appear at either end. These overlapping conflicts include (a) dependence-independence, (b) security in the status quo-demand for growth and change, and (c) impulsive satisfaction of needs-delay of gratification. Developmental conflicts occur and are resolved through the child overassimilating new competencies and opportunities, the adult placing social constraints on the child, the child accommodating the social constraints, the child identifying with the adult and internalizing the social constraints, and then the child retreating toward the other end of the continuum. When the conflict is managed destructively, instead of internalizing the social constraints and accepting them as internal guidelines, the child dissociates the social constraints and overtly conforms while internally resisting. Since developmental conflicts are repetitious, they must be faced over and over again. Adults such as teachers need to be consistent in enforcing social constraints but should also support growth and risk-taking. Perhaps the most important key to ensuring that developmental conflicts are well managed is to teach students how to negotiate to solve problems.

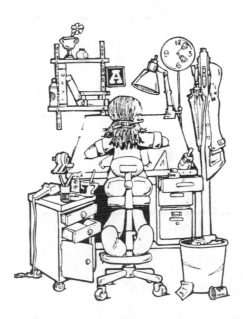

⚜ Creative Conflict Contract ⚜

Major Learnings	Implementation Plans

Date _____ Date of Progress Report Meeting _____

Participant's Signature _____

Signatures of Other Group Members _____ _____

_____ _____ _____

EXERCISE

MATERIALS

CHAPTER VOCABULARY

Working with a partner, learn the definitions of the following words.

1. Define each word in two ways.
   First, write down what you think the word means.
   Second, look it up in the book and write down its definition.
   Note the page on which the definition appears.

2. For each word write a sentence in which the word is used.

3. Make up a story in which all of the words are used.

4. Learn how to spell each word. They will be on your spelling test.

Dictionary

Word List

- developmental conflict
- accommodation
- integration
- social constraints
- overassimilation
- identification
- dissociation

8 Peacemaking

The Lure Of Going For The "Win"

No logic or wisdom or will-power could prevail to stop the sailors. Buffeted by the hardships of life at sea, the voices came out of the mist to the ancient Greek sailors like a mystical, ethereal love song with tempting and seductive promises of ecstasy and delight. The voices and the song were irresistible. The mariners helplessly turned their ships to follow the Sirens' call with scarcely a second thought. Lured to their destruction, the sailors crashed their ships on the waiting rocks and drowned in the tossing waves, struggling with their last breath to reach the source of that beckoning song.

Centuries later, the Sirens still call. Educators seem drawn to competitive learning, crashing their teaching on the rocks due to the seductive and tempting attractions of trying to find out which student is "best." Students are also captured by the seduction of wanting to build their successes on the failures of their classmates. And when conflicts occur, going for the "win" has an irresistible call to many. Striving to solve the problem so both sides benefit may seem idealistic but undoable. Cooperative learning provides a far more effective alternative to competition and creates the foundation within which conflicts may be managed constructively. Problem-solving negotiations provide an alternative to the "win-lose" approach to resolving conflicts and teach students the procedures and skills required to work effectively with classmates and faculty to maximize their education and cognitive and social development.

Peer Mediation

Suzzane, who is a new student from another country, sits down to eat lunch with several classmates. Pam says, "This is 'invitation only.' No foreigners allowed." Suzzane, her feelings obviously hurt, says, "Sorry" and walks away. "That's terrible," Mary says to Pam. "You shouldn't have done that." "You're such a 'goody-goody'," Pam replies. "We don't want you here either!" Mary and Pam get more and more angry and begin yelling at each other. Things come to a head when Pam pushes Mary.

Conflicts occur all the time in school. They are a natural, inevitable, potentially constructive, and normal part of school life. While in extreme cases conflicts erupt into violence, most conflicts among students are far milder, involving disagreements over rumors, name calling, boyfriends/girlfriends, and the like. Some of the conflicts are resolved. Many, if not most, are not. In most cases, students either escalate conflicts in destructive ways or disengage harboring anger and resentments that continue to simmer underneath the surface. Covert conflicts then exist in which students sit in classrooms and "fester" about their perceived grievances. Until covert conflicts are made overt and resolved, students cannot focus their attention on learning.

Several factors contribute to students' failures to resolve their conflicts constructively. Students often are from different cultural, ethnic, social class, and language backgrounds. Different students often have quite different ideas about how conflicts should be managed. The procedures and strategies students use to manage their conflicts are quite often inadequate and destructive, making things worse rather than better. Students may get angry, fight, hurl verbal abuse at each other, verbally harass each other, ignore the conflict, take their anger out on someone/something else, play head-games, or fantasize how to get revenge. These methods generally provide little chance of resolving any problems and often result in alienating students from their peers and the school staff. Most students simply do not know how to manage their conflicts constructively.

Under these circumstances, conflict can produce chaos. Teachers can respond by being police officers, arbitrators, or mediators. Ideally, however, **teachers will co-orient students by teaching them the procedures and skills required to manage conflicts constructively.** Conflicts, no matter what, occur all the time in school and only students themselves can restore order and peace. What is needed is a training program that creates a shared set of procedures and strategies for negotiating solutions to joint problems and mediating conflicts among classmates.

In the above example, Mary and Pam need a peer mediator to help them resolve their conflict (so do Pam and Suzzane). Roger is a class mediator for that day. He approaches Mary and Pam, separates them, helps them cool down. He then meets with them and ensures that they are committed to mediating their conflict. He asks if they want to solve the problem and does not proceed until both answer "yes." Since the role of mediator is rotated through the class, both Pam and Mary have themselves been mediators and will be again. This increases their willingness to participate in the process. Then Roger explains:

"Mediation is voluntary. My role is to help you find a solution to your conflict that is acceptable to both of you."

"I am neutral. I will not take sides or attempt to decide who is right or wrong. I will help you decide how to solve the conflict."

"Each person will have the chance to state his or her view of the conflict without interruption."

"The rules you must agree to are (a) agree to solve the problem, (b) no name calling, (c) do not interrupt, and (d) be as honest as you can."

"If you agree to a solution, you must abide by it. You must do what you have agreed to do."

"Anything said in mediation is confidential. I will not tell anyone what is said."

Roger reminds Mary and Pam that they are friends, are in many of the same classes, and participate in many of the same activities. He then leads them through the negotiation procedure. Each states what she wants. Each states how she feels. Each states the reasons for her wants and feelings. Each summarizes her understanding of what the other wants, how the other feels, and the reasons underlying both. Roger helps Mary and Pam invent three optional plans to resolve their conflict. They then choose the one they like the best and shake hands.

Finally, Roger closes the mediation session by formalizing the agreement and stating he would check in with them in a few days to see if the agreement was working.

Conflict management procedures and skills are too important to leave to chance. Children and adolescents need to be directly taught in school the negotiation procedures and skills and given the mediation experiences that will help them live happy and successful lives. When students are taught how to manage conflicts constructively, they become peacemakers. Part of every student's responsibilities is to manage his or her conflicts constructively and help schoolmates do likewise.

Nature Of Conflict

To manage conflict constructively, and to help classmates mediate their conflicts, students have to understand what conflicts are. Whenever the actions of one person frequently prevent, block, or interfere with another person's attempts to achieve his or her goals, a **conflict** exists. There are four major types of conflicts. When one person's ideas or conclusions are incompatible with those of another person, and the two must reach an agreement, a **controversy** occurs. If John believes that Byron is the greatest romantic poet while Jane thinks Elizabeth Barrett Browning is, John and Jane are in a controversy. When a person has two incompatible ideas, a **conceptual conflict** exists. If Jack believes that a rock will fall faster than a feather but that gravity operates uniformly on all objects, he has a conceptual conflict. When one person strives to achieve his or her goals and another person blocks him or her from doing so, a **conflict of interests** exists. If Jan wants to use a computer to do her homework and Jill wants to use the same computer to practice keyboarding, they have a conflict of interests. When recurrent incompatible actions occur between a child and an adult as part of the child's social development, a **developmental conflict** exists. When Jacob asserts his independence by stating that to his teacher only he can know what is best for him, Jacob and his teacher are engaged in a developmental conflict. These **conflicts are managed constructively** when an agreement is reached that solves the problem, strengthens the relationships among participants, and increases their ability to resolve their conflicts constructively in the future.

Value Of Conflict

Juan is eating lunch with several friends when Peter strolls up to the table, grabs the cake from Juan's tray, and eats it before Juan can move. The next hour the history teacher is explaining how world interdependence has increased dramatically during the past 50 years. Juan is not listening. He is seething with anger, planning how to "get" Peter for eating his cake. After class a friend invites him to a party. Juan does not hear. He is too preoccupied with his angry at Peter.

Knowing how to negotiate and how to mediate has far ranging effects on students. Without the ability to negotiate solutions to joint problems it is difficult to maintain caring and committed relationships over a long period of time. Resolving many of the developmental imperatives requires negotiating with parents and other adults. Conflicts with others, when managed constructively, help clarify one's values, attitudes, and identity and how one needs to change. Knowing how to negotiate and mediate teaches students both interpersonal and academic skills, improves cooperative work, increases students' commitment to education, and prepares students to be citizens in a complex and conflict-filled world. The more students learn how to take a cooperative approach to managing conflicts through joint problem- solving, the healthier psychologically they tend to be and the better able they are to deal with stress and adversity and cope with life's challenges and unforeseen adversity. There are few things more important for future quality of life and career success than teaching students how to manage conflicts constructively. **Negotiation procedures and skills are carried with the student wherever he or she goes and, once acquired, cannot be taken away.** They are a gift of incalculable value.

Not only does learning how to manage conflicts constructively benefit students in many personal ways, it is also good for the school. When students learn how to manage their conflicts constructively the learning climate of the classroom and school change dramatically. Discipline problems are reduced as students resolve their problems without needing help and assistance from faculty and staff. Teachers have more time to teach. Time-on-task increases. A better life within the school and a more peaceful classroom begins with each individual student being better able to face conflicts and find ways to ensure that all participants benefit by the solution of underlying problems.

Steps Of Managing Conflicts Constructively

The value of conflicts is maximized when (a) a cooperative context for relationships is created through the extensive use of cooperative learning, (b) academic controversies are structured by the teacher, (c) all students learn a basic negotiation procedure, (d) all students learn how to mediate their classmates' conflicts, and (e) teachers arbitrate as a last resort.

The Context Of Conflict

Conflicts can only be managed constructively within a cooperative context. The first step to ensuring that students learn how to deal with their conflicts in helpful and beneficial ways is to make the classroom and school a cooperative enterprise. This will only happen when cooperative learning is used the majority of the time.

There are two possible contexts for conflict: cooperative and competitive (in individualistic situations individuals do not interact and, therefore, no conflict occurs). In a **competitive context** a valued commodity (such as grades) is scarce and individuals work against each other to win. Each person tries to defeat others. Within such a context individuals do not share information and are as likely to mislead as to clarify. Competitors are likely to misperceive the other's intentions and distort rival's actions. Competitors tend to be suspicious of and hostile toward each other. They tend to deny the legitimacy of the rival's goals and consider only their own interests. The overuse and inappropriate use of competitive (and individualistic) learning procedures should be avoided. The more competitive the relationships among students, and the more students are focused on their own self-interests, the more destructive conflicts will be. In a competitive context you go for the win and then walk away.

In a **cooperative context** individuals work together to achieve shared goals. The more honestly they communicate with each other, the more accurately they perceive each other's actions, the more they trust each other, and the more committed they are to each other's interests, the better able they are to achieve their mutual goals. In a cooperative context you solve the problem so that the joint effort to achieve mutual goals can continue.

The constructive resolution of conflict within the classroom and school requires students and staff to recognize that their long-term relationships are more important than is the result of any short-term conflict. In order for their long-term mutual interests to be recognized and valued, individuals have to perceive their interdependence and be invested in each other's well-being. To teach students the procedures and skills they need to manage conflicts constructively, furthermore, a cooperative classroom environment must be established. Classroom conflicts may be prevented, reduced, and managed constructively through the establishment of a cooperative context characterized by a supportive and caring classroom community. The easiest way to do so is to use cooperative learning procedures the majority of the day. Since cooperative learning increases achievement and promotes a number of other important instructional outcomes, there will be little objection to doing so.

Learning To Negotiate

You negotiate to resolve conflicts of interests. **Negotiation** is a process by which persons who have shared and opposed interests and want to come to an agreement try to work out a settlement. There are two types of negotiations. **Win-lose negotiations** occur when participants want to make an agreement more favorable to themselves than to the other persons. It is appropriate primarily when participants will never have to work with each other in the future. Such situations are rare. The majority of the time individuals negotiate within an ongoing relationship. That requires **problem-solving negotiations** where the goal is to reach an agreement that benefits everyone involved. To negotiate a solution to a mutual problem students have to:

1. Agree on a definition of the conflict by stating what they want and how they feel, listening carefully to the other person, and agreeing on a definition of the conflict that specifies it as a small and specific mutual problem to be solved--TUD (tell, understand, and define).

2. Exchange reasons for positions by expressing cooperative intentions, exchanging reasons, focusing on interests not positions, exploring how interests are incompatible and compatible, and empowering each other by giving choices.

3. Understanding of the other person's perspective by paraphrasing and checking perceptions of the other person's interests and reasons.

4. Invent options for mutual gain by both inventing creative options and avoiding the obstacles to creative problem solving.

5. Reach a wise agreement that meets the legitimate needs of all participants, when it is based on principles that can be justified on some objective criteria, when students' ability to work cooperatively with each other has been enhanced, and when students' ability to resolve their future conflicts constructively has been strengthened.

Negotiating wise agreements is not always easy. Sometimes students have to try, try again until a wise agreement is reached. To negotiate in good faith students need to build a reputation of being honest, truthful, and trustworthy. Not all issues, however, are negotiable. Students must know the difference between a negotiable and a nonnegotiable issue. And they must be able to say "No, I will not negotiate on this issue" when it is appropriate to do so.

Deciding Whether Or Not To Negotiate

Within any conflict students have two concerns: to achieve their goals and to maintain effective working relationships with each other. Those two concerns result in five possible strategies for managing conflicts: withdrawal, forcing, smoothing, compromise, and confrontation. In deciding which of the five strategies to use within any one conflict, there are six rules to consider:

1. Do not withdraw from or ignore the conflict unless the goal and the other person are unimportant.

2. Do not engage in "win-lose" negotiations. Only go for a win when you will never see the other person again.

3. Assess for smoothing. When the other person's goal is very important to him or her, and your goal is not important to you, smooth.

4. Compromise when time is short.

5. Confront to begin problem-solving negotiations.

6. Use your sense of humor.

Managing Anger

One of the most difficult aspects of confronting another person and initiating problem-solving negotiations is managing emotions. Managing anger is especially problematic. If you try to hide it, very likely the problem will not be correctly identified and a wise agreement will not be reached. But if you express your anger destructively, the relationship may be severely damaged if not ruined.

Anger is a defensive emotion reaction that occurs when a person is frustrated, thwarted, or attacked. Students get angry when other people obstruct their goal accomplishment, frustrate their attempts to accomplish something, interfere with their plans, make them feel belittled and rejected, or indicate that they are of no value or importance. When students get angry at each other the results can be either destructive or constructive. **Anger tends to be destructive** when (a) students express anger in a way that creates dislike, hatred, frustration, and a desire for revenge on the part of the other person or (b) anger is repressed and held inside (which tends to create irritability, depression, insomnia, and physiological problems such as headaches and ulcers). **Anger tends to be constructive** when students feel energized, motivated, challenged, and excited, and the other person feels friendship, gratitude, goodwill, and concern.

To manage anger constructively students need to recognize and acknowledge that they are angry. They decide whether or not to express the anger. The anger can be expressed directly and descriptively when it is appropriate to do so. The anger could also be expressed indirectly or students could move to an alternative feeling when direct expression of anger is not appropriate. During it all, students should stay task oriented. They analyze, understand, and reflect on their anger. They congratulate themselves on managing anger constructively and express any other emotions (such as respect or appreciation) directly and descriptively.

Developmental Conflicts

One of the major sources of conflicts of interests is the demands that physical, social, and cognitive development make on children and adolescents. As students get older, they get taller, stronger, smarter, more skilled in relating to others, more able to see issues from a variety of perspectives, and more able to be an equal in relationships with a wide variety of people of many different ages. The maturation and development process requires that relationships change with adults as well as with peers. Conflicts of interests result. Such developmental conflicts reoccur over and over again and cycle in and out of peak intensity as students mature physically, socially, and cognitively. A developmental conflict comes to the fore at a particular time, reaches a peak intensity, is worked through or put aside as another developmental conflict builds up, and reappears in a new form later on. Students work to establish and understand their dependence versus independence, security in the status quo versus demand for growth and change, and impulsive satisfaction of needs versus delay of gratification. Students overassimilate and push their demands to the extreme. Adults such as teachers and/or peers are forced into placing social constraints on the student. The student accommodates the social constraints and either identifies with the adult and internalizes the social constraints or dissociates the social constraints and overtly conforms while internally resisting.

Implementing A Peer Mediation Program

Once students have mastered establishing a cooperative context, negotiating to solve a mutual problem, confronting constructively to initiate negotiations, and managing their own and classmates' anger, they are ready to help classmates resolve their conflicts by being a mediator. To implement a peer mediation process the teacher selects each day two students to be the class mediators. Any conflicts that students can not negotiate resolutions to are referred to class mediators. The role of class mediator is rotated through-

out the class so that each student serves as class mediator an equal amount of time. Students need to know how to arrange for a mediator when they need one. Periodically, once or twice a week the teacher should teach a refresher lesson on negotiation and mediation to improve continuously students' skills in using the procedures.

When Mediation Fails

When mediation fails the conflict is referred to the teacher. The teacher first tries to mediate. If that fails, the teacher has to decide through arbitration. Both students present their best case. The teacher carefully listens and then decides how the conflict is to be resolved. Arbitration seldom satisfies anyone, leaving at least one student with resentment and anger toward the arbitrator. More importantly, it reinforces students' beliefs that they are not capable of working out future disputes themselves. For these reasons, arbitration is the last resort for resolving conflicts within the classroom and school. In a way, arbitration is a threat to encourage the success of negotiations and mediation.

Use Of Academic Controversies

A peer mediation program is not the only way teachers can ensure that students learn how to manage conflicts constructively. Teachers should also frequently promote intellectual controversies to increase the quantity and quality of academic learning. In order to maximize student achievement, student critical thinking, and student use of higher-level reasoning strategies, teachers need to engage students in intellectual conflicts within which they have to prepare intellectual positions, present them, advocate them, criticize opposing intellectual positions, view the issue from a variety of perspectives, and synthesize the various positions into one position. The frequent use of academic controversies allows students to practice their conflict skills daily.

A detailed program to train teachers in how to structure academic controversies to ensure that all students are intellectually challenged within the classroom is presented in **Creative Controversy: Intellectual Challenge In The Classroom** (Johnson & Johnson, 1987/1992).

Table 8.1

Constructive	Destructive
Cooperation, mutual interests, and community predominate	Competitive and individualistic self-interest predominate
Conflicts are faced, expressed, and resolved openly	Conflicts are avoided, repressed, and suppressed
Intellectual conflicts structured and promoted	Intellectual conflicts suppressed and squelched
Students are taught negotiation procedures	Open expression of conflicts discouraged and not allowed
Students are taught mediation procedures	Teacher arbitrates all conflicts
Developmental conflicts are viewed as natural and healthy	Developmental conflicts are viewed as pathological
Conflict skills are taught, practiced, and used	Conflicts skills are not taught or practiced
Student autonomy in managing conflicts constructively encouraged	Teacher arbitrates all conflicts

Looking Forward

Now that you have reached the end of this book you are at a new beginning. Years of experience in using the negotiation and mediation procedures and skills are needed to gain real expertise in managing conflicts constructively. The more you negotiate, the more you mediate, the more you will learn. Your understanding of how to build a cooperative context, how to negotiate, how to initiate negotiations, how to manage anger constructively, and how to mediate will deepen as you carefully apply each to new conflict situations. In the end you may find that conflicts offer the chance to see a problem more clearly, get new ideas, achieve new perspectives, and make better friends. It is through conflict that we grow, develop, learn, progress, and achieve. In the end you may find that conflicts enrich rather than disrupt your life.

⮞⟦ Creative Conflict Contract ⟧⮜

Major Learnings	Implementation Plans

Date _____ Date of Progress Report Meeting _____

Participant's Signature _____

Signatures of Other Group Members _____ _____

_____ _____ _____

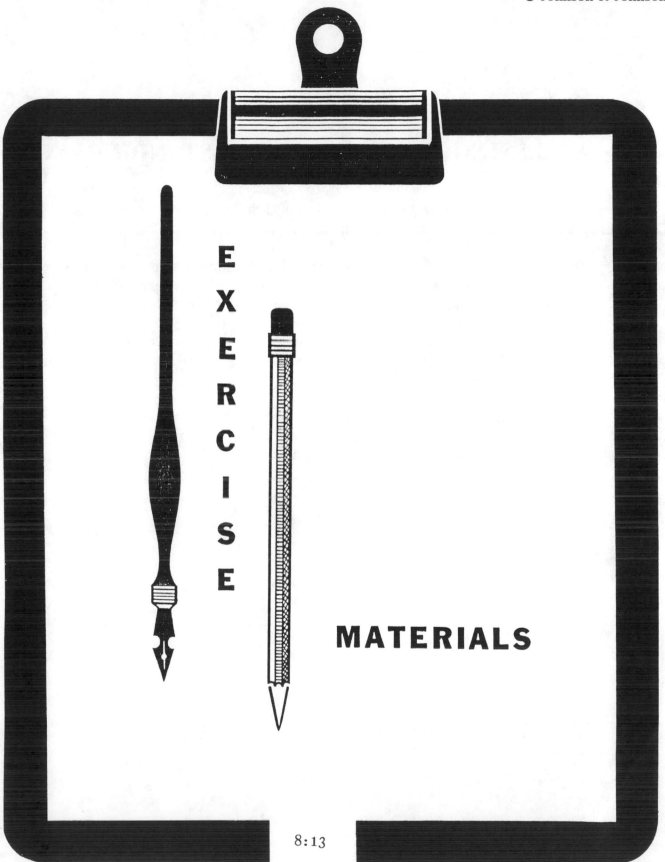

EXERCISE

MATERIALS

8:13

ASSESSING STUDENTS' UNDERSTANDING

You will benefit from assessing your understanding of each chapter and then reviewing the parts you do not fully understand. Your **tasks** are to:

1. Review the first seven chapters and write out three questions for your classmates to answer that will test their understanding of the content of the chapter. Write each question on a 3x5 index card. You will write out twenty-one questions in all.

2. Place the questions for each chapter in a bowl. There will be seven bowls (one for each chapter). Randomly draw three questions from each bowl. Write out answers to the questions you have drawn.

Work **cooperatively**. Form a pair. Agree on the questions you write for each chapter. Agree on one answer to each question you answer. One member of your pair will be randomly selected to present your answers to the class as a whole.

Qualities of Good Mediation

Make two columns on a sheet of paper. Label one "Is" and the other "Is Not." Think of what a student mediator is and is not. Write your ideas in the appropriate column. Work **cooperatively** in a pair to complete this task. Make one list for the two of you, both of you must agree, and each must be able to explain your answers.

What Is Good Mediation?

Place a "yes" for each quality of good mediation and a "no" for each quality of poor mediation. Work **cooperatively** in a pair. Agree on each answer. Each must be able to explain why you answered the question as you did.

_____ A good listener.

_____ A police officer.

_____ A good team member.

_____ A person who interrupts or focuses attention on him- or herself.

_____ A fair person who does not take sides.

_____ A judge.

_____ A helper.

_____ A person who gives orders or advice.

_____ A dependable person.

_____ A person who talks about other students' conflicts.

_____ A person you can trust.

Steps in Mediating

Read each of the statements given below. Number the stage of mediation each statement belongs to (1 = End Hostilities, 2 = Ensure Commitment, 3 = Facilitate Negotiations, 4 = Formalize Agreement). Work **cooperatively** in a pair. Agree on each answer. Each must be able to explain why you answered the question as you did.

_____ Will you describe your view of the conflict?

_____ Do you agree to follow these rules?

_____ Hello. My name is xx. I'm your mediator.

_____ What are three ways this problem could be solved?

_____ What happened?

_____ Tell me what xx wants, how xx feels, and the reasons why xx wants and feels as he/she does.

_____ Stop fighting! Stop fighting!

_____ Can you repeat back what xx has said?

_____ What do you want? How do you feel?

_____ Go to opposite corners in the room. Fill out the Conflict Form. Then we will talk.

_____ Do you agree to solve the problem?

_____ I have written your agreement down. Sign here. I will check back with you in two days to see if the agreement is working.

TRUE o^r FALSE ?

Answer each question "true" or "false." Work **cooperatively** in a pair. Agree on each answer. Each must be able to explain why you answered the question as you did.

_____ Mediators do not say who is right and who is wrong.

_____ There are at least two sides in every conflict.

_____ Once the two students feel better about each other, the conflict is over.

_____ Most students cannot say what they want.

_____ Conflict is a natural part of life.

_____ All conflicts end in violence.

_____ Feelings are irrational and confuse negotiations.

_____ It is important to learn not to get angry.

_____ Letting students interrupt and correct each other helps clarify what the conflict is.

_____ A wise agreement is one that allows both students to achieve their goals.

_____ When you are angry it is OK to embarrass or humiliate the other person.

_____ Decide who is right and have the other person apologize.

_____ Once an agreement has been reached, the job of the mediator is over.

_____ We should eliminate all conflict in our classroom.

_____ Reasons do not matter. Just focus on what each person wants.

_____ Only conflicts where physical fighting is involved need to be mediated.

_____ Humor often helps students resolve their conflict.

TRUE or FALSE? (continued)

_____ Mediation works best when students are really angry, because then they will tell the truth.

_____ Conflicts can escalate or de-escalate, depending on what is said or done.

_____ Once a mediator has both students tell what happened, then his or her job is done.

_____ In conflicts people are so upset that it is a waste of time trying to get them to understand each other's point of view.

_____ Mediators help students think of several possible optional agreements before they decide on how best to resolve their conflict.

_____ Fighting fair shows respect for oneself and for others.

_____ Part of the final agreement is that the students should avoid contact with each other in the future.

MEDIATION RULES

List the four rules students must agree on:

1.

2.

3.

4.

Evaluation of Mediation Programs

You may wish to evaluate the effectiveness of your peer mediation program. There are two things you will wish to find out:

1. Was the peer mediation training conducted effectively?

2. Is the peer mediation program achieving its goals?

To answer these questions you need to collect information systematically. Included in this chapter are a several instruments to help you do so.

1. **Conflict Report Form:**

   a. Pick a time that the form can be given regularly.

   b. Have students work in pairs to fill out the form.

   c. Classify conflicts into categories such as:

   d. Weekly record the frequency of each type of conflict on a class chart.

   e. Make sure that students understand it is not the frequency of conflicts that matters, it is how they are managed. Conflicts should occur frequently and be managed skillfully.

2. **What do you do when you negotiate a problem?** Ask students to list the steps.

3. **What Would You Do?** Tell students that here is a conflict that two of your classrooms had. They are to think about what is happening in the conflict and, as a mediator, write what they would do to help these two classmates resolve their problem.

4. **Conflict Essay:** Ask students to write an essay (create a skit or puppet show) about what they have learned about managing conflicts.

5. **Favorite Story:** Ask students to analyze a conflict in one of their favorite stories.

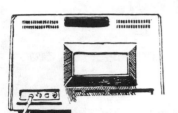

What Would YOU Do?

Here is a conflict that two of your classrooms had. Think about what is happening in the conflict. As a mediator, what would you do to help these two classmates resolve their problem? Write your answer below.

Today in school each student is given a chance to work at the computer. When your turn comes you go over to the computer and one of your classmates is still using it. You tell the person working at the computer that it is your turn, but they tell you that they have not finished yet and keep working. It is important that you use the computer during your assigned time to get your work done. What should you do?

If it was my turn to use the computer I would:

My Favorite Story

Choose one of your favorite books, movies, or short stories. Analyze it:

1. What is the conflict the book or movie revolves around?

2. Who is involved, when does it happen, where does it happen, and how is it managed?

3. What strategies do the characters use to manage or resolve the conflict? How successful are those strategies?

4. How would you manage the conflict? Describe your procedures, strategies, and skills in detail.

Assessing Students' Understanding of Mediation

Qualities Of Good Mediation

Make two columns on the blackboard, one labeled "Is" and the other "Is Not." Ask students what they think a student mediator is and is not. Write their responses in the appropriate column. Add any they do not mention.

What Is Good Mediation?

Place a "yes" for each quality of good mediation and a "no" for each quality of poor mediation.

_____ A good listener.

_____ A police officer.

_____ A good teamworker.

_____ A person who interrupts or focuses attention on him- or herself.

_____ A fair person who does not take sides.

_____ A judge.

_____ A helper.

_____ A person who gives orders or advice.

_____ A dependable person.

_____ A person who talks about other students' conflicts.

_____ A person you can trust.

Student Recruitment Sheet

1. **What is mediation?** Mediation is cooperatively resolving your conflict with the help of a trained mediator.

2. **Who?** Anyone in conflict with another student.

3. **Why?** Because you work out your own solution to your conflict instead of having a decision handed down by a teacher or principal.

4. **Where?** Right in your school.

If you like to try new things, help others with their conflicts, be in the middle of things, or gain valuable skills, volunteer to be trained as a mediator. Before the end of the year every student in the class may take their turn being a mediator. You will be asked to:

1. Take part in 15 hours of training.

2. Attend regular meetings with the teacher and the other mediators.

3. Be available for one mediation a week during lunch or study hall.

Volunteer to Learn To Mediate

Conflict Reporting Form

Date: _____ Reporter: _____

Others Taking Part:

_____

_____

What It Was All About: _____

_____

_____

How Did You Feel About the Way the Conflict Was Resolved?

(Circle one number)

1	**2**	**3**	**4**	**5**
Very Unhappy	*Unhappy*	*OK*	*Happy*	*Very Happy*

Drill and Review Game

1. **Mediation Catch:** Form groups of five members each. Each group stands in a circle and is given a tennis ball. Display the steps of mediating (ending hostilities, ensuring commitment to mediation, facilitating negotiations, formalizing the agreement). Throw a tennis ball. Whoever catches it has to give a statement from some aspect of the next step of mediating. Keep the game up until the mediation procedure has been covered several times.

MEDIATOR

has learned new ways to mediate conflicts between people

at

School in

and shall from this day be accorded the title and responsibilities of

OFFICIAL MEDIATOR

Teacher _____

Special Mediation Advisor _____

Date _____

Glossary

Accommodation: Adjusting behavior to conform to social constraints.

Aggression: Attempt to hurt someone or destroy somthing.

Aggressive-Passive Mentality: Students believing that either they (a) must dominate through force or (b) are passive victims unable to defend themselves or act in their own best interests. The resulting resentment powers resistance to learning.

Anger: A defensive emotional reaction that occurs when we are frustrated, thwarted, or attacked. Anger is a righteous but defensive reaction to frustration and aggression based on a unidimensional perceptual focus, a physical demand to take action, and a belief that we must get our way.

Assertiveness: Describing feelings, thoughts, opinions, and preferences directly to another person in an honest and appropriate way that respects both oneself and the other person.

Arbitration: The submission of a dispute to a disinterested third party who makes a final and binding judgment as to how the conflict will be resolved.

Behavioral Description: A statement that includes a personal statement (referring to "I," "me," or "my") and a description of the specific behaviors observed.

Blame: Believing that the cause of frustration is wicked people (including yourself) who deserve to be punished for their evil acts.

Carve-Outs: Carving an issue out of a larger context, leaving the related issues unsettled. This is the opposite of a tie-in.

Catharsis: The release of pent-up emotion experienced either by talking about feelings or by engaging in very active emotional release such as crying, laughing, or shouting.

Catastrophizing: Believing that one must have his or her way and that it is awful not to get everything wanted.

Common Fate: When one cannot succeed unless the other person succeeds and the other person cannot succeed unless one succeeds. You sink or swim together.

Competitive Learning: Students working against each other to achieve a goal that only one or a few can attain. You can attain your goal if and only if the other students involved cannot attain their goals.

Compromising: Giving up part of your goal while the other person does the same in order to reach an agreement. You seek a solution in which both sides gain something and settle on an agreement that is the middle ground between your two opening positions.

Conceptual Conflict: Conflict that exists when incompatible ideas exist simultaneously in a person's mind or when information being received does not seem to fit with what one already knows.

Conciliation: People involved in a conflict are brought together to discuss the problem. The Latin root "conciliare" means "to call or bring together, to win over" and is derived from "conilium" which is "a meeting or assembly."

Conflict: The occurrence of incompatible activities. An activity that is incompatible with another activity is one that prevents, blocks, or interferes with the occurrence or effectiveness of the second activity. Incompatible activities may originate in one person, between two or more people, or between two or more groups.

Conflict of Interests: When the actions of one person attempting to reach his or her goals prevent, block, or interfere with the actions of another person attempting to reach his or her goals.

Confronting: Directly expressing your view of the conflict and your feelings about it while at the same time inviting the other person to do the same so that negotiations may be begun. The negotiations are aimed at ensuring that you and the other person both fully meet your goals and maintain the relationship at the highest level possible.

Controversy: Conflict that exists when one person's ideas, information, conclusions, theories, and opinions are incompatible with those of another and the two seek to reach an agreement.

Cooperative Base Groups: Cooperative learning groups used to provide long-term support and assistance for academic progress.

Cooperative Learning: Students working together to accomplish shared goals. Students perceiving that they can succeed if and only if the other persons with whom they are cooperatively linked achieve their goals.

Co-Orientation: Operating under the same norms and adhering to the same procedures.

Counter-Conditioning: Conditioning students to respond in a way that is counter to destructive actions such as being hostile.

Developmental Conflict: A recurrent conflict that cycles in and out of peak intensity as the person develops socially. When recurrent incompatible activities between adult and child based on the opposing forces of stability and change within the child cycle in and out of peak intensity as the child develops cognitively, socially, and physically.

Disputant: Person involved in a conflict of interests.

Dissociation: The internalization of social constraints and adult values but rejecting them by seeing them as alien to one's own value structure. There is outward compliance to the social constraints while inner resistance continues. Direct or "real" solutions to the conflicts are abandoned for fantasy, pretend, or imaginary solutions.

Divergent Thinking: Generating a variety of ideas about how to solve a problem.

Egocentrism: The embeddedness in one's own viewpoint to the extent that one is unaware of other points of view and of the limitation of one's perspective. Being unaware that other perspectives exist and that one's own view of the conflict is incomplete and limited.

Expand the Pie: Adding new resources so that increased options for agreement are available.

Feelings: Internal physiological reactions to your experiences.

Feeling Description: A combination of a personal statement (referring to "I," "me," or "my") and specifying the feeling by name or by action-urge simile or some other figure of speech.

Fight Form: A form disputants fill out before mediation that requires them to reflect on the conflict, define it, and think of alternative ways of resolving the conflict.

Fixation: A mind set fixed on one thing so that the person is unable to think of or see alternatives.

Forcing: Overpowering opponents by requiring them to accept your solution to the conflict. You seek to achieve your goals at all costs and without concern with the needs of others.

Formal Cooperative Learning Groups: Cooperative learning groups used to teach specific academic content and social skills.

Fundamental Attribution Error: Belief that other people's behavior is caused by their personalities and nature while one's own behavior is caused by circumstances and situational factors.

Goal: An ideal and desired state of affairs that people value and are working to achieve.

Goal structure: The type of social interdependence specified among individuals as they strive to achieve their goals.

Groups Processing: Discussion of how well group members are achieving their goals and maintaining effective working relationships among members.

Hit-And-Run: You start a conversation about the conflict, give your definition and feelings, and then disappear before the other person has a chance to respond.

Identification: When a person tries to be like someone he or she loves, admires, or fears by incorporating their qualities and attributes into him- or herself.

Individual Accountability: When the performance of each individual student is assessed and the results given back to the group and the individual.

Individualistic Learning: Students work by themselves to accomplish learning goals unrelated to those of their classmates.

Informal Cooperative Learning Groups: Cooperative learning groups used to ensure active cognitive processing of information during a lecture or direct teaching.

Interests: The potential benefits to be gained by achieving goals. An individual's wants, needs, values, and goals.

Integration: The internalization of social constraints and adult values and accepting them into one's own value structure.

Irrational Assumption: A belief that makes you depressed, anxious, or upset most of the time.

Joint Outcome: Sum of benefits for everyone involved.

Manipulation: It is influencing others in ways they do not fully understand with consequences that are undesirable for them but highly desirable for oneself.

Mediation: When a neutral and impartial third party actively assists two or more people (called disputants) to negotiate a constructive resolution to their conflict. The Latin root "mediare" means "to divide in the middle."

Mote-Beam Mechanism: Students see small misbehaviors of opponents while ignoring one's own large misbehaviors.

Mutual Causation: When whether you succeed or fail depends both on your own efforts and the efforts of the other person. You must depend on the other person to help you succeed and he or she must depend on you to help him or her succeed.

Negotiation: A process by which persons who have shared and opposed interests and want to come to an agreement try to work out a settlement.

Nonnegotiable Norms: Norms individuals are expected to follow without exception, such as those outlawing physical violence against oneself or another person, public humiliation and shaming, and lying and deceit.

Nonassertiveness: You say nothing in response to a provocation, keeping your feelings to yourself, hiding feeling from others, and perhaps even hiding your feelings from yourself.

Norm of Mutual Responsiveness: Rule that you should be committed to fulfilling each other's goals and concerned about each other's interests.

Norms: Shared expectations about the behavior that is appropriate within the situation.

One-Step Negotiations: Each person (a) assesses the strength of his or her interests, (b) assesses the strength of the other person's interests, and (c) agrees that whoever has the greatest need is given his or her way.

Oppositional Interaction: Students discouraging and obstructing each other's efforts to achieve. Students focus both on increasing their own achievement **and** on preventing any classmate from achieving higher than they do.

Overassimilation: Pushing new skills and opportunities to beyond socially defined limits.

Package Deals: When several issues that are considered part of the agreement are settled.

Paraphrasing: Restating, in one's own words, what the person says, feels, and means.

Perception-Checking: Asking for clarification or correction to make sure your understanding is accurate. It involves describing what you think the other person's feelings are, asking whether or not your perception is accurate, and refraining from expressing approval or disapproval of the feelings.

Personal Statements: Statements that refer to "I," "me," "my," or "mine."

Perspective: A person's way of viewing the world and his or her relation to it.

Positive Interdependence: Students perceive that they are linked with others in a way that one cannot succeed unless the other members of the group succeed (and vice versa) and/or that they must coordinate their efforts with the efforts of their groupmates to complete a task. They perceive that they "sink or swim together."

Problem-Solving Negotiations: When each negotiator has as his or her goal the reaching of an agreement that benefits everyone involved. You negotiate to solve the problem when you have an ongoing cooperative relationship with the other person, must negotiate an agreement to resolve the current conflict, and then will continue the cooperative efforts and the relationship.

Promotive Interaction: Students helping, assisting, encouraging, facilitating, and supporting each other's efforts to learn, achieve, complete tasks, and produce in order to reach the group's goals.

Relationship Statements: Personal statements that describe some aspect of the way the two of you are interacting with each other.

Restitution: Making amends for injury, mistreatment, or insult.

Role Reversal: Having two participants in a conflict reverse roles and play each other during a role play.

Self-Blame: When you judge your basic self-worth on the basis of your inadequate or rotten behavior.

Self-Fulfilling Prophecy: Perceiving another person as being immoral and hostile and behaving accordingly, thus evoking hostility and deceit from the other person.

Single Step Solution: When you, after assessing how important your goals are to you and how important the other person's goals are to him or her, decide to give up your goals and help the other person achieve his or her goals. In a relationship it is important that each person gives in to the other about 50 percent of the time.

Smoothing: Giving up your goals and letting the other person have his or her way in order to maintain the relationship at the highest level possible. When the goal is of no importance to you but the relationship is of high importance, you smooth.

Social Constraints: Limits placed on a person's behavior by other people that define what is realistic and unrealistic behavior within the relationship and setting.

Social Perspective Taking: The ability to understand how a situation appears to another person and how that person is reacting cognitively and emotionally to the situation.

Tie-Ins: When an issue considered extraneous by the other person is introduced and you offer to accept a certain settlement provided this extraneous issue will also be settled to one's satisfaction.

Trade-Offs: The exchange of two different things of comparable value.

Win-Lose Negotiations: When each negotiator has as his or her goal making an agreement more favorable to oneself than to the other negotiator.

Wise Agreements: An agreement fair to all participants, based on principles, that strengthens participants' abilities to work together cooperatively, and improves participants' ability to resolve future conflicts constructively.

References

Bach, G., & Wyden, P. (1969). **The intimate enemy.** New York: William Morrow.

Berlyne, D. (1966). Notes on intrinsic motivation and intrinsic reward in relation to instruction. In J. Bruner (Ed.), **Learning about learning** (Cooperative Research Monograph No. 15). Washington, D.C.: U.S. Department of Health, Education, and Welfare, Office of Education.

Bigelow, R. (1972). The evolution of cooperation, aggression, and self-control. In J. Cole and D. Jensen (Eds.), **Nebraska symposium of motivation** (pp. 1-58). Lincoln: University of Nebraska Press.

Blake, R., & Mouton, J. (1969). **Building a dynamic corporation through grid organization and development.** Reading, MA: Addison-Wesley.

Boulding, E. (1964). Further reflections on conflict management. In R. Kahn and E. Boulding (Eds.), **Power and conflict in organizations**. New York: Basic Books, 146-150.

Burke, R. (1969). Methods of resolving interpersonal conflict. **Personnel Administration**, 48-55.

Burke, R. (1970). Methods of resolving superior- subordinate conflict: The constructive use of subordinate differences and disagreements. **Organizational Behavior and Human Performance, 5**, 393-411.

DeCecco, J., & Richards, A. (1974). **Growing pains: Uses of school conflict**. New York: Aberdeen Press.

Deutsch, M. (1962). Cooperation and trust: Some theoretical notes. In M. Jones (Ed.), **Nebraska symposium on motivation**. Lincoln: University of Nebraska Press, 275-319.

Deutsch, M. (1969). Conflicts: Productive and destructive. **Journal of Social Issues, 25,** 7-43.

Deutsch, M. (1973). **The resolution of conflict**. New Haven, CT: Yale University Press.

DeVries, D., and Edwards, K. (1973). Learning Games and Student Teams: Their Effects on Classroom Process. **American Educational Research Journal**, **10**, 307-318.

Erickson, E. (1950). **Childhood and society.** New York: Norton.

Erickson, E. (1968). **Identity: Youth and crisis.** New York: Norton.

Fisher, R., & Ury, W. (1981). **Getting to yes**. Boston: Houghton Mifflin.

Freud, S. (1930). **Civilization and its discontents.** London: Horgarth.

Glasser, W. (1984). **Control theory**. New York: Harper & Row.

Johnson, D. W. (1969). Students against the school establishment Crisis intervention in school conflicts and organization change. **Journal of School Psychology, 9.** 84-92.

Johnson, D. W. (1971). Role reversal: A summary and review of the research. **International Journal of Group Tensions**, **1**, 318- 334.

Johnson, D. W. (1974). Communication and the inducement of cooperative behavior in conflicts. **Speech Monographs**, **41**, 64-78.

Johnson, D. W. (1972/1990). **Reaching out: Interpersonal effectiveness and self-actualization** (4th Ed). Englewood Cliffs, NJ: Prentice-Hall.

Johnson, D. W. (1991). **Human relations and your career** (3d Ed). Englewood Cliffs, NJ: Prentice-Hall.

Johnson, D. W., & Johnson, F. (1975/1991). **Joining together: Group theory and group skills** (4th ed). Englewood Cliffs, NJ: Prentice-Hall.

Johnson, D. W., & Johnson, R. (1974). Instructional goal structure: Cooperative, competitive, or individualistic. **Review of Educational Research**, **44**, 213-240.

Johnson, D. W., & Johnson, R. (1978). Cooperative, Competitive, and Individualistic Learning. **Journal of Research and Development in Education**, **12**, 3-15.

Johnson, D. W., & Johnson, R. (1983). The socialization and achievement crises: Are cooperative learning experiences the solution? In L. Bickman (Ed.), **Applied social psychology annual 4**. Beverly Hills, CA: Sage Publications.

Johnson, D. W., & Johnson, R. (1975/1991). **Learning together and alone: Cooperative, competitive, and individualistic learning** (3rd ed.). Englewood Cliffs, NJ: Prentice-Hall.

Johnson, D. W., & Johnson, R. (1989a). **Cooperation and competition: theory and research**. Edina, MN: Interaction Book Company.

Johnson, D. W., & Johnson, R. (1989b). **Leading the cooperative school**. Edina, MN: Interaction Book Company.

Johnson, D. W., Johnson, R., & Dudley, B. (1991a). Effects Of Peer Mediation Training On Elementary School Students. Minneapolis, MN: University of Minnesota, article submitted for publication.

Johnson, D. W., Johnson, R., & Dudley, B. (1991b). An Evaluation of A Peer Mediation Training Program On Elementary School Students. Minneapolis, MN: University of Minnesota, article submitted for publication.

Johnson, D. W., Johnson, R., & Holubec, E. (1984/1990). **Circles of learning**. Edina, MN: Interaction Book Company.

Johnson, D. W., Johnson, R., & Maruyama, G. (1983). Interdependence and interpersonal attraction among heterogeneous and homogeneous individuals: A theoretical formulation and a meta-analysis of the research. **Review of Educational Research**, **53**, 5-54.

Johnson, D. W., Maruyama, G., Johnson, R., Nelson, D., & Skon, L. (1981). Effects of cooperative, competitive, and individualistic goal structures on achievement: A meta-analysis. **Psychological Bulletin**, **89,** 47-62.

Johnson, D. W., McCarty, K., & Allen, T. (1976). Congruent and contradictory verbal and nonverbal communications of cooperativeness and competitiveness in negotiations. **Communication Research**, **3,** 275-292.

Kohn, A. (1986). **No contest: The case against competition.** Boston: Houghton Mifflin.

Kreidler, W. (1984). **Creative conflict reslution.** Glenwood, IL: Scott, Foresman.

Kouzes, J., & Posner, B. (1987). **The leadership challenge.** San Francisco: Jossey-Bass.

Lawrence, P., & Lorsch, J. (1967). **Organization and environment: Managing differentiation and integration**. Cambridge, MA: Division of Research, Graduate School of Business Administration, Harvard University.

Mayer, A. (1903). Uber Einzel-und Gesamtleistung des Schul kindes. **Archiv fur die Gesamte Psychologie**, **1**, 276-416.

Pepitone, E. (1980). **Children in cooperation and competition**. Lexington, MA: Lexington Books.

Piaget, J. (1948). **The moral judgment of the child** (2nd ed.). Glencoe, IL: The Free Press.

Piaget, J. (1950). **The psychology of intelligence.** New York: Harcourt.

Resenberger, B. (1984, April). What made humans human? **New York Times Magazine**, 80-81, 89-95.

Rosenshine, B, & Stevens, R. (1986). Teaching Functions. In M. Wittrock (Ed.), **Handbook of research on teaching** (3rd Ed., pp. 376-391). New York: Macmillan.

Schmidt, F., & Friedman, A. (1985). **Creative conflict solving for kids.** Miami Beach, Fl: Grace Contrino Abrams Peace Education Foundation.

Sharan, S. (1980). Cooperative learning in teams: Recent methods and effects on achievement, attitudes, and ethnic relations. **Review of Educational Research**, **50**, 241-272.

Tjosvold, D., & Johnson, D. W. (Eds.). (1983). **Productive conflict management: Perspectives for organizations.** New York: Irvington.

Tjosvold, D., Johnson, D. W., & Fabrey, L. (1980). The effects of controversy and defensiveness on cognitive perspective-taking. **Psychological Reports**, **47**, 1043-1053.

Triplett, N. (1898). The dynamogenic factors in pacemaking and competition. **American Journal of Psychology**, **9**, 507-533.

Walton, R. (1986). **Interpersonal peacemaking** (2nd Ed.). Reading, MA: Addison-Wesley.

Watson, G., & Johnson, D. W. (1972) **Social psychology: Issues and insights**. Philadelphia: Lippincott.

Wilson, R. (1987). Toward Excellence in Teaching. In L. Aleamoni (Ed.), **Techniques for evaluating and improving instruction** (pp. 9-24). San Francisco: Jossey-Bass.